STATES IN DISGUISE

States in Disguise

CAUSES OF STATE SUPPORT FOR REBEL GROUPS

Belgin San-Akca

OXFORD
UNIVERSITY PRESS

OXFORD
UNIVERSITY PRESS

Oxford University Press is a department of the University of Oxford. It furthers
the University's objective of excellence in research, scholarship, and education
by publishing worldwide. Oxford is a registered trade mark of Oxford University
Press in the UK and certain other countries.

Published in the United States of America by Oxford University Press
198 Madison Avenue, New York, NY 10016, United States of America.

Library of Congress Cataloging-in-Publication Data
Names: San-Akca, Belgin, author.
Title: States in disguise : causes of state support for rebel groups / Belgin San-Akca.
Description: New York, NY : Oxford University Press, 2016. | Includes bibliographical references and index.
Identifiers: LCCN 2016015938| ISBN 9780190250881 (hardcover : alk. paper) |
ISBN 9780190250904 (pbk. : alk. paper)
Subjects: LCSH: Non-state actors (International relations) | Insurgency. | State, The. |
Alliances. | International relations.
Classification: LCC JZ4059 .S36 2016 | DDC 355.02/18—dc23
LC record available at https://lccn.loc.gov/2016015938

9 8 7 6 5 4 3 2 1

Paperback printed by WebCom, Inc., Canada
Hardback printed by Bridgeport National Bindery, Inc., United States of America

To my true supporters:
Erkan, Teoman, and Kenan

Contents

List of Maps

List of Figures

List of Tables

List of Abbreviations

AMB	Al-Aqsa Martyrs' Brigades
AN	National Alliance (Chad)
ANC	African National Congress
APF	Alliance of Palestinian Forces
AQIM	Al Qaeda in the Islamic Maghreb
ATOP	Alliance Treaty Obligations and Provisions
BLA	Balochistan Liberation Army
BRA	Balochistan Republican Army
CINC	Composite Index of National Capability
COW	Correlates of War
CPN/M	Communist Party of Nepal-Maoist
CPT	Communist Party of Thailand
DCP	Dangerous Companions Project
DRC	Democratic Republic of the Congo
ELF	Eritrean Liberation Front
EPLF	Eritrean People's Liberation Front
EPR	Ethnic Power Relations
ETA	Basque Homeland and Freedom
FAN	Armed Forces of the North (Chad)
FARC	Revolutionary Armed Forces of Colombia
FAT	Chadian Armed Forces
FLN	National Liberation Front

FMNLF	Farabundo Marti National Liberation Front of El Salvador
FROLINAT	National Liberation Front of Chad
FSA	Free Syrian Army
GAM	Free Aceh Movement
GDP	Gross Domestic Product
GIA	Armed Islamic Group of Algeria
IG	al-Gama'a al-Islamiyya (Islamic Group)
IGO	Intergovernmental Organization
IRA	Irish Republican Army
ISI	Inter-Services Intelligence (Pakistan)
ISIS	Islamic State of Iraq and Syria
ITERATE	International Terrorism: Attributes of Terrorist Events
KDPI	Kurdistan Democratic Party of Iran
KIO	Kachin Independence Organization
KNU	Karen National Union
KR	Khmer Rouge
LRA	Lord's Resistance Army
LTTE	Liberation Tigers of Tamil Eelam
LURD	Liberians United for Reconciliation and Democracy
MAR	Minorities at Risk Project
MDD	Movement for Democracy and Development
MEK	Mujahedin-e Khalq
MENA	Middle East and North Africa
MERIP	Middle East Research and Information Project
MIPT	Memorial Institute for the Prevention of Terrorism
MODEL	Movement for Democracy in Liberia
MOSANAT	Movement for the National Salvation of Chad
MPLA	People's Movement for the Liberation of Angola
MPS	Patriotic Salvation Movement (Chad)
NAGs	Nonstate Armed Groups
OLF	Oromo Liberation Front
PFLP	Popular Front for the Liberation of Palestine
PFLP-GC	Popular Front for the Liberation of Palestine – General Command
PIJ	Palestinian Islamic Jihad
PITF	Political Instability Task Force
PKK	Kurdistan Workers' Party
PLA	People's Liberation Army (China)
PLF	Palestine Liberation Front
PLO	Palestine Liberation Organization

PRG	Politically Relevant Group
RSM	Rebels' Selection Model
RUF	Revolutionary United Front
SAVAK	Sazeman-e Ettelaat va Amniyat-e Keshvar (Organization of Intelligence and National Security)
SCIRI	Supreme Council for the Islamic Revolution in Iraq
SMC	Supreme Military Council (Syria)
SRG	Strategic Reference Group
SSM	States' Selection Model
START	National Consortium for the Study of Terrorism and Responses to Terrorism
TKB	Terrorism Knowledge Base
UCDP/PRIO ACD	Uppsala Conflict Data Program/The Peace Research Institute Oslo Armed Conflict Dataset
UFDD	Union of Forces for Democracy and Development
UN	United Nations
UNITA	National Union for the Total Independence of Angola
UTO	United Tajik Opposition
WRP	World Religion Project

Acknowledgments

THIS BOOK HAS been eight years in the making. It is based on four years of research for my dissertation at the University of California, Davis, and four years of research funded by a Marie Curie Reintegration Grant from the European Commission between 2011 and 2015, while I was a faculty member in the Department of International Relations at Koç University, Istanbul. The empirical analysis in this book is based on the Dangerous Companions Project (DCP), funded by the Marie Curie Reintegration Grant. Throughout the years, I benefited from the support of several individuals and organizations.

During my doctoral study at the University of California, Davis, I had the opportunity to work with two amazing mentors: Miroslav Nincic and Zeev Maoz. I thank them for their unwavering enthusiasm for this project throughout my graduate school years and for keeping me motivated to complete the book afterward. Miko dedicated many Starbucks sessions to help develop the project initially. He taught me that completing any scholarly work successfully requires a balance between reading and writing. I have been privileged to enjoy countless scholarly interactions with Zeev when I was at Davis. Without him, I would not have turned my scattered ideas about state support for non-state violence into the current organized structure. His influence on my scholarship is best expressed by the two periods in my academic career: Before-Zeev and After-Zeev. I take pride in having the opportunity to continue working with such an intellectually engaging scholar after I moved from Davis.

The Department of Political Science at the University of California, Davis, provided teaching and research assistantships that made the long years of dissertation research materially viable. I received the Institute of Government Affairs Dissertation Improvement Grant, which made it possible to hire Arash Khosrowshahi and Kris Inman as research assistants for data collection. I also thank Elissa Alzate, Monti Data, Jennifer Ramos, and Matthew Weiss for their friendship and support.

Koç University, where I currently teach, has provided an intellectually stimulating environment with extraordinary research support. The summer research program, which allows faculty members to spend time abroad to undertake research, made it possible to conduct part of the research while in residence at the Center for Middle Eastern Studies at Harvard University, during the summer of 2011. The sabbatical leave gave me the opportunity to devote long hours to the manuscript and the underlying data collection effort during the fall semester of 2012. I especially thank Umran İnan, the president of Koç University, and Barış Tan, the Vice President for Academic Affairs, for instituting a sabbatical leave policy for young faculty members. Ali Çarkoğlu, the dean of the College of Administrative Sciences and Economics currently, covered my courses, when I was on sabbatical leave, and motivated me to complete the book.

The Office of the Vice President for Research and Development at Koç University coordinated summer research programs, which allowed interested students from Turkey and around the world to be employed for data coding in 2014 and 2015. I thank Arzu Yılmaz for her enthusiasm in matching the students' research interests with the project. My gratitude to Zeynep Neyza Akçabay, Meltem İşanlar, and Ebru Tan from the Research, Project Development and Technology Transfer Directorate, for their help during the grant proposal preparation stage and the grant management process after securing the funding. My colleagues in the Department of International Relations provided a friendly environment, which alleviated the many hours spent in seclusion during this project. I enjoyed the friendship and support of Şener Aktürk, Özlem Altan-Olcay, Selim Erdem Aytaç, Reşat Bayer, Ahmet İçduygu, Ziya Öniş, Bahar Rumelili, Murat Somer, and Şuhnaz Yılmaz-Özbağcı. I thank Güneş Ertan for her help with the network figures and Caner Bakır for helping me to develop the idea for the image on the book cover. Arif Akca helped with finding the images and making them suitable for a book cover.

In addition, the Marie Curie Reintegration Grant of the European Commission made it possible to hire many research assistants to collect data. It also allowed me travel abroad on various occasions to present papers related to the project and receive feedback from many valuable colleagues in Europe. İlayda Bilge Önder and Efe Can Çoban have been as enthusiastic about this project as myself. Their passion for data collection and coding kept me motivated during the final stages of writing.

İlayda stayed with me until the end and has shown extraordinary resilience and self-discipline, far beyond what is expected from an undergraduate student. Gizem Türkarslan coordinated the team of research assistants, in addition to collecting and coding data. Emine Arı and Fatih Erol helped with the final touches on the manuscript.

I owe a special debt of gratitude to Angela Chnapko for her trust in this project and her professionalism as an editor. Two anonymous reviewers at Oxford University Press provided invaluable feedback, which inspired me to add the case studies on Israel and Chad. The final manuscript also benefited from copyediting by Paul Slate and Mari Christie.

Most significantly, I will always be grateful to my parents, Beyhan and Şeref, who supported me in pursuing an academic career. Without my parents' strong belief in the virtues of education, I would have never made it this far. They never interfered in the paths I chose to pursue throughout my life. I am indebted to them for their unconditional love and support. I was never quite clear how they managed to maintain such faith in me despite all my complaints. Now that I have my own kids, I realize the sacrifice they made, letting me go all the way to the other side of the world to pursue my dream.

Throughout the years required to complete my PhD study, and this project, I have been fortunate to have one person who has always been there for me, sharing the frustrations and joys of academic life. My greatest acknowledgement is to my husband, Erkan Akca, whose unconditional support helped soothe my conscience about taking time away from him and our two sons. Words cannot express my gratitude to him. Our marriage has endured the challenges of academic life because of the sacrifices he has made over the years. Without my husband's love and support, I would have never completed this book. My older son, Teoman, who was four years old when I started this project, is now twelve years old and has a brother. When he saw my name on the title page of the manuscript, he opened his eyes wide and said: "Mom, you have a book?" It was then that I decided to complete the book. I am sorry for missing playtime with my younger son, Kenan. But I know that he will forgive me once he realizes how dedicated his mother is to completing the projects she undertakes. And building a great future for him and his older brother are my lifetime projects. I hope this book will serve as a small step toward a brighter future for generations to come. I dedicate it to my true supporters, my husband and our two sons.

STATES IN DISGUISE

For a prince should have two fears: one internal, concerning his subjects; the other external,
concerning foreign powers. From the latter, he can defend himself by his effective arms and
his effective allies. . . . Internal affairs will always be stable when external affairs are stable,
provided that they are not already disturbed by a conspiracy.
THE PRINCE, Niccolò Machiavelli[1]

1 Introduction
BRINGING NONSTATE ARMED GROUPS INTO THE STUDY
OF INTERNATIONAL RELATIONS

WE LIVE NEITHER in the times of the *Thugs*,[2] who paid off the sovereigns of
neighboring states to find external sanctuaries around India, nor in the times of
the *Assassins*,[3] who belonged to the first historically recorded international armed
organization directed and maintained by a state. Though no longer in return for
money, states constitute the major sources from which nonstate armed groups acquire support in the form of sanctuaries, funds, weapons, and logistics. These two
historical cases also reflect the two major trends that exist today in the complex
web of relations between states and nonstate armed groups: (1) states select, if not
form, nonstate armed groups to which they provide support, and (2) nonstate armed
groups select the countries from which they extract and acquire resources regardless
of whether the state in a given country deliberately creates channels to aid them.

The current international environment faces an unprecedented challenge from
nonstate armed groups, including ethnic and religious insurgents and terrorists,
which fight a government within the borders of a given country. These groups not only
threaten the states they primarily target, but also collaborate with some states against
others. Indeed, 41 percent of all armed groups fighting against states in the post–
World War II period emerged in the past several decades. While almost 60 percent
of these groups were purposefully supported by states that provided troops, safe

havens, weapons, funds, training, and logistics aid to sustain their violent operations, approximately 45 percent of rebel groups managed acquiring resources within the borders of a country without the sponsorship of the state within the given country.[4] These figures indicate that the upsurge of nonstate violence in world politics does not seem to be a problem particularly related to the absence of state and, therefore, a lack of governance in certain territories and locations. Rather, to a great extent, it is a problem generated by states themselves, mostly through covert means.[5]

The resilience of nonstate armed groups in world politics along with states is further reinforced by the recent upsurge of armed violence led by terrorist groups such as al-Shabaab, Islamic State of Iraq and Syria (ISIS), al-Qaeda, and Boko Haram. Considering these groups operate in parallel to—both with and against—the conventional state order in the international system, their complex interactions with states can no longer be reduced to the idea of proxy war. The state-centric view of proxy war, which dominated international relations studies until recently, treats nonstate armed groups as subordinate entities, with no autonomous decision-making capacity. Yet, various historical cases prove that armed rebel groups make deliberate choices in aligning with certain states in their search for external resources. In addition, their objectives do not always overlap with those of the states that support them.

Yasser Arafat, the chairman of Fatah and the Palestine Liberation Organization (PLO), managed to escape decisively from the influence of strong regimes under the leadership of Hafez al-Assad and Gamal Abdel Nasser in Syria and Egypt, respectively. Instead, he looked for support from states such as Libya, Tunisia, Sudan, and China (Mann 2007). Palestinian Islamic Jihad (PIJ) relocated its offices multiple times, first from Gaza to Lebanon—though this was due to forced expulsion—and then from Lebanon to Damascus upon the invitation of the Syrian regime (Strindberg 2000). The Kurdistan Workers' Party (PKK) operated offices and training camps in several Western states, such as Germany and Belgium, and it conducted violent attacks against various Turkish businesses across Europe in the early 1990s.[6]

This neglected dimension of the relations between states and armed rebel groups is to some extent captured by some recent work employing the principle-agent theory to explain state support of rebel groups (Bapat 2007; Byman and Kreps 2010; Salehyan 2010; Salehyan et al. 2011). The principle-agent theory offers that states (principles) will covertly delegate rebel groups (agents) to conduct some of their foreign policy business to save cost. Yet we still need to refine our theories through systematic empirical analysis to capture the full domain of interactions between states and rebel groups. States that provide support to certain rebel groups do not always support them to achieve specific benefits. Occasionally, they support rebels because they have some ideational attachment to them. In addition, principle-agent approach does not capture the cases in which a state does not create deliberate channels to aid a rebel group, but the latter manages acquiring resources within its territories.

It is the purpose of *States in Disguise* to explain the complex patterns of inter-actions between states and nonstate armed groups, both in terms of the processes leading to external state support and the motives of the actors behind such support. Thus, it attributes an active role to rebel groups as equally autonomous actors that, like states, possess decision-making capacity. It, does not confront, but advances our knowledge of state and rebel group relations beyond the insights we have learnt so far. It adopts an approach that goes beyond focusing on interactions only between rebel groups and their state supporters, but also between their supporter states and target states. This approach yields novel testable implications about the patterns in state and rebel group relations from the perspective of inter-state relations.

I present a selection theory to systematically examine the diverse patterns that exist in the interactions between states and rebel groups. I argue that these diverse patterns can be captured to a great extent if we take into account the nature of inter-state environment, which determines the kind of rebels states intentionally support and the kind of states rebel groups seek to acquire resources from. The interactions between states and rebel groups are only meaningful if we examine them through the relations between target states and supporter states.

The study of armed violence and its influence in world politics can no longer be lim-ited to state-centric views and theories. We need to develop more nuanced theories, tested with empirical analyses, to explain the causes and consequences of the complex web of relations between states and armed rebel groups. This book examines state-rebel group interactions to explain the domestic and international political factors, as well as material and ideational motives, driving diverse patterns in these intrigu-ing networks of relations. Material benefits, also called strategic interests, refer to the pursuit of some foreign policy objectives, such as joining forces against an enemy and achieving concessions in bargaining with rivals. On the other hand, ideational motives refer to actors' behaviors driven by the specific ideas, norms and identities they adhere to (Lebow 2010). Ideas, norms and identity are key in determining the ideational con-tiguity among states. In examining the systematic effect of inter-state ideational con-tiguity, we have surprisingly little work using inter-state ideational contiguity as an explanation behind state behavior and testing its implications with a large dataset.[7]

The theoretical framework builds on the premise that there are various paths to collaboration between states and rebel groups. When seeking support from each other, both go through a decision-making process, which ends with specific prefer-ences. As states select the rebel groups to which to provide support, rebel groups also select the states from which to seek support. In this respect, the multi-layer pat-terns of interactions between states and rebel groups are classified under two main categories: (1) state-rebel group alliance or cooperation and (2) de facto support. The first type of interaction emerges because states are motivated to support rebels. The resulting support is intentional in the sense that states deliberately create channels to aid rebels. On the other hand, the second type stems from one-sided selection by rebel groups, which states do not necessarily knowingly abet. These two types of interaction can be further clarified with the following examples.

In March 2011, Ecuadorian security forces detained a suspected Revolutionary Armed Forces of Colombia (FARC) arms smuggler during a raid on a house in Quito, the capital. During the raid, they captured many rifles, machine guns, manufacturing equipment, and notebooks, which detailed the training of the 48th and 29th fronts of FARC (Gilmour 2011a). In the following year, Ecuadorian security forces uncovered a military arsenal suspected to belong to FARC near the border with Peru (Gilmour 2011b; Hurst 2012). No evidence suggested that the Ecuadorian government was involved in creating channels to abet FARC militants. In other words, FARC militants managed to raise funds and smuggle arms within Ecuador without any deliberate act on the part of Ecuador's government to aid them.

The second example is related to the intentional support of rebels by states. On December 12, 2003, a public law titled "Syria Accountability and Lebanese Sovereignty Restoration Act of 2003" was passed by the U.S. Congress. This law was intended to compel the Assad regime to change its policy of support for terrorism and meddling in Lebanon and Iraq, as well as the development of weapons of mass destruction and ballistic missile programs. One specific demand from the Syrian regime was to close the offices and headquarters of Hamas and PIJ in Damascus and cease support for terrorism in general (Marquis 2004; Schenker 2006). Syria had historically formed and supported various militant Palestinian groups against Israel, its major external adversary, ever since Israel's foundation, and especially after the loss of the Golan Heights to Israel in the end of the Six-Day War.

These examples accentuate two main selection processes in state-rebel interactions. From the perspective of states, armed rebel groups serve as a means to avoid direct confrontation with other states. This is because use of military force has gradually evolved into a very costly tool to realize foreign policy objectives. Furthermore, supporting rebels is also a means of catering to the domestic populace, especially if rebels have common ideational ties with major ethnic and religious groups and minorities within their territories. This was the case with the Syrian-PIJ-Hamas relations. From the perspective of rebel groups, acquiring state supporters is a prestigious undertaking, proving their ability to extract human and material resources within the borders of other countries, without the intentional sponsorship of these countries' states and/or governments. This is illustrated by the case of Ecuador and FARC.

The theoretical framework of this book, then, is based on a series of hypotheses about the factors that motivate states to support rebel groups intentionally to pursue certain foreign policy objectives, and the motives of rebel groups in selecting certain countries as major grounds of resource acquisition and operation. This latter form of support is referred as de facto support.

1.1 Why Study External Support for Rebel Groups?

On October 7, 2001, the United States launched Operation Enduring Freedom against Afghanistan, to capture the perpetrators of the September 11, 2001, attacks and punish the Taliban regime, which had provided support to al-Qaeda. Although 9/11 is not unique in terms of the level of violence committed by nonstate armed groups, it stimulated a new debate about the root causes of nonstate violence, specifically terrorism. The gravest threat to the United States and world security was no longer from rival great powers but, rather, from poorly governed states, such as Pakistan and Afghanistan.[8]

The idea that weak states are hospitable to, and harbor, armed rebel groups, specifically terrorists, has been commonly accepted among both political scientists and policymakers (Lesser 1999; Rotberg 2002; Patrick 2006; Rice 2008). These views have been based largely on the resurgence of fundamentalist groups, such as al-Qaeda in the Middle East, and their use of weak states, such as Afghanistan, as safe havens. Although continuing violence and territorial hold by ISIS in Syria recently reinforces this view, historically, the most prominent cases of support—such as Iran's support of Hezbollah, Syria's support of Hamas and PIJ, Libya's support of the Irish Republican Army (IRA), and Pakistan's support of various Kashmiri groups—cannot be explained by ineffective state governance.

Historian Walter Laqueur points out that in the forty-nine countries designated by the United Nations (UN) as the least developed, hardly any nonstate violence occurs, most specifically terrorism.[9] Weak state capacity could be one factor making some states natural candidates from whom such groups acquire resources, but it is definitely not the only one. Considering that rebel groups need various resources, including but not limited to safe havens, weak states are not the best resources for infrastructure, funds, arms, and other logistical support. In weak states, rebels occasionally end up exploiting a power vacuum to freely recruit, raise funds, smuggle weapons, and find safe havens. But when examining the major sources of support for rebel groups, it is found that almost 50 percent of all the rebel groups, operating in the post–World War II period, received support from states, which were not necessarily weak. Indeed, they purposefully provided them with funds, arms, logistics, safe havens, training, and training camps.

Among these groups, several are worth highlighting. The Liberation Tigers of Tamil Eelam (LTTE) fought the Sri Lankan government between 1983 and 2009, demanding a separate state for the Tamil people. The LTTE violence was blamed for a dozen high-level assassinations and more than 200 suicide attacks, at a cost of more than 60,000 lives (Perry 2006). In Colombia, the FARC has engaged in kidnappings, drug trafficking, and hijacking, as well as guerrilla warfare against Colombia's military forces. More than 200,000 people have died since 1966, as a result of armed clashes between the Colombian government and FARC.[10] Colombia spends 2 percent of its Gross Domestic Product (GDP) annually to fight this group (McLean 2002). The al-Gama'a al-Islamiyya (Islamic Group) of Egypt (IG), a Sunni fundamentalist group with aspirations to found an Islamist government, became prominent after the assassination of Egyptian president Anwar Sadat in 1981, and fought an insurgency against the Egyptian government between 1989 and 1998.[11]

All of these groups have three things in common: (1) they are not formally affiliated with the armed forces of a state; (2) they primarily use violent means; and (3) they have state supporters that provide them with arms and logistics aid, funds, safe havens, training camps, and, occasionally, troops. The LTTE received support from India, Cambodia, and Thailand in the form of arms, sanctuary, and training camps. Although FARC's main source of funding is drug trafficking, it has used neighboring states to obtain arms, funds, and, occasionally, safe havens. The IG of Egypt received funds from Sudan and Iran, which also provided training camps to the group's militants and leaders. Examining these groups through the lenses of international politics, one can see their endurance is, to a great extent, facilitated by states, not by a lack of state capacity. Frequently, these groups operate freely in spaces and territories, where state governments declare and maintain considerable autonomy.

Traditionally, the mainstream paradigms, such as realism, liberalism, and constructivism, position states as the major actors in international relations. International security can be promoted or disturbed by states alone. Though liberalism suggests that international organizations, such as the UN, can serve as a platform to resolve disputes among states, they can do so only to the extent that states agree to work through them in resolving their disagreements. So, in testing existing paradigms or developing new ones, nonstate armed groups are not included as autonomous actors by scholars of international relations. My secondary purpose here is to develop such a framework, to test the applicability of existing paradigms in the unconventional setting of state-rebel group relations.

Since states are sovereign equals of each other, from the perspective of interstate relations, it is *normal* to help a state that is targeted by a rebel group. What is unusual for a state is to support the rebel group, which operates in an illegitimate sphere, against one of its *equals*. This illegitimacy stems from the commonly held idea that the state holds a monopoly over the legitimate use of violent means (Weber

1946). Especially perplexing is that if a rebel group fails to achieve its objectives, external states, which abet them have the risk of souring their relations with the rebels' targets. Such has been the experience of several states, including the United States and Turkey, in the recent conflict between the Assad regime in Syria and the rebels trying to bring it down. *What, then, motivates states to provide support to a rebel group fighting another state?*

With the understanding that supporting a rebel group targeting another state constitutes an act of interstate animosity, this book seeks an answer to this question through the lenses of interstate relations. It uncovers the nature of relations between states A and B, that is whether they share a conflict history and/or have common ideational ties, to discover a systematic explanation for state A's support of a rebel group against state B. By the same token, it uncovers the nature of relations between A and B that drives a rebel group fighting B to seek support from A. In general, it seeks to uncover the nature of the international environment that gives rise to the emergence of cooperative relations between states and armed rebel groups.

1.2 Rebel Groups and Their Characteristics

I define rebel groups by the means they employ—in this case, "violence"—and the goals they pursue—"political objectives."[12] "Political objectives" refer to the demands of the group from its target state, such as territory, regime change, and/or leadership change. Defining rebels in terms of both their means and their objectives is useful in generalizing across various types, including ethnic, religious, and national insurgencies; revolutionary movements; and terrorists and guerrilla organizations. Although examining each type separately would provide leverage in a different research context, such an overall treatment of various types of nonstate armed groups facilitates generalization, which is useful within the context of the current book's research agenda, regardless of their sphere of influence. While the influence of groups, such as al-Qaeda and the PLO, reaches beyond their particular region, groups, such as the FARC and Basque Homeland and Freedom (ETA), are largely limited to the country that they target.

In general, six main caveats must be noted for the nonstate armed groups or rebel groups that make up the subject matter of this book:

1. Rebel groups included here comprise only groups that primarily resort to violence to pursue their objectives. Groups that spread their propaganda solely via peaceful means are not included among the population of nonstate armed groups in this analysis.[13]

2. They do not have a formal affiliation with a sovereign state actor within the international system. The fact that a sponsor allowing its troops to fight alongside the members of a nonstate armed group does not qualify for formal affiliation with a state.[14]
3. "Rebel group," in this context, refers to an organized group of people. Spontaneous protest movements do not meet that criterion.
4. A "rebel group" pursues political goals, such as secession, regime change, or leadership change, within its target state. As such, criminal organizations, such as the Mafia, are not a part of the nonstate armed groups included in this study.
5. They use various tactics ranging from guerrilla tactics directed at only military and security apparatus, to terrorist tactics that involve civilians.
6. Not all rebels reside within the countries against which they fight. Different scenarios are possible for interaction with their targets and supporters. For instance, Jemaah Islamiyya (JI) aspires to found an Islamic state in Southeast Asia and targets more than a single state. It has bases in Malaysia, Thailand, Singapore, and the Philippines, and wants to establish an Islamic state that includes these countries, as well as Brunei.

State support of rebels takes various forms. In principle, this might be examined on two dimensions: whether it contributes directly or indirectly to the violent activities of a rebel group, and whether it is intentionally provided by a state, its government and/or its leader(s) through deliberately created channels. Table 1.1 presents a few possible scenarios in terms of the types and causes of state support for rebel groups.

TABLE 1.1 Types and Causes of State Support for Rebel Groups

Types		Causes	
Direct	Indirect	Intentional	De Facto
• Safe Haven	• Political support	• Conflict escalation	• Weak or low
• Weapons	• Peaceful propaganda	• Bargaining chip	capacity
• Training camps	• Fundraising	• Regional influence	• Democratic
• Troops	• Trade activities	• Instigate instability	countries
• Funds	• Transport of		
• Logistics aid	weapons		
• Greece: PKK	• European states:	• Iran: Hezbollah	• Pakistan: Taliban
• Syria: PIJ	PKK	• Syria: PIJ	• Some European
	• USA: IRA		states: PKK

"Direct forms of support" refer to the types by which states directly contribute to the violent conduct of a rebel group. They include providing training and training camps, funds, arms, logistics aid, and/or troops. "Indirect forms of support" include allowing leaders and/or members of such groups to live within state territory, engage in propaganda via peaceful means, and fundraise, as well as the question of whether a state actor publicly acknowledges a rebel group's objective as just. Several armed rebel groups, such as Fatah, Hamas, the Free Aceh Movement (GAM), LTTE, and PKK, have enjoyed extensive support from many states throughout their existence. While allowing troops to fight alongside rebels, or giving them arms, can directly influence their capability to fight, allowing them to open offices, or publicly acknowledging their objectives as "just," are less direct, but equally important, forms of support. The empirical analysis in this book focuses on the following forms of support: providing safe havens to leaders and/or members of a group, training camps, training, weapons and logistics aid, funds, transport points for military equipment and military advice, maintain offices, and troops.

1.3 The Book's Approach

Although it has been five decades since the UN General Assembly passed a resolution, on December 21, 1965, stating that "no State shall organize, assist, foment, finance, incite or tolerate subversive, terrorist, or armed activities directed towards the violent overthrow of the regime of another State, or interfere in civil strife in another state,"[15] subsequent decades have witnessed numerous proxy wars, military interventions, and significant state support for terrorism, in order to shape the internal politics of other states by abetting rebels fighting against them. Of the rebel groups that emerged in the period following World War II, almost 65 percent received some form of support from external states, either as a result of states' selection or the rebel selection processes described above. A total of 45 percent of the entire support occurred in the post–Cold War period, which is a significant indicator that such a strategy is not limited to a period characterized by proxy wars of the superpowers.[16] Since the French Revolution, which marked the onset of the modern nation-state, states have supported nonstate armed groups targeting other states, as a strategy to realize specific foreign policy objectives. The international community's continuous efforts to agree on a set of principles for response to nonstate violence—such as questions of self-determination, intervention, nonintervention, and sovereignty—point to the intrinsic problems of the issue embedded within the idea of the nation-state, which seems frequently at odds with itself (Buchanan 1992; Heraclides 1992, 1997; Herbst 1989; Little 1985; Little 2013; Moore 1969).

The regularity of ethnic and religious insurgencies challenging nation-states, and the increase of internal armed conflicts galvanized by ethnic, religious, and ideological differences, can be compared to a decline in interstate armed conflict. This fact calls for exploration of the causes and effects of nonstate violence. Explanations can be found only if we examine the inciting roles of international and domestic political factors in nonstate violent acts, given that rebels find and extract an extensive amount of resources from states themselves. Therefore, to add to the study of why and how nonstate armed groups emerge, endure, and disappear in world politics, the empirical analyses yield novel implications for not only explaining the reasons behind state support, but also for revealing the conditions under which states are dissuaded from supporting rebel groups. Furthermore, the formulation of state support within the context of triadic relations among rebels, their targets and supporters allows for a central and active role to nonstate armed groups in shaping international relations, a type of actor that has long been denied or ignored in mainstream security studies (Deutsch 1964; Morgenthau 1967; Owen 2010).

The theory of state support for rebel groups is built on the basis of three assertions: (1) rebel groups, or nonstate armed groups, are purposive and autonomous agents; (2) state support of rebels should be framed in a way to allow for the examination of the effect of inter-state relations on the relations between rebels and their state supporters; (3) many historical examples of rebel groups, who managed to survive for a long period, confirm that they learnt how to bypass their principles (state supporters). This last point deserves further elaboration. When Yasser Arafat founded Fatah in 1959 as an armed movement to fight against Israel, he hardly had any difficulty finding support from surrounding states, including Jordan, Iraq, Egypt, and Syria. All of these states had suffered military defeat by Israel after the latter's foundation in 1948. Yet one major issue Arafat had to address with Syria and Egypt was autonomy in Fatah's conduct of operations against Israel (Mann 2007). Once he realized that it would be difficult to obtain a high degree of autonomy under the sponsorship of Syria and Egypt, he turned to new supporters, including Libya and Lebanon, who would oppose relatively less against operations targeting Israel.

The story of Fatah shows that the insights derived from the principle-agent theory, though very valuable, is not sufficient when rebel groups (agents) manages to bypass the constraints imposed on them by their sponsors. Intentional and de facto support emerge as a result of two distinctive selection processes on the part of states and rebel groups. States are perceived to "select" rebels if evidence exists that a government or its official affiliates purposefully create channels to help them. Rebels are considered to get de facto support if they manage acquiring funds, weapons, safe havens and other forms of support without any evidence that the government or its formal affiliates within a country provides such support.[17] The motives behind intentional and de facto support is argued to be in line with the logic of explanations offered by major theories of International Relations in explaining inter-state conflict and cooperation. Insights of Realism, Liberalism, and Constructivism are utilized in a complementary manner to deliver a full picture of the diverse patterns prevalent in the relations of states and rebel groups.

The armed rebel groups included in this study do not have any official affiliation to a state, or a state's armed wings, and all challenge their target states for territorial and political concessions primarily by means of violence as I mentioned earlier. Thus, the groups included in this study range from terrorists, such as the Red Brigades in Italy, to insurgents, such as the GAM in Indonesia, to revolutionary groups, such as the FARC. It may not be immediately evident why all three types should be in the same book. They each have distinct objectives and identities, that is, religious, ethno-nationalist, and/or revolutionary. This is exactly why I include them in the same study: to go beyond a divisive intellectual categorization. Studying them separately allowed us to better understand the conditions under which each occurs and the grievances their adherents try to address. We now accumulated large bodies of research on civil war, terrorism, ethnic strife, rebellion, and revolution. Nonetheless, I argue that a unified picture of nonstate violence from the perspective of interstate relations is only possible if we simply treat them as armed opposition groups fighting against states within the borders of various countries.

1.4 Why State Selection and Rebel Selection as Separate Processes?

State selection and rebel selection are separate processes pointing out two divergent, but intermingled, paths, leading rebels to acquire resources from states other than their targets. Such a framework allows one to go beyond the limited view of mainstream security studies, with respect to proxy wars and the post-9/11 treatment of nonstate violence as instigated mainly by weak or failed states.

The United Opposition Front of Tajikistan (UTO) was founded in 1992 against the pro-Russian government in Dushanbe, and supported by Iran, which was trying to expand its sphere of influence in the region at that time (McElroy 1998). The Communist Party of Nepal-Maoist (CPN/M), founded in 1996 with a goal of toppling the monarchy in Nepal, used India as a weapons transport point. In this second case, the Indian government did not create channels to help the CPN/M but rather, was used by the rebel group due to its geographical contiguity to Nepal. Examining both in the same study helps to reveal whether the underlying international and domestic political factors influence external support for rebels differently across state selection and rebel selection processes.

What is it about the relations between states A and B that state A chooses to support a rebel group targeting state B, while the rebel group in question chooses state A from which to seek support? Disclosing the systematic international effects is possible only after controlling for foreseeable factors, such as geographical proximity, and by means of an overarching study that includes a variety of rebel groups—without excluding some of them on the basis of their objectives and identity.

In this respect, external state support is treated as a dependent variable, shaped by interstate relations, rather than an independent variable influencing interstate relations, though the latter circumstance is not denied.[18] The nature of interstate relations determines, to a great extent, the motives of both states and rebel groups in aligning with each other. It is then required to identify the parameters that shape the patterns of interactions between states. In addition to distinguishing between two selection processes, the theoretical framework builds on the motives states and rebels are driven by in cooperating with each other.

The main paradigms of international relations suggest states cooperate with each other out of several motives. Realism stipulates that states ally with each other on the basis of common interests, that is, against rising powers (the logic of balance of power) and/or common threats (the logic of balance of threat). Liberalism asserts that states cooperate with each other on the basis of specific ideational affinities, such as domestic regime type, commonly shared values, norms, and worldview, despite not denying the role of common interests in uniting states. The conventional theories of International Relations identify two major motives behind the behavior of states: material/strategic and ideational interests. In forming alliances with their equals, states are driven both by material/strategic and ideational motives. The empirical analyses in the coming chapters reveal that rebel groups select certain states as support bases due to their ideational affinity with them rather than shared material interests.

This book offers the first book-length treatment of external support of rebel groups building on these motives. I develop a selection framework that distinguishes between state selection and rebel selection processes. The States' Selection Model (SSM) develops hypotheses about the conditions under which supporting rebels is a viable option from the perspective of states, while the Rebels' Selection Model (RSM) develops hypotheses about the conditions under which rebels seek resources within some countries. Each process ends with the emergence of external support for rebels, in the form of intentional and de facto support, respectively.

The SSM argues that the calculus on whether to support a rebel group by states or, more specifically, leaders is based on three factors: whether the rebel group's target is an external adversary, whether they have to deal with domestic problems, and whether they share common ideational ties with the rebel group. The RSM argues that rebels are motivated by their need for resources and autonomy, both of which are vital for their survival and continued operations against their targets. Therefore, they perceive the adversaries of their targets and/or ideationally contiguous states as potential supporters. Rebels' calculus for seeking safe havens within the borders of other states is driven by the perceived ability of those states to deal with possible retaliation from target states. Hence, weak states are not ideal for rebels' maintenance of their operations, due to the risk of failure in front of possible retaliation from rebels' targets. This contrasts with the commonly held view in the post–Cold War period with respect to the role of weak states in the rise of terrorism and insurgency.

The literature on third–party intervention in civil wars offers valuable insights about why states choose to intervene in certain internal conflicts, and on whose side—rebel groups or the target governments—but its focus remains mostly on overt military intervention. Recent efforts have been made to include other types of intervention, such as diplomatic and economic intervention. Developing a new theoretical framework, Regan and Aydin (2006) offer some insights into the influence of various other forms of intervention on conflict outcome. An earlier work by Cunningham (2010) also examines the role of biased mediators in internal conflict—whether they keep to the side of a government or a rebel group. The academic debate, thus, has shifted from intervening in a conflict by resorting to military force, to other forms, such as economic and diplomatic intervention (Regan et al. 2009).

The problem with this recent expansion of the literature, though, is that there is a theoretical and empirical mismatch when it comes to applying their findings to explain state-rebel group interactions in the context of covert support. Theoretically, intervention is an overt, rather than covert, act. In other words, when a state decides to intervene in an ongoing internal conflict, it does not attempt to hide its act. On the other hand, when states choose to support rebel groups, they frequently go undercover in doing so. Therefore, empirically, the data used for the analysis of what makes states intervene in ongoing internal conflicts were collected, initially, for a different purpose. Even if an outside state intervenes in a conflict on the side of a rebel group, it is not equivalent to what covert support implies, which often goes unnoticed in the international arena and is the subject matter of the current book.

1.5 Existing Research and the Book's Contribution

Debates over the future direction of international politics have evolved around two main themes, represented by two major camps. One is that international politics is characterized by embedded interactions between states and nonstate actors, including violent and nonviolent actors. This view holds that the international system progresses toward more peaceful relations. The second camp positions states as the major actors in international politics and asserts that international politics is characterized by competition between equally sovereign territorial units. This view suggests that the nature of security concerns, such as conflict over territory and resources, has not changed much and will continue to remain central in international politics.

This book builds a theoretical bridge between the two approaches by treating nonstate actors as potential partners of states. Conventionally, students of international relations investigate the patterns of alliances and alignments between states, as they cooperate with each other to achieve common benefits or against common threats. The same logic can be applied to explain external support for rebel groups. Similar to alliances, both sides gain some good when exchanging such support. Despite the fact that patron-client networks emerge in an asymmetric and hierarchical environment—that is, states do not perceive rebels as their equals, and there is power asymmetry between states and rebels—these issues are also common in interstate alliances.

States may choose to compensate for their lack of state allies with rebels. In choosing other states as allies, states might act to get on the bandwagon or achieve a balance, depending on the international power distribution. In addition, the repertoire of empirical researchers delving into how states display an act of animosity against another state has to move beyond direct use of force. States fight each other directly, yet they also employ indirect use of force that can be characterized as an act of animosity. Supporting a rebel group fighting another state is an act of animosity and requires as much analysis as the decision about whether to use force against a state.

The selection theory of state-rebel group relations presented here argues that state support of rebels is driven by three main motives: strategic interest, ideational affinity, and domestic incentives. Each of these is derived from three main schools of thought in the study of international politics: realism, constructivism, and liberalism.[19]

Material interest refers to the presence of a foreign policy benefit by a state that supports a rebel group against another state. It could be related, but not limited, to the presence of a rivalry or conflict history between the rebel group's target and supporter. Ideational affinity refers to the presence of ethnic, religious, and ideological ties between a rebel group and its supporter as well as between a rebel group's target and supporter. In comparison to the attention given to geographical contiguity, the studies of interstate conflict and cooperation has given surprisingly little attention to ideational contiguity between states. Finally, *domestic incentive* refers to domestic political instability, which constrains extraction and mobilization of human and material resources required to deal with external threats through conventional means.

The concept of material/strategic interest is derived from the realist paradigm, which denotes foreign policy as a product of changes in the external environment of states (Waltz 1959, 1979; Morgenthau 1963).[20] While "strategy" refers to a broader spectrum of policies formulated by states in dealing with their external environment, it is used in a very restricted sense in this book. States make foreign policy choices in consideration of the relative capabilities and motives of their rivals. They are conventionally assumed to balance against their adversaries by forming alliances with other states (Waltz 1979; Walt 1987, 1985)[21] or mobilize internally to build military power in an attempt to catch up with their adversaries (Jervis 1989; Art 2000). The insight of realism related to the support of some rebel groups by states is that states ally with rebels to balance against their adversaries (Saideman 2002).[22] Similarly, a rebel group selects a state that is an adversary of its target.

Ideational affinity is derived from the teachings of both liberalism and constructivism, concerning the influence of norms, identity, and culture on foreign policy. Constructivism assumes a mutual construction of the agent and structure (Kubalkova et al. 1998; Hopf 2002; Klotz and Lynch 2007; Lebow 2008, 2010). The agent refers to the states in the international arena, and the structure refers to the international system in general. Ideational identity shapes the perceptions of states with respect to others' motives and interests (Wendt 1992; Jepperson et al. 1996; Checkel 1998). Foreign policy outcomes are a function of a state's perception of its international environment, which is shaped by its ideational characteristics. Based on this line of argument, one would expect that states support rebels with whom they share a common ideational identity, such as ethnic kinship, religious affinity, worldview, and/or belief system. By the same token, a rebel group selects a state with which it shares similar ideas and worldviews. Furthermore, the ideational contiguity between a rebel group's target and supporter is also significant. For instance, states might avoid supporting rebels against ideationally contiguous states. The well-known democratic peace argument rests on the idea that common domestic political norms and institutions drive states to see benefit in a common future characterized by cooperation rather than conflict (Maoz and Russett 1993).

The insights built on the domestic incentives related issues mostly imply that the division between domestic and international political spheres are ambiguous (Bueno de Mesquita 2002).[23] Domestic political factors determine international outcomes to a great extent. Within the context of state support for rebels, considering domestic incentives helps to refine the systematic explanations about the relations between states and rebel groups. Since not all states support rebels that target their adversaries, we need to further specify the conditions under which they do. A domestic incentive for allying with a rebel group emerges when states face constraints in extracting and mobilizing domestic resources to deal with their adversaries abroad. A domestic incentive for a rebel group to select a particular state emerges when a state's domestic capacity diminishes to an extent that it is no longer able to protect its borders from penetration by rebels who seek safe havens, arms, funds, recruitment, and other resources.

The existing research on the external support of rebels has relied on one of these explanations, while ignoring the others (Saideman 2001, 2002; Bapat 2007; Braithwaite and Li 2007; Salehyan 2007, 2010). Bapat's work (2007) considers strategic interaction between a supporter and a target, but it does not take into account ideational affinity and domestic factors. Saideman (2001, 2002) focuses on ethnic minorities, arguing that ethnic ties matter the most in explaining a state's support of ethnic rebel groups within a neighboring country, without making a reference to the nature of relations between a target and a supporter. Braithwaite and Li (2007) and Piazza (2007) argue that weak states are most likely to serve as safe havens for terrorists. Especially in the post–Cold War period, weak states, and their selection by rebels as safe havens, have been at the center of research on state sponsorship of terrorism (Lesser et al. 1999; Campbell and Floumoy 2001; Rotberg 2003; Piazza 2007). Focusing on a single factor leads to empirical findings that apply only to the cases they study. A full and systematic analysis of the conditions under which states and rebels choose each other as partners requires an examination of state support in the context of the network of interactions within a triad of a rebel group, its target state, and its supporter state.

State support for rebels emerges as a result of a selection process by both states and rebels. Rebel groups have as much potential to form alliances with states as states do. Frequently, rebel groups emulate states through declaration of a name and a leader. Although states and rebels do not sign written agreements to establish a partnership, some do resemble interstate alliances, such as Hezbollah and Iran, Syria and PIJ, and the National Union for the Total Independence of Angola (UNITA) and Zaire. Similar to interstate alliances, the alliances between states and rebels do not last forever. The empirical analysis presents parallels between interstate alliances and alliances between states and rebels in terms of the factors driving them.

State support is also perceived to be endogenous to interstate relations. It shapes international politics as much as it is shaped by it. Hence, state support should be examined in a triadic context, taking into consideration the interactions among rebels, their targets, and their supporters. Interactions among the three actors are displayed in Figure 1.1. In a triad, the conflict history and ideational contiguity between a rebel group's target and an outside state (labeled as supporter in the figure) are expected to influence the rebel group's calculation about whether the outside state is likely to provide resources for its operations against the target. By the same token, the degree to which an outside state shares ideational ties with a group, and both conflict history and ideational ties with the group's target, are shown to influence the outside states's decision to support a given rebel group.

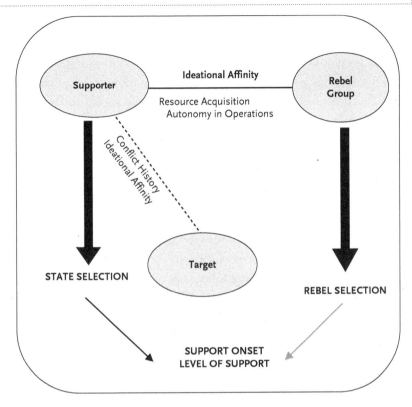

FIGURE I.I A Selection Model of State-Rebel Group Relations

Work on state support has so far relied on dyadic analysis, which refers to interactions between rebels and their supporters or between rebels and their targets without taking into consideration the interactions between target and supporter states (Saideman 2001, 2002; Bapat 2006, 2007; Salehyan 2007; Salehyan et al. 2011).[24] This is especially problematic for cases in which more than one rebel group targets the same state, or an outside state ends up supporting more than one rebel group fighting against the same state. Focusing either on the interactions between a supporter and a rebel group or a target state and a rebel group misses the big picture, which can be completed only by looking at the interactions between target and supporter states.

The approach of the current project further differs from previous work by incorporating ideational factors and rebels' characteristics.[25] The conflict history and ideational ties between a supporter and a target, and between a supporter and a rebel group, all play a role in determining support onset and support level. States that share a conflict history with a rebel group's target, and/or share ideational ties with a rebel group, are potential supporters, from the perspective of rebels. Rebels that target a state's adversaries, and/or are ideationally contiguous, are potential partners, from the perspective of states.

1.6 Alternative Explanations

Three other possible explanations can be cited for the formation of state-rebel group alliances. First is that both states' and rebels' selection is a matter of opportunity. Therefore, the process of state-rebel group alliance formation is associated with stochastic and random effects, rather than deliberate choices by states and rebels. If the Chechen separatists had been active during the Cold War period, the United States and other Western nations would probably have supported them. However, counterfactual analysis is rather difficult in our field, and we could hardly know if a state would support a rebel group against an external adversary, the group's target, regardless of the other considerations, such as ideational ties and the ability to deal with possible retaliation from the rebel group's target. All we can tell from the empirical analysis is that not every incidence of state support is directed toward adversaries; not all rebels who target adversaries of a state are selected by the state as a partner. This makes sense if we think about real world examples, such as Iran and Hezbollah. Despite the fact that Hamas, PIJ, and the Popular Front for the Liberation of Palestine (PFLP) all target Israel, Iran provided rather extensive support to Hezbollah, which is an ideationally contiguous group, more so than any other militant Palestinian group.

Second, state support is concentrated in regions plagued with high levels of nonstate violence. The research on the geography of nonstate violence is still evolving (Li and Schaub 2004; Enders and Sandler 2006; Braithwaite and Li 2007; Stohl 2007), and further research might pursue this question specifically. The empirical evidence collected under the Dangerous Companions Project (DCP), which is the basis of this book's empirical analysis, does not find any region that especially stands out in terms of the number of states which support rebel groups or from which rebel groups manage to acquire resources, except those in sub-Saharan Africa. Though sub-Saharan Africa has the highest number of rebel groups (36 percent) and supporter states (33 percent), the proportion of support provided to these groups by sub-Saharan African states is approximately 15 percent. In other words, it does not seem to correlate that regions plagued by nonstate violence also host the most dedicated state supporters.

A third explanation is that state support for rebels is driven by ethnic groups that often share ties with their kin across the borders of neighboring states. Empirical findings reveal that it is not only ethnic ties that matter, but also religious and ideological ones. The empirical results in Chapters 4 and 5 explain the conditions under which ideational ties matter, going beyond transnational ethnic ties as the main driver behind state support of rebels. I find many examples in which states support ideationally noncontiguous rebels against their adversaries: Greece's support of the PKK, Libya's support of the (IRA), and support of various Afghani groups by the

United States and several western European states during the Cold War period. Yet I also find that, in about 40 percent of the total state years of support, states supported ideationally contiguous rebel groups despite the fact that rebels were not fighting against their adversaries. Overall, ideational affinity between rebels and supporters drive support for almost 48% of the total support years.

These alternative explanations do not discount the value of the explanation proposed by the theoretical framework in this book. Rather, the purpose is to capture the complexity of state-rebel group interactions. Whether supporters are geographically concentrated or simply utilize random opportunities, there is still a nonrandom component that needs to be addressed by a systematic analysis of what makes the modern international environment so conducive to the recent rise and endurance of nonstate armed groups.

1.7 Methodology

The theoretical framework proposed here requires a large-N dataset, which is essential to test the hypothetical propositions. The widely held post–Cold War view that nonstate violence is a problem aggravated by ungoverned territories or weak states is mostly an artifact of the post–1990 developments with respect to al-Qaeda and Afghanistan. A large-N analysis provides a test of this view within a broader context of rebel groups. I collected new data on covert state support for rebel groups, which have been active in the post-1945 period, to test for the empirical implications outlined in this book. The decision to collect data has been prompted by three factors:

1. There are no data on the characteristics of rebels that would allow me to test for the influence of ideational factors, that is, ethnic and religious ties and political and ideological views.
2. There are no data on covert state support that cover the entire post-1945 period.[26]
3. There are no data that clarify whether a state creates deliberate channels to support a rebel group or a rebel group obtains de facto support from a country without any sponsorship of that country's government or state. Without additional data collection and coding, it is not possible to capture the two different selection processes proposed here.

I collected data on state supporters, type and period of support, and the objectives and ideational characteristics of 455 Nonstate Armed Groups (NAGs) that have been active in the post-1945 period (NAGs dataset).[27] Using thousands of news reports, and secondary sources,[28] I identified approximately 352 SSM cases, where states purposefully cooperated with rebels, and 342 RSM cases, where rebels selected countries within which to run their activities, without the governments of these countries creating channels to abet them.

Findings from the empirical analysis of the NAGs dataset are complemented by two detailed case study analyses. Chapter 4 presents an analysis of all the militant groups targeting Israel since its foundation in 1948, and their interactions with outside states. Chapter 5 presents an analysis of all rebel groups targeting Chad since it achieved independence from France in 1960, and their de facto supporters. The goal is to illustrate the mechanisms through which intentional and de facto support emerge.

1.8 Outline of the Book

Subsequent chapters introduce the theoretical framework, then present and test the hypotheses on the basis of two selection models. In general, I argue that states might be driven by strategic and/or ideational motives in supporting rebels. Yet their calculus is mostly a function of domestic troubles that leaders face and their expectations about dealing with possible retaliation from a rebel group's target. When states face internal and external threats simultaneously, they are more likely to resort to rebel groups against their external adversaries. On the other hand, weak states are not necessarily the most preferred sources of support by rebels for two reasons: they do not have the ability to deal with a possible retaliation, and they lack the infrastructure and resources required for maintaining persistent operations against their targets.

In chapter 2, I present a selection theory of support onset and support level. I argue that the formation of state-rebel group alliances is not random; rather, it is based on rational calculations on the part of both states and rebels. I develop a theoretical model that examines state support within the context of interactions among three actors: rebels, targets, and supporters. From this model, I derive hypotheses about the conditions that make states most likely to support certain rebels, and the factors that drive rebels to seek resources within certain countries.

Chapter 3 lays out the research design, including selection of cases, data collection and coding procedures, and operationalization of the key variables. In addition, it presents the findings with respect to the main trends in state-rebel group interactions, building on the empirical research from the DCP and the NAGs dataset.

Chapter 4 briefly presents the hypotheses from the SSM laid out in chapter 2 in light of a case study of militant groups fighting against Israel. It further presents findings from a series of quantitative multivariate analyses using the new data. My primary goal in this chapter is to test for the direct and interactive effects of conflict history and ideational factors on the support onset and level. In addition, I investigate the effects of external and internal threats on external state support of rebels.

Chapter 5 starts with a case study of rebel groups fighting against Chad and the mechanisms through which they manage acquiring resources within the borders of other countries without any state sponsorship. It, then, poses the hypotheses for the RSM laid out in chapter 2. This chapter also tests models of specific types of support, since it is more meaningful to talk about rebels moving across the borders of an outside state, rather than to talk about the level of support. Across both models, the results suggest that a supporter's relative strength (vis-à-vis target state) and supporter-rebel group ideational affinity prevail as the two most significant predictors of de facto support.

Chapter 6 presents the main trends in the formation of state-rebel group alliances, without distinguishing between the two selection processes. Additionally, I present a summary of the theory of state-rebel group selection outlined in chapter 2 and discuss the implications of the empirical findings for the five main theoretical propositions summarized at the end of chapter 2. I conclude with the implications of the current research for policymaking and future venues of research on this topic.

2   A Selection Theory of State Support for Rebel Groups

DESPITE UNPRECEDENTED INNOVATIONS in military technology, states continue to suffer from violence generated by armed rebel groups. In the post–World War II period, 89 percent of armed conflicts have been caused by ethnic and religious insurgencies, guerrilla groups, terrorists, and revolutionary movements.[1] Militarily superior states, such as Russia, the United States, France, and Israel, have all been targeted by rebel groups seeking political and territorial concessions. Several factors contribute to the decades-long endurance and increasing lethality of armed rebel groups. In the post–Cold War period, scholarly attention has been directed toward the active role played by states that support nonstate armed groups. States provide armed rebels with sanctuaries, access to their territories, transport of arms and logistics aid, funds, and training camps, as well as military advice, arms, and troops. Despite the fact that the strategy of supporting nonstate armed groups against other states is older than the history of the nation-state, we lack a systematic analysis of the conditions under which states and rebels select one another in their pursuit of specific goals.

The theory of state-rebel group selection proposed herein argues that states are most likely to support rebels when they face simultaneous threats on the domestic and international fronts. In addition, states are expected to provide a higher level of support to rebels groups, which are fighting against their adversaries if they also have to deal with a domestically unstable environment. A state experiencing domestic turmoil and instability has limited capacity to mobilize the masses to fight against an external enemy, since such mobilization might provoke further domestic unrest. On the other hand, rebels see rival or enemy states of their targets as potential supporters since they have a higher chance of acquiring resources from the governments of these states. Those governments are also more likely to grant higher levels of autonomy to rebels in operations against the common enemy.

Bapat (2007) and Salehyan (2010) offer similar insights to explain state support of rebel groups as well as rebel groups' decision to go transnational. Similar to their findings, the NAGs dataset reveals that 65 percent of the total observations related to intentional state support occurs in the context of inter-state enmity. The theoretical framework and empirical analyses offered in this book advances our knowledge of the conditions under which states choose to support rebels against external adversaries and the factors that motivate them to provide lower or higher levels of support. In addition to interstate rivalry or enmity between targets and supporters, when it comes to granting autonomy to rebels, other factors also come into play, such as domestic incentives for supporting rebels and ideational ties with rebel groups. If rebels are affiliated with the domestic opposition in a supporter state or cause internal turmoil within the supporter, as Fatah did in Lebanon, Jordan, and Egypt, then states might hesitate to provide a high level of autonomy to such groups. Therefore, I develop and test theoretical arguments about the role that inter-state and state-rebel group ideational ties play in support onset and level.

The selection theory of support hypothesizes about state-rebel relations in a triadic context of interactions among rebels, target states, and supporter states of rebels. Only then is it possible to apply and test the teachings of liberalism and constructivism with respect to shared norms, ideas, and identities not only between supporter states and rebels groups, but also between supporter and target states. Furthermore, this framework allows testing for the inter-state factors that discourages states from supporting rebel groups against other states. The dyad-level characteristics of the relations between rebels and their target state, such as a group's size vis-à-vis its target state, and these between rebels and their supporters, such as whether they have common ethnic ties, are significant for determining whether a rebel group receives external support (Saideman 1997, 2001; Salehyan et al. 2011). Yet, an analysis going beyond dyad-level variables is required to capture the effects of the full set of interactions among rebels, their target states, and their supporter states on external state support of rebels.

If shared norms , ideas, and identities influence how states devise foreign policy, then, from the perspective of supporter states, it is not just a matter of ideational ties with rebel groups, but also those with target states, when deciding on whether or not to support rebels. The existing research so far has focused on relative strength of supporter states vis-à-vis target states and inter-state enmity to explain the effect of inter-state relations on state support of rebels (Saideman 2002; Salehyan et al. 2011; Bapat 2012; Maoz and San-Akca 2012). Yet we know that inter-state relations are characterized with friendship and cooperation as much as enmity and conflict. For example, one of the reasons why rebel groups, such as ETA, did not acquire extensive support from states adjacent to Spain, the target of the ETA, could be traced to the ideational environment within Europe.

ETA, for many years after its foundation in 1959, considered the Basque region in France a safe haven for Basque militants, mostly due to the unwillingness of the French government to take serious action against ETA militants so as not to provoke its own Basque minority (Encarnacion 2007, p. 954). In 1984 France made its first gesture with regard to Spain's fight against ETA, when the French government extradited several ETA militants who were on the Spanish government's blacklist (Linnee 1985; Morgan 1985). Finally, in May 1987 France and Spain signed an antiterrorism agreement, which marked the onset of more decisive actions against ETA's territorial presence within France. It is not surprising that cooperation between the two governments against terrorism came after the death of Spanish dictator Francis Franco in 1975 and the subsequent foundation of a democratic regime in Spain. At that time, the democratic government granted some autonomy to various minorities within Spain, including the Basque people. In other words, it would be difficult for France to justify a loose policy in handling infiltrations of a rebel group into its borders, especially a rebel group fighting a neighboring democratic state. France faced a decision: whether to prioritize its ideational affinity with the Spanish government or its ideational ties to the ETA. It seems they have chosen the former.

In developing the state-rebel selection theory, I begin with four assumptions. First, state support emerges as a result of two selection processes: state selection and rebel selection. Rebels choose their supporter states, and states choose rebels to abet. The fact that rebels select some countries to acquire resources from is referred to as de facto support. It means that a state itself, or its associated organs, does not intentionally create channels to provide safe havens, training camps, funds, arms, logistics aid, and training for a given rebel group. However, the group manages to acquire these resources within its borders by its own means and efforts. In other words, rebels manage acquiring resources from governed spaces or territories despite the absence of the sponsorship of states in these countries. Second, the emergence of state support, whether as a result of state selection or as a result of rebel selection, is endogenous to interstate relations. Specifically, the enmity or friendship ties between states serve as an explanation behind the increase or decrease of the likelihood of the support as a result of both selection processes. Third, it is a costly strategy to pursue, due to the risk of a direct confrontation with a rebel group's target. Fourth, if rebels are supported by states intentionally, it constitutes an act of animosity against the targets of rebel groups in the form of the indirect use of force.

This theory further asserts three main drivers of state support for rebels: material interest, ideational affinity, and domestic incentives. Material interest points to the presence of a history of conflict between a rebel group's supporter and target. Ideational affinity refers to the presence and configuration of ethnic, religious, and ideological ties among rebel groups, their targets, and supporters. Lastly, domestic incentives refer to domestic political instability and constraints to extraction and mobilization in supporter states. As explained in the previous chapter, each of these is derived from three main schools of thought in the study of inter-state relations: realism, constructivism, and liberalism.

When making decisions about whether to support a rebel group, states are driven by both material and ideational motives. Rebels, on the other hand, in seeking external supporter states, are primarily interested in resource acquisition and autonomy in operations against their target states. The material and ideational motives of states provide them with hints about whether to seek support from them, and the type of support to pursue. The theoretical framework offers insights for the following questions:

1. *Under which conditions are states more likely to support rebel groups, which fight against their external adversaries?*
2. *What are the systematic patterns in rebels groups' selection of some countries to acquire resources from despite that the states or governments in these countries do not create channels to intentionally abet them?*
3. *Under what circumstances do material interest, ideational motives, and domestic troubles motivate states and rebels to seek support from one another?*
4. *What is the effect of inter-state ideational ties on state support of rebels?*

Next, I present a review of the literature on the role of domestic and international factors in foreign policy, with respect to external adversaries. It has two purposes: (1) placing state support of rebels among the foreign policy instruments that states utilize strategically, and (2) specifying the conditions under which this becomes a viable option for states. The following section presents the general theoretical framework and discusses the main assumptions and hypotheses that underpin the SSM and RSM. The conclusion presents a summary of the arguments tested in chapters 4 and 5.

2.1 State Support as a Foreign Policy Instrument: Internal and External Determinants

Not all foreign policy related to a state's security is devised to deal with external issues, and, often, its nature is determined by both the external and the internal political settings within which leaders make decisions (Putnam 1988; Maoz 1990).[2] Thus, the utility of a foreign policy decision should be evaluated on two dimensions: its success in meeting domestic political objectives and its effectiveness in managing external threats. In other words, a foreign policy decision should incur minimal cost at home and maximum cost to one's external rival (Nincic 1982). Experts of international politics argue that states develop foreign policy as a result of two stimuli: threat perception and opportunity perception (Maoz 1990; Brecher 1993). A foreign policy decision is either directed toward an external actor from whom a state perceives a threat, or it is triggered by the perception of an opportunity that changes cost-benefit calculus, or both.[3] Yet threat perception needs to include the perception of domestic threats to the survival of a leader or a government. For any foreign policy to be carried out, under any sort of political system, it is critical that the leadership and/or government retain the ability to extract and mobilize human and material resources at home.

Scholarly work on foreign policy has long since surpassed the idea of the external security environment as the main driver of foreign policy behavior. Research by scholars who examine domestic influences on interstate relations, has shown that foreign policy decisions are also triggered by internal threats (Bueno de Mesquita and Lalman 1990; Maoz 1990, 1996; Bueno de Mesquita 2002). This body of literature generated two lines of argument on the influence of internal threats on foreign policy. One argument centers on the consequences of domestic instability on a state's external behavior. It claims that leaders who face threats to their survival in the domestic realm may initiate wars to create a "rally 'round the flag" effect at home (Rosecrance 1963; Wilkenfeld 1968; Levy and Vakili 1992; Maoz 1996; Walt 1996; Gelpi 1997).[4] These scholars identify two causal paths from domestic turmoil to external war: diversionary and opportunistic. The diversionary theory argues that a state experiencing domestic threat may try to channel public anger against an external adversary to acquire domestic support for the present regime; the opportunistic attack theory argues that domestic turmoil creates an opportunity to resolve longstanding problems with external enemies (Levy 1988, 1989; Starr 1994). Thus, a state experiencing domestic unrest is vulnerable to external enemies, who wait for an opportunity to attack their enemy in the pursuit of enduring problems.

The other line of argument uses the rational choice approach and emphasizes the political survival motive of leaders as the main determinant in initiating war (Bueno de Mesquita and Lalman 1990; Fearon 1994; Bueno de Mesquita and Siverson 1995; Fearon 1997; Bueno de Mesquita et al. 2003).[5] These scholars build on the assumption that the leaders of democracies have a shorter time horizon, facing periodic elections, whereas the leaders of authoritarian regimes are not subject to preset rules and regulations with respect to their policy decisions. As a result, the leaders of democracies initiate conflict early in their tenure to avoid losing elections, whereas leaders in autocracies initiate conflict later in their tenure, after they consolidate their power.

Neither the diversionary/opportunistic theory nor the political survival approach takes into consideration various challenges states face to their extraction and mobilization of domestic resources. It is commonly accepted that wars are costly and last longer than initially predicted (Fearon 1995; Wagner 2000), and that states primarily depend on domestic resources for addressing external threats (Carr 1954; Morgenthau 1963; Mintz 1989; Powell 1993; Clark 2001).[6] The diversionary use of force theory assumes that leaders already perceive some risks to their survival at home before they decide to channel domestic anger toward an external target. It is not clear, then, why engaging in a war leads to a "rally 'round the flag" effect rather than an increase in domestic grievances and opposition against extraction and mobilization of domestic resources. In addition, it is not clearly identified under what circumstances a state needs a resurgence of belligerence around nationalist sentiments, except in the works of Walt (1996) and Maoz (1996), who looked explicitly at states that went through a "revolution," characterized by a drastic regime and leadership change, or an "evolution," characterized by a lesser-scale change in the domestic political setting.

It is hard to deny that leaders consider both internal and external threats when they decide how to respond to external adversaries (Azar and Moon 1988; Simon and Starr 1996). However, the scholarly work is not clear about how leaders weigh the various threats posed by internal and external adversaries, when acting to address them. Leaders who face domestic survival risk might put their regime under further jeopardy by engaging in a prolonged conflict against a relatively strong external adversary, in contrast to the assumption of the diversionary theory.[7]

Supporting rebel groups fighting other states is a foreign policy strategy more frequently employed by states that face domestic unrest than researched by students of international politics. The demise of the Soviet Union in the beginning of the 1990s put an end to the study of interstate relations dominated by power rivalry among superpowers. The rise of nonstate violence in the post–Cold War period has finally directed scholarly attention toward the interactions between states and rebel groups and the transnational effects of these interactions. The limited amount of research on state support of rebel groups also emerged in this period.

One strand of research centered on counterinsurgency and counterterrorism by addressing how to deal with threats posed by nonstate armed groups, in general

(Brophy-Baermann and Conybeare 1994; Posen 2001; Bueno de Mesquita 2005; Byman 2005a; Bapat 2006). Another line of research emerged, mostly in the field of Comparative Politics, which emphasized the international dimension of nonstate violence (Zartman 1995; Brown 1996; Jackson 1996; Reno 1999; Mackinlay 2000; Rothchild 2002; Piazza 2007). These scholars argue that violence generated by rebel groups often spills over into neighboring states—and the international environment as a whole—thus undermining global security and stability.

A relevant body of work examines outside state support for rebels as a form of external intervention in internal conflicts. Regan (1996, 1998, 2000, 2002) and Balch-Lindsay and Enterline (2000) examined both the factors driving outside states to intervene on the rebel or government side of an internal conflict, and the effect of external intervention on internal conflict duration and outcome. A newly evolving body of research addresses the question of state support for rebel groups more directly. It examines the conditions under which states support rebels, as well as the implications of state support for international stability (Byman et al. 2001; Byman 2005b; Gleditsch et al. 2008; Salehyan 2009, 2010).

Some scholars examine how to stop host states from serving as safe havens to these groups (Collins 2004; Schweitzer 2004; Atzili & Pearlman 2012). Others examine how state support influences the onset and escalation of international conflict (Salehyan and Gleditsch 2006; Salehyan 2008a, 2008b; Gleditsch et al. 2008; Schultz 2010). In the context of state support for rebel groups, Salehyan (2007), Cunningham et al. (2009b), and Cunningham (2010) examine how civil wars are influenced when rebels find external safe havens. Although these works have been pioneering new lines of research in the discipline, and shifting scholarly attention to external support for rebels, to achieve more nuanced explanation of state support for rebel groups, we need further focus on state support *specifically*, developing testable hypotheses and engaging in systematic data collection, moving beyond the post–Cold War period.

Despite increased scholarly attention, we have yet to catch up in developing an overall theoretical framework and collecting the required data to test myriad empirical implications about the emergence of state support for rebel groups. Such a theory and data are also necessary to explore whether there are distinct patterns in state and rebel group interactions across Cold War and post–Cold War periods, as claimed by some scholars, but not empirically tested due to the absence of large-N datasets on covert support of rebel groups (Hartzell et al. 2001; Kalyvas and Balcells 2010).[8] Invaluable recent work (Bapat 2007, 2012; San-Akca 2009; Salehyan et al. 2011; Maoz and San-Akca 2012) has examined why and how external state support emerges by focusing on interstate rivalries and the interstate power balance. Specifically, Bapat (2007) examines the conditions under which terrorists seek external sanctuaries, thus attributing an active role to terrorists themselves, which is similar to the approach I adopt in this book, but applied to rebel groups in general.

This book builds on this recent work in the following ways:

- it expands beyond material interests by developing and empirically testing a theory of support that takes ideational motives of states and rebels into consideration,
- it broadens the defined types of external state support, beyond safe havens or external sanctuaries, and
- it acknowledges the extensive scope of methods rebels use in finding outside resources by incorporating cases in which not states, but rebels, actively seek and acquire support from certain countries in an effort to systematically evaluate the patterns through which rebel groups diversify their resource bases.

This last point is important, since we have increasingly come to live in an interdependent world, where individuals can travel and live freely within the borders of any country they choose to do so. The recent problem of foreign fighters joining ISIS from the European states, such as Belgium, France, and the United Kingdom is mostly a result of this interdependence, which allows individuals to benefit from the free environment in European democracies.

2.2 A Selection Theory of State-Rebel Group Cooperation

I argue that a state spots an opportunity in the rise of a rebel group targeting its adversary, especially if the state is experiencing domestic unrest. Domestically troubled states can allocate more of their limited resources to dealing with domestic troubles by using rebels as proxies against their external adversaries. This was the case of the newly established Ba'ath regime in Syria and the Free Officers regime in Egypt, when they provided support to several militant Palestinian organizations against Israel during the 1950s and 1960s.

A domestically troubled state needs to extract and mobilize resources at home to address domestic threats. Regardless of its political system; a state has to rely on its domestic populace to extract and mobilize resources against internal and external threats. If stretched between enemies on both domestic and international fronts, a rebel group fighting against the external enemy turns out to be a convenient partner. By reducing dependence on domestic populace, these proxies prevent a state from provoking further internal unrest. Facing constraints to extraction and mobilization of domestic resources, which could be allocated for direct use of force against the Saddam regime in Iraq, Mohammad Reza Shah's regime in Iran supported Kurdish rebels within Iraq throughout the 1960s and first half of the 1970s.

By the same token, a rebel group perceives the adversaries of its target state as potential supporters. Various militant Palestinian groups elicited and secured support from Egypt and Syria continuously. However, not every state supports every rebel group that targets its external adversaries, and not every rebel group will necessarily choose the adversary of its target as a supporter. Therefore, I argue that material interest, ideational factors, and domestic incentives all have their own separate, but intertwined path, leading to state-rebel cooperation.

The following sections divide the formation of state-rebel group cooperation into the two selection processes and specify the variables and hypotheses related to material, ideational, and domestic determinants of state-rebel group cooperation. The purpose of the state-rebel selection theory is not to develop competing hypotheses of the material, domestic, and ideational determinants of state-rebel group alliances. Rather, it aims to explore where and how these three types of incentives converge—and diverge—to result in intentional or de facto state support.

2.2.1 STATES' SELECTION MODEL

The calculation of states as to whether to provide support to a rebel group is based on whether the rebel group targets an adversary (strategic or material interest), whether it is an ideationally contiguous group (ideational motive), and whether leaders and/or government face risk to survival at home (domestic incentive), leaving them vulnerable to an external adversary.

Realism sees foreign policy as a product of changes in the external environment of states (Waltz 1959, 1979; Morgenthau 1963). States or leaders choose from available foreign policy options by considering the relative capabilities and motives of their rivals. A derivation from realism is the idea that states support rebel groups to balance against their adversaries, when they are unable or unwilling to achieve parity through conventional means; that is to say, through external and internal balancing. External balancing means that a state founds an alliance with another state against a common threat, whereas internal balancing means that a state turns to its domestic populace to extract and mobilize resources in dealing with this threat. Thus, strategic cooperation occurs when a state and a rebel group ally with each other against a common adversary. This is in line with the theory of balancing, which argues that states are more likely to form alliances with the enemies of their enemies.

An ideational cooperation occurs as a result of shared ethnic and religious ties, worldview, and belief system between a state and a rebel group. Constructivist scholars argue that these ideational characteristics influence states' perceptions of others' motives and interests (Wendt 1992; Jepperson et al. 1996; Checkel 1998). Based on this line of argument, one expects states to support rebels with whom they have common ideational ties, such as ethnic kinship, religious affinity, worldview, and/or belief system. For ideational factors to prove significant for state-rebel relations, they need to drive cooperation in the absence of strategic or material concerns.

In light of the discussion so far, I begin with two basic hypotheses:

H_1: A state is more likely to support a rebel group that targets an adversary, rather than a group that targets a non-adversary. The level of support also tends to be higher if a rebel group targets its adversary.

H_2: A state is more likely to support an ideationally contiguous rebel group than a rebel group with which it does not share any ideational ties. And, the level of support tends to be higher for these groups.

Strategic Cooperation

A state's decision to initiate an overt confrontation against an external adversary depends on its domestic extraction and mobilization capacity and its relative strength vis-à-vis the adversary. Externally, the relative capacity of a state determines its expectation of victory in a potential conflict(Morrow 1985, 1989). Internally, by channelling anger against an external target, a leader might improve his or her domestic support (the "rally 'round the flag effect") (Levy 1988, 1989; Morgan and Bickers 1992; Maoz 1996). The diversionary theory assumes scapegoating an external target automatically translates into full mobilization of domestic resources, yet the circumstances that create the need for such a rally might also turn into an impediment to achieving such full-scale domestic mobilization. As mentioned earlier, majority of the intentional support occurs within the context of inter-state enmity. In this section, I try to refine the conditions under which states are most likely to support rebels against their external adversaries.

Extraction and mobilization potential is a function of both real human and material resources a state can extract from its domestic population, combined with the degree of domestic opposition the leadership faces (Buzan 1983; Mastanduno et al. 1989; Jackman 1993; Wendt and Barnett 1993; Simon and Starr 1996). The degree of domestic opposition determines how much a leader might extract from its domestic population without risking his own (or his government's) survival. Figure 2.1 presents scenarios of different foreign policy outcomes associated with various levels of domestic and external threat a state might face. Testing all four

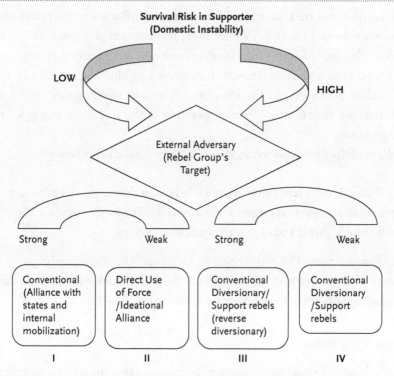

FIGURE 2.1 Interaction between Domestic Instability and External Threat

scenarios presented in the figure is beyond the scope of this book. However, it serves to extrapolate and demonstrate the thesis that supporting rebels is a likely course of action pursued by states dealing with various levels and combinations of internal and external threats.[9]

I start the discussion of the four scenarios and the conditions under which supporting rebels is a viable option. If a target retaliates or pursues the group within the borders of the state where it enjoys safe havens, this might lead to a direct confrontation between supporter and target states (Gleditsch and Beardsley 2004; Gleditsch 2007; Gleditsch et al. 2008; Saideman 2001; Salehyan 2008a, 2008b). Such cases are not scarce. Lebanon and Israel, Thailand and Myanmar, and Turkey and Iran all skirmished with each other in pursuit of rebels in the others' territories. Considering these risks, supporting rebels is not necessarily trouble-free for states in every circumstance. Therefore, it is the purpose of the theoretical framework to determine the conditions that make supporting rebels a viable option. To further complicate matters, none of the alternatives is mutually exclusive; they might co-exist. Here, I am interested only in those scenarios in which leaders and/or states make the decision to support a rebel group—as opposed to other policies they may pursue against their adversaries.

In the first scenario, the risk to survival is low domestically, while a state faces a strong external enemy. Whether an external adversary (the target of rebel group) is strong or weak is a function of its relative capacity vis-à-vis a supporter state. Conventional means of dealing with an adversary are viable options in this scenario. Alliance formation is traditionally perceived as a balancing behavior motivated by the strategic incentives that politicians face (Gulick 1955; Morgenthau 1959; Waltz 1979; Walt 1985; Mearsheimer 1994; Schweller 1994; Smith 1995; Reiter 1996). In facing a relatively strong external adversary, a state's support of a rebel group involves a risk of retaliation, whereas forming an alliance with other states might help deter the same external adversary. In this scenario, we do not expect a state to support an ideationally contiguous rebel group either, since the risk of retaliation is high.

H_{1a}: The likelihood of a state's support for a rebel group increases as the relative strength of the external adversary (the rebel group's target) decreases.

In the second scenario, the domestic threat to survival is low and the external adversary (the rebel group's target) is weak. This scenario demonstrates the idea that initiators win wars most of the time (Maoz 1983). If an external adversary is weak, then confronting it conventionally involves a high likelihood of achieving the desired outcome. However, this scenario provides an ideal situation, where a state decides to support a rebel group due to its ideational characteristics. Since the external adversary is weak, the expectation of retaliation is low, so support would be provided to an ideationally contiguous rebel group that targets one's adversary. The elaboration of the hypotheses related to this scenario is postponed to the following section.

The third and fourth scenarios involve situations in which leaders have to deal with internal and external threats simultaneously. Supporting a rebel group is a feasible option in both scenarios. In the third scenario, supporting a rebel group might lead to a reverse diversionary effect (Nincic 2005),[10] helping the state avoid being labeled the initiator, but still garnering domestic support through a rally 'round the flag effect.

In the fourth scenario, supporting rebels is a viable option since the external adversary is not expected to retaliate and there are domestic troubles confronting a supporter state. In this case, the leaders might delegate their external wars to rebels.[11] Doing so helps them minimize demands from their domestic population to deal with the external adversary (Art 2000; Jervis 1989). It is also possible for a state to engage in a diversionary attack, since the adversary is relatively weak and an easy victory might be achieved. Still, supporting a rebel group against an adversary, that is indirect use of force, would help a state to further undermine its rival's power. A state dealing with domestic disturbances cannot divert all of its resources toward external adversaries.

H_{1b}: The likelihood of supporting a rebel group against an adversary increases if leaders have to deal with internal and external threats simultaneously.

Facing a relatively strong adversary, a state might choose to ally with other states per the logic of balance of power and/or threat (Waltz 1979; Walt 1985). Therefore, one can expect that when states lack such conventional state allies, they are in relatively higher need of proxies, and so more likely to delegate their wars to rebel groups.

H_{1c}: States are more likely to support rebels against their external adversaries if they do not have conventional state allies to fight alongside with them. In the event of an attack from their adversary rebels serve as substitutes for regular state allies.

Ideational Cooperation

Some states support rebels that do not necessarily target their adversaries. Indeed, the NAGs dataset reveals that in 35 percent of total cases of intentional support, states provide support to ideationally contiguous rebel groups, which do not necessarily fight against their adversaries. Ideational identity of a state consists of ethnic, religious, and ideological attributes of its society and political regime.[12] This builds on the constructivist and liberal schools of International Relations. Constructivist scholars argue that norms, beliefs, and ideas, which are the components of ideational identity, have as much influence on the foreign policy behavior of states as strategic or material interest, although they do not agree on how and why norms, beliefs, and ideas matter (Goldstein and Keohane 1993; Katzenstein 1996; Checkel 1998). The debate over material interests versus ideational identity, and how each defines the other, has long occupied scholars.[13] My purpose in this section is to discuss how different components of ideational identity help define states' interests in domestic and international affairs,[14] and under what circumstances ideational motives drive a state to support a rebel group, even when the target of the rebel group is not a rival or an external adversary.

Ideational identity is also examined as a variable in research on the alliance patterns among states. Scholarly work on the subject has produced mixed evidence on ideational identity in alliance formation among states. In his study of alliances in the Middle East, Barnett (1996) argues that the construction of a common "Arab national identity" helps to define common threats and explain alliance patterns. Stephen Walt's (1987) balance of threat theory argues that ideology, a component of ideational identity, is a less powerful motive for alliance formation among states than threat perception.[15] In this book, ideational identity is considered to represent more than the ideological tendency of a government or state. The identity of a state encompasses the broader ideational characteristics of its society, such as ethnolinguistic characteristics and religious beliefs as well as the political ideology its government adheres to.

Ideational affinity with both a rebel group and the rebel group's target influences the likelihood of support by a state. There are two ways through which ideational affinity with a rebel group drives state support. One is the convergence point, when strategic interest and ideational affinity are both present. The presence of a strategic interest (i.e., target is an adversary) determines the decision to start supporting a rebel group in the first place, while ideational affinity guides a state's decision to support a particular rebel group out of many that fight against its adversary. As demonstrated in the first scenario in Figure 2.1, when a rebel group's target is a weak external adversary, it creates further incentive for the state to support an ideationally contiguous group.

H_{2a}: The likelihood of a state's support for an ideationally contiguous rebel group increases if it is relatively strong vis-à-vis the rebel group's target.

The other likely, and similar, scenario is at the divergence point, wherein ideational affinity is present, but strategic interest is not. Although the target is not an adversary, the presence of ideational affinity puts an obligation on a state to support a rebel group. This is in line with the findings of scholarly work on transnational ethnic ties and their influence on international intervention in ethnic conflict (Saideman 2001, 2002).

H_{2b}: Common ideational ties between a state and a rebel group increase the likelihood of support, even if the rebel group's target is not an adversary.

Figure 2.2 demonstrates the convergence and divergence points between strategic interest and ideational affinity, and the pattern of alliances between state and rebel groups. Ideational identity and strategic interest are not mutually exclusive; both may drive support simultaneously. This is illustrated by the convergence point in Figure 2.2. Iran's support of Hezbollah in southern Lebanon is a good example of an ideational alliance. Iran has been in a protracted rivalry with Israel since the 1979 Iranian Revolution, which was driven by a religious doctrine decidedly unfriendly to the idea of an independent Jewish state. Therefore, Iran provides support to an ideationally contiguous rebel group, against the common enemy (of Iran

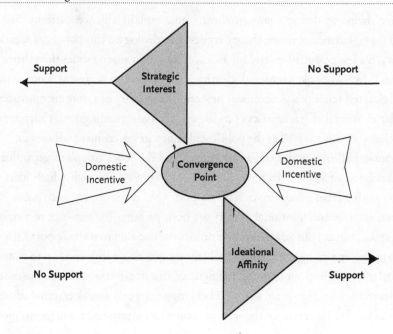

FIGURE 2.2 Convergence and Divergence of Strategic Interest and Ideational Affinity

and Hezbollah). When it comes to other militant Palestinian groups, such as Fatah, PFLP, and PIJ, affiliated with the Sunni sect of Islam, not the Shi'a (as is Hezbollah), Iran's support has historically remained limited by comparison.

Domestic incentives are significant in both strategic alliances and ideational alliances between states and rebel groups. In the former, the presence of domestic opposition and risk to survival reduces a state's ability to engage in overt confrontation with an adversary. In the latter, the ideational affinity with the members of the elite, or some segments of society, might lead a state to support a rebel group to avoid alienating members of some segments of society). India provided safe havens, training, and arms to various Tamil separatists in Sri Lanka, including the LTTE, to meet the demands of the Tamil minority living within its own borders (Crenshaw 2001).

H₃: The level of support increases if a state has ideational ties with a rebel group that targets its adversary (interaction effect of material and ideational motives).

This expectation is also in line with the findings of Maoz et al. (2007) with respect to the disproportional influence of indirect relations on international outcomes. They found that the "enemy of my enemy" assumption of realism is more valid among states that are jointly democratic or are joint members of an intergovernmental organization (IGO). In other words, states are more likely to form alliances with the enemies of their enemies if they also share ideational ties with them.

Furthermore, ideational ties between the target and the supporter of a rebel group matters as much as these between the rebel group and its supporter. Several studies identified state support of terrorism as an ideologically motivated phenomenon during the Cold War period and attributed the emergence of international terrorism to the ideological divide between the United States and the Soviet Union (Cline and Alexander 1984; Crenshaw 1990; Kegley 1990). Both states supported insurgencies in various parts of the world to expand their sphere of influence, despite the fact they did not perceive a threat from the targets of these insurgents.

While ideational affinity between a rebel group and its supporter increases the likelihood of support, one expects to see a negative influence of ideational ties between supporters and targets on support for rebels. Huntington's clash of civilizations thesis holds culture as the main explanation of inter-state conflict (Huntington 1993, 1996). Despite its fame, the clash of civilizations thesis has been criticized extensively due to its shallow categorization of civilization groups in the world (Russett et al. 2000; Henderson 1997; Huntington 1993, 1996). Going beyond categorizing countries into broad civilization groups, the analyses in this book test the role of a diverse set of shared ideational ties in encouraging or discouraging state support of a rebel group, within a triad where the target and supporter shares ideational ties.

H_4: The likelihood of support decreases if a rebel group's supporter and target are ideationally contiguous states. In addition, the level of support also declines if two states share ideational ties.

Four different scenarios are possible, based on different combinations of supporter-rebel and target-supporter ideational ties. In the first scenario, the supporter has ideational affinity only with the rebel group (hypothesis 2). In the second scenario, the supporter shares ties only with the target (hypothesis 4). In the third scenario, the supporter has ties to both a rebel group and its target. In this case, if the target is an external adversary, a state is not expected to care much about its ideational ties to the target (hypothesis 2). If it is not an adversary, though, the decision to support the rebel group depends on the level of domestic pressures that leaders have toward providing support. In this scenario, states provide support to their ethnic or religious kin. In other words, sharing common ties with the target state of a rebel group does not have influence on the likelihood of support, if a state also shares ties with the rebel group.

H_{4a}: When having common ties with both rebels and targets, supporters tend to value their ties with target states more than the ones with rebels (interstate ideational affinity).

2.2.2 REBEL GROUP SELECTION MODEL

The calculus of rebels in selecting their supporters is based on their need for two things: autonomy and resources. Rebels need autonomy in their operations against their targets. Therefore, one of the most significant forms of external support is acquiring safe havens in another state, especially if the target is a strong state with the ability to repress the group. Gaining an external host state has multiple implications for a rebel group that lives within the borders of its target. On the one hand, it provides rebels with more leverage when bargaining with their target governments (Bapat 2007). It is difficult for a target state to trace and attack a rebel group within the borders of another state. In addition, it serves as a resource pool from which rebels can arrange logistics support and recruit people.

On the other hand, by moving across the borders of another state, a rebel group makes a sacrifice in its autonomy, since it now subjects itself to the supporter state, which has the discretion to cease its support at any time. Therefore, rebels prefer states, which are likely to give them a high level of autonomy in operations against their targets. Logically, the external adversaries of a rebel group's target and states with which rebels have ideational ties, are perceived as potential supporters who are more likely to grant such autonomy.

> H_5: Rebels are more likely to select the adversaries of their targets to acquire
> safe havens and other forms of support than the non-adversaries.
>
> H_6: Rebels are more likely to select ideationally contiguous states as
> supporters than states with which they do not have common ties.

Regardless of whether they stay inside their target states or fight them from external safe havens, rebels' selection is inherently motivated by survival. As a result, they like to secure continual access to human and material resources, as well as the ability to escape from the repression of their targets (Sandler and Lapan 1988; Byman 2005c; Siqueira and Sandler 2006; Bapat 2007). A factual piece of information related to the rebel groups' motivations of survival is proposed by Hoffman (1998), who found out that most terrorist groups do not survive more than one year. Thus, it is essential to have access to resources outside of their target states, even at the cost of some autonomy.

> H_7: A rebel group is more likely to choose a relatively strong state vis-à-vis its
> target, as a safe haven than a weak one, since a strong state has the ability to
> repel possible retaliation from the rebel group's target. This is also true when
> it comes to other forms of support.

H_8: The likelihood that a rebel group will seek external safe havens is higher if it targets a domestically strong state, rather than a domestically weak one, due to the rebel group's concern for securing itself from repression by its target.

The hypotheses discussed so far have been examined in the context of terrorist groups' and ethnic rebels' decision to seek external safe havens (Bapat 2006, 2007; Salehyan 2009). The selection theory of state support for rebels advances our knowledge of the systematic determinants of support beyond the decision of rebel groups to acquire external safe havens. De facto support, as is conceptualized here, emerges when a rebel group selects certain states from which to extract various sorts of resources including arms and funds, and logistics support, without deliberate action on the part of that state's government to create direct or indirect channels to help the rebel group. The selection theory of support suggests that it is possible to systematically examine various motives rebels have in seeking specific sorts of support in some countries without sponsorship of states in those countries.

States such as Cambodia, Zambia, and Ecuador are selected by rebels to obtain different types of support, due to the inability of these states to effectively protect their borders from infiltration by rebels. Weak states reduce the cost of operations for rebels, which are in need of autonomy. This has also been the commonly held view in the aftermath of the 9/11 attacks in the United States.[16] Weak states or failed states have come to be perceived as the main facilitators of international terrorism (Piazza 2007; Rice 2008; Braithwaite and Li 2007). In contrast, I argue that weak states are the least of the issues, when it comes to addressing the root causes of rebels acquiring resources from external states. Hastings (2010) proposed similar insights about weak states in his research about several Southeast Asian groups, such as GAM. He argues that these groups need to use the infrastructure of the states that serve as safe havens. Therefore, failed or collapsed states, like Somalia, are not the best breeding grounds for the rebels.

H_9 (weak state assumption): A rebel group is more likely to choose a weak state as a safe haven since it has the opportunity for a high level of autonomy in operations against its target.

As mentioned previously, a rebel group's calculus for securing safe havens in a state is also driven by the relative strength of the potential supporter, vis-à-vis a target. A state with weak domestic capacity is also expected to be more vulnerable to potential retaliation from the target states of rebels.[17] This was also the case when various militant Palestinian groups preferred to establish safe havens within Jordan,

Lebanon, Egypt, and Syria, with whom they shared both a common enemy in Israel and similar ideational ties.

H_{10}: The level of de facto support a rebel group pursues in a country increases if the latter is the adversary of the rebel group's target and it is ideationally contiguous to the rebel group (interaction of external threat and ideational contiguity).

Most recently, an excellent example of de facto support is found in ISIS' free operations within the borders of many European states. It was a shocking finding that several ISIS militants faced no constraints and challenges in organizing the Paris attacks from Belgium (Chann 2015). This attests to the vulnerability of democratic states for rebel groups, which raise funds, recruit militants, and plan attacks within their borders. Democratic states are convenient grounds, where rebels can enjoy a high level of autonomy. An extensive body of research finds that there is a positive relationship between democracy and terrorism (Eyerman 1998; Li 2005; Chenoweth 2010). The institutions, which constrain the policy makers and the norms related to individual freedoms and liberties embedded in democracies present an opportunity that terrorists can exploit (San-Akca 2014). Building on this line of argument, it is logically consistent to argue that democratic states are selected by rebel groups to acquire specific sorts of support, such as offices for fundraising and other activities and/or safe havens for leaders of rebels.

H_{11}: Rebel groups are more likely to seek de facto support within democratic countries in comparison to autocratic states.

A rebel group's decision to operate within the borders of a state, or to seek other types of support from external states, is not random or coincidental. Rather, it depends on a calculation by the rebel group about the expected ability of the potential supporter to manage possible retaliation from the target state and its willingness for providing the desired level of support. The willingness is measured by whether a given group has common ideational ties to the potential supporter state, and whether its domestic political environment provides opportunity for exploitation. Such an opportunity might be present if there is a domestic turmoil within a country or it is governed by an advanced democratic political system. Furthermore, rebels do not necessarily choose weak states, despite the fact that they might provide a great deal of autonomy in conduct of operations against target states.

2.3 Conclusion

In the preceding sections, I proposed a general theory to explain the patterns in state-rebel group interactions. I pursued two steps to develop a theory of state-rebel selection. First, I developed two models to examine the formation of a state-rebel group alliance from the perspective of both a supporting state and a rebel group. Strategic and ideational drives in the SSM influence the cooperation patterns between states and rebels. I argue that diversionary theory produces misleading results for a state's external behaviour, if we do not take into consideration the relative strength of the external adversary toward whom internal aggression is redirected. Supporting rebels fighting other states is a foreign policy instrument that states resort to under various circumstances.

In the RSM, the desires for survival, autonomy, and resources are identified as the main drivers behind the search for external state supporters by rebel groups. This does not mean that rebels are not driven by strategic and ideational motives. Rather, they act as mediating variables between interstate relations and a rebel group's decision to select a certain state. I argue that external adversaries and ideationally contiguous states are both perceived as potential supporters by rebels, since they might grant a high level of autonomy to rebels and rebels can easily extract human and material resources within their borders. However, this does not tell the whole story since rebels like to secure their survival by choosing externally strong states, vis-à-vis their targets, as supporters. Thus, this might make them forgo strong demands for autonomy from supporter states.

The following testable arguments are yielded in general:

1. States intentionally support rebels who target their adversaries if they are troubled domestically and face constraints to extraction and mobilization of resources through externally allying with other states or internally mobilizing their domestic populace.

2. States support ideationally contiguous rebels whether the latter targets an adversary or not. Furthermore, ideational factors reinforce a state's decision, if a state has to choose one rebel group to support among many that target its adversary.

3. States are less likely to support rebels against their adversaries if they have conventional state allies that they can trust in times of emergency.

4. States are less likely to provide support to groups that target ideationally contiguous states. Inter-state ideational ties dissuade state support of rebel groups.

5. The highest level of support occurs when a state and a rebel group have a common adversary (i.e., a rebel group targets a state's adversary) and share ideational ties, and the state is relatively strong vis-à-vis the target state.

6. Rebels do not necessarily choose weak states as supporters. Weak states do not necessarily make the best supporters, due to their inability to deal with possible target retaliation, poorly developed infrastructure, and limited resources on which rebels can rely to maintain operations against their targets.

7. Rebels are more likely to choose democratic states to acquire specific sorts of support, such as offices and safe havens for leaders due to the embedded normative and institutional constraints in democratic systems that make it difficult to formulate policies to restrict rebels' free movement and activities within their borders.

8. Rebels are more likely to seek de facto support from countries, which are internally troubled and with which they share ideational ties.

3 Dangerous Companions

RESEARCH DESIGN, DATA COLLECTION,
AND CODING PROCEDURES

THE THEORETICAL FRAMEWORK outlined in the previous chapter suggests two models for explaining how rebel groups acquire resources from states: the States' Selection and Rebels' Selection Models, SSM and RSM, respectively. I test the implications of these models by using a new dataset on 455 rebel groups that have been active in the post-1945 period. Next, I describe the data collection and coding procedures and discuss what the state-Nonstate Armed Groups Cooperation dataset (NAGs dataset) reveals about the patterns of state-rebel group relations in the past decades.

The NAGs dataset is a part of the Dangerous Companions Project (DCP), which I developed and managed as the principle investigator. In addition to data collection and coding, DCP consists of an online platform containing the profiles of each rebel group, major regional and world trends in external state support of rebel groups, and the corresponding datasets.[1] Most importantly, the project is unique in terms of its online data portal, which lists all the sources used to code the variables related to each NAG. The goal is to contribute to research transparency in scholarly work. Especially if the subject matter is covert support of rebel groups by states, it is even more important in addressing questions related to coding observational data about state behavior. The empirical analysis in the following chapters is based on the findings of this project.

The rest of this chapter is organized as follows. In the first section, the unit of analysis and the criteria used for selection of cases are discussed, as well as the differences with other existing datasets on external state support for rebels. Second, the definition and operationalization of state support are reviewed. In addition to presenting key variables and descriptive statistics, this section describes in detail the coding procedures used to determine state supporters, the types of support, and the period during which each type of support is given. Last, the operationalization and measurement of the key explanatory variables that are included in the specification of the SSM and the RSM are introduced.

3.1 Case Selection

3.1.1 UNIT OF ANALYSIS

The unit of analysis is a triad-year. A triad includes a rebel group, a target (a state that is the subject of nonstate violence), and a potential supporter (a state that is likely to support a rebel group when an opportunity arises). Each triad has as many observations as the number of years a rebel group is active. The opportunity for state support arises with the formation of a rebel group and continues as long as it is active, that is, engages in violent conduct against its target. The assumption is that a state might support a group from inception to demise, or only for a temporary period.

The fluid and complex nature of state-rebel group interactions requires a triadic approach to tracing these interactions—over time and across space. And not only must rebel group and supporter interactions be reviewed, but also target state and supporter state relations. Only then is it possible to examine the influence of strategic and ideational factors on intentional and de facto support. Including target state-supporter state relations as an explanatory variable also allows for an examination of state-rebel group relations through the lens of interstate relations. The analytical approach, therefore, advances the scholarly debate in two ways: (1) going beyond the approach of the existing literature, which is limited to the dyadic-level analysis of rebel group-target state relations; (2) bringing in interstate ideational ties to explain the emergence of outside state support for rebel groups. The population of triads has been constructed at three stages. First, I identify the states that have been consistently targeted by one or more rebels in the post-1945 period. Then I identify the group(s) that targets them. Last, I identify the potential supporters for each target-rebel group pair.

Identifying Target States and Rebel Groups

The first step is identifying incidents of armed conflicts between a state and a rebel group. I use the Uppsala Conflict Data Program (UCDP)/Peace Research Institute Oslo (PRIO) Armed Conflict Dataset (ACD) to identify such incidents (Gleditsch et al. 2002; Pettersson and Wallensteen 2015). The ACD provides information on four different types of armed conflicts: (1) interstate conflict; (2) internal conflict between a government and opposition group; (3) internationalized internal conflict between an opposition group and a government, with external intervening states; and (4) extrasystemic conflict between a state and an opposition group, outside the territory of the given state.

An opposition group is defined as "any non-governmental group of people having announced a name for their group and using armed force to influence the outcome of an incompatibility."[2] The subject of a conflict between a government and an opposition group could be a piece of territory, the government, or both territory and government. A territorial dispute is when a group issues demands for secession or autonomy. An incompatibility related to the government might be about the type of political system, the replacement of central government, or the change of its composition.

The ACD criteria about the rebel groups to include in the dataset are quite pragmatic: groups involved in a conflict that reached, at minimum, twenty-five battle-related deaths for at least one year, that have an organizational structure (i.e., declared a name), and that use arms to fight the government. Spontaneous violent protests do not count as politicized organized violence according to the ACD criteria. Using the ACD list of the opposition side of conflicts between governments and nonstate armed groups, the NAGs dataset collects information on 455 rebel groups, determined to be targeting 105 states between 1945 and 2010. The total number of such groups is approximately 530, as of 2014. The armed opposition groups that emerged after 2010, or were pure military factions trying to conduct a military coup, are not included in the NAGs dataset.

The NAGs dataset includes more detailed information about the objectives of these groups, going beyond the dichotomous coding of the ACD. The rebel objectives include toppling an existing leadership, demands for policy change, claims related to autonomy or secession, and change of political system in addition to the specific claims for a new regime including a military, theocratic and democratic regime. Various types of groups are coded. They include secessionist/national liberation movements, which demand territorial secession or adherence to another state. The examples of such groups are the IRA, which fought the United Kingdom for several decades, Oromo Liberation Front (OLF), which have ongoing secessionist claims from Ethiopia, and GAM, which led an insurgency against Indonesia for almost three decades.

Among other groups are there rebels, which demand a change of political system (such as founding an Islamic state, a democratic state, or a socialist state), the leadership, and/or the composition of the government. Some examples of groups with such objectives are the Lord's Resistance Army (LRA), which fought the Ugandan government to establish political system ruling the country according to Christian theology, the Supreme Council for the Islamic Revolution in Iraq (SCIRI), which tried to bring an Islamic regime in Iraq), and the Shining Path, which wanted to establish a socialist regime in Peru.

Furthermore, the NAGs dataset contains variables on rebel groups' ideational attributes, whether they have political parties representing them in the domestic political arena of their targets, and whether they have a support base among the populace in their target and/or supporter states. It is found that 14 percent of the groups had political party wings, which were actively participating in the political life of their target states at some point during their lifetime. And, 20 percent garnered support from the domestic populace of their targets and/or potential supporters.

Identifying Potential Supporters

After identifying the rebels, their targets, and the periods during which rebel groups are active, I determined the potential supporters of various rebel groups. The list of potential supporters for a group is constructed by using the politically relevant group (PRG) of a focal state, for the purposes of this book, the "target state." The PRG of a state includes geographically contiguous states, regional powers with the ability to exert regional influence, and global powers whose influence goes far beyond their regions.[3] Each state that is the target of a rebel group is paired with other states in its PRG.

There are some disadvantages to using politically relevant dyads (Maoz and Russett 1993; Maoz 1996; Lemke and Reed 2001). For instance, Saudi Arabia has been supporting various armed rebel groups within Afghanistan. In the dataset, this information is not included as Saudi Arabia is not a member of Afghanistan's PRG. Instances also exist in which a sponsor assists a rebel group financially or diplomatically even though they are located far away from a target. For instance, Cuba provided assistance to the leftist rebels in Angola prior to 1975 allowing the leftist People's Movement for the Liberation of Angola (MPLA) to gain power in Angola. Still, the benefit of limiting the number of potential supporters to be examined for each target exceeds the benefit of including every state. The reliability of the politically relevant dyads in interstate conflict studies has also been proven by Lemke and Reed (2001). They conducted an empirical analysis both with the entire set of dyads of countries in the world, and with the politically relevant dyads, and found that the results were not significantly different across findings.

Time Frame: "The Opportunity Period"

The opportunity to support a rebel group arises as soon as it starts engaging in violence against its target. We hardly hear about the sub-state groups, which use peaceful means to pursue their objectives from their target states. Therefore, each triad is listed as many years as the rebel group actively uses violence against its target state. Each observation is then coded for whether an activity of state selection or rebel selection is observed.[4]

The ACD data includes three dates for the start of each armed conflict between a state and a group: the date when the first battle-related death is observed in a given conflict, the date when an armed conflict reaches twenty-five battle-related deaths, and episode start date when violence stops for one year or more and restarts. I use the date when the first battle-related death occurs (regardless of whether it reaches the twenty-five battle-related death threshold in that year) although the NAGs dataset starts coding support as soon as a group is found to declare a name. The opportunity to support a group emerges as soon as it starts engaging in violence against its target, regardless of the number of casualties suffered by either side.

When it comes to determining whether a rebel group has terminated its activities, I relied on the UCDP Termination dataset, which codes the end date of episodes, rather than the entire conflict (Kreutz 2010). A new episode starts every time a group's name changes or violence escalates to reach the twenty-five battle-related death threshold after it stops for at least one year. When an episode does not meet the armed conflict dataset criteria in terms of fatality, organization level, or the group's objective, for at least one year, it is coded as the end date of the episode according to the UCDP Termination dataset. However, this does not mean that the group is entirely inactive. It might reinstate its armed activities in the future. As long as an episode is told to end with "no or low activity", rather than an agreement, according to the termination data, I assume that the group is active and the opportunity to support it continues to exist, from the perspective of a potential supporter. The only cases for which conflict is determined to terminate are the ones where both parties sign an agreement. If a rebel group is inactive during a period and returns to the use of violence after a while, the years in between are included as part of the opportunity period, during which, external state support might emerge. For example, the Karen National Union (KNU) started its activities against Myanmar

(Burma) in 1948. Four episodes of violent conflict have been recorded between the KNU and Myanmar: 1948–1992, 1995, 1997–2003, and 2005–present. For the purposes of the NAGs dataset, I take 1948 as the start date and include all the years until 2010, which is the cutoff point for the NAGs dataset.

3.1.2   A NEW DATASET ON STATE SUPPORT FOR REBEL GROUPS: *WHY COLLECT NEW DATA?*

This book is primarily concerned with the determinants of state support for non-state armed groups and, specifically, the influence of target-supporter relations on the likelihood and level of support. The international aspect of internal conflict has been extensively studied when it comes to ethnic conflict with a focus on the role of transnational ethnic kin and refugees and diaspora in neighboring states in the acquisition of external safe havens and the spread of internal conflict to international arena (Kalyvas and Balcells 2010; Saideman and Jenne 1992; Saideman 1997, 2001; Salehyan 2009; Stavenhagen 1996). In an effort to explain how transnational ethnic ties, refugees and diaspora influence civil war in a given state, the primary focus of these scholars has been on the ethnic ties of rebels within state A with ethnic groups that live in state B (Cederman et al. 2009, 2013).

The analysis in this book presents an assessment of state-rebel group relations posed through the lens of interstate politics, while bringing in ideational ties between not only rebel groups and states that support them, but also between target and supporter states. Ideational characteristics are not limited to ethnic identity. Thus, the NAGs dataset collects detailed information on the religious identity and political ideology of rebels since such data is not yet available. Furthermore, no existing dataset contains the required information on de facto support.

Earlier efforts to collect data on armed groups have been concerned mostly with addressing the root causes behind the instigation of ethnic and religious insurgency, revolution, and terrorism (MAR[5], GTD[6], ITERATE[7]). These datasets are designed to address different theoretical questions. As a result, they are either about the main attributes of groups, such as size, objectives, and fatalities caused, or about the individual attacks conducted by them.

Another related body of data is found in the study of civil war and external interventions. Several scholars collected data on external military, economic, and diplomatic intervention in civil war, and the side on which outside states choose to intervene (Regan 1996, 1998, 2000; Aydin and Regan 2011). Regan (2002) identifies whether a foreign state provided military or economic aid to one of the sides in an intrastate war. Yet he did not specify the multiple actors involved in the opposition side of a conflict. Thus, we do not have information on external state support of each rebel group involved in a civil war if there are multiple groups involved in the same conflict. The updated version of the intervention data continues focusing on intrastate conflicts as one single unit, and does not distinguish between different parties and nonstate actors included in an intrastate conflict (Regan et al. 2009). Saideman (2001, 2002) distinguishes between states that support the government side of an armed conflict and those that support the opposition groups, yet, he does not specify the type of support provided. His data is also limited to ethnic insurgents. Thus, it does not allow for testing the arguments related to rebel groups overall.

Furthermore, in these data, it is about overt intervention by states and not necessarily covert support, in the sense covered in this book. Therefore, the focus was more on the decision of outside states to intervene in a civil war, and on whose side the intervention occurred, that is to say, the government or opposition side. Data collection efforts, thus, focused more on the nature, type, and timing of intervention, the number of outside states intervening in a given conflict and the relations among the interveners, and the type and duration of intervention rather than the complex relations between states and rebel groups (Aydin 2012; Aydin and Regan 2011; Balch-Lindsay and Enterline 2000; Findley and Teo 2006; Regan 1996, 1998, 2000).

Recently, two attempts were undertaken to collect data on nonstate armed groups and their supporters. One of them is Nonstate Actor Data (Cunningham et al. 2009a). The Non-State Actor (NSA) dataset is a dyadic dataset with information on each NSA's military strength and capacity, leadership characteristics, popular support, and political linkages, as well as external sponsorship. However, external state support is not broken into diverse types. We know only if there was explicit or implicit support by external states.

Similarly, UCDP's External Support Data is another dyadic dataset, containing information on external supporters that give support to a rebel group in a given year from 1975 to 2010, also coding for different types of support (Högbladh et al. 2011). This dataset, on the other hand, is limited in its temporal domain, which does not go back beyond 1975. Armed groups, such as the Khmer Rouge (KR), the National Liberation Front (FLN), and the Eritrean Liberation Front (ELF) existed prior to 1975, yet the data on supporters are only collected for the post-1975 period. The total number of observations in the external support dataset is about 7,900, whereas the total number of observations in the NAGs dataset is about 17,250. Furthermore, neither the NSA dataset nor the UCDP External Support Dataset contains information on de facto support and the ideational characteristics of rebel groups, which are required to test the main hypotheses outlined in this book.

The fluid nature of state-rebel group relations requires a new way of conceptualization, which goes beyond treating rebel groups as passive partners of states. The theoretical framework developed in the previous chapter is based on such a new conception that points out the unprecedented rise of nonstate armed groups across the world in recent decades. Scholars of international politics are scrabbling to keep pace with this new group of actors that influence international politics as much as states do. The state-centric view of international politics, which presumes a role for nonstate armed groups only when they are used as proxies in advancing the strategic interests of their state patrons, is an artifact of the Cold War period thinking. This view ignores, and occasionally denies, any primary role that other actors can assume in world politics besides the nation-state (Holsti 1996; Lebow 2010).

Indeed, almost 50 percent of the cases in the NAGs dataset belong to the rebel selection category described in the previous chapter. Rebels manage to acquire resources from countries without states in these countries creating channels to aid them. In other words, rebel groups are autonomous entities, which can find external resources without states necessarily allowing them to acquire resources within their borders. Furthermore, the NAGs dataset reveals that while 64 percent of observations with intentional state support fall in the Cold War period, 50 percent of observations with de facto support fall in the post–Cold War period. Given that only two-and-a-half decades have passed since the end of the Cold War, which lasted for almost five decades, these figures reveal new patterns in state-rebel group interactions. While there is a decline in intentional support during the post–Cold War period, de facto support is on the rise comparing the duration of both periods. Supporting rebels is not a strategy limited to major powers or a specific period in world history. Moreover, rebel groups seem to learn how to diversify their sources of support by reaching beyond major powers and not depending on state sponsors. Rebels manage to acquire resources in some countries despite the absence of any sponsorship of the states, which govern these countries.

3.2 State Support: Operationalization

3.2.1 STATE SELECTION CASES

State support for rebels takes various forms, ranging from providing bases for operations and training to recognition of their cause as "just" (O'Neill 1980; Byman 2005c). I am interested in those types of support that directly or indirectly contribute to the violent activities of rebel groups. In addition to determining the type of support, the NAGs dataset also contains information on whether states intentionally create channels to assist rebels. This is essential for distinguishing between the state selection and rebel selection processes. Data on rebel selection is particularly timely, given that rebel groups have managed to acquire resources within the borders of various countries through alternative means, without any state sponsorship.

Determining the type and date of support is a challenging task, since the states that provide assistance to rebels often deny that they do so. Various sources are used to determine the type of support provided, including major news sources, scholarly case study analysis of individual conflicts and rebel groups, and primary sources, when available.[8] Mere allegations by the targets of rebels are not sufficient to determine whether a state provides the alleged assistance to a rebel group.

The NAGs dataset[9] includes information on nine types of intentional support for rebels by states:

- Safe havens for rebel group members
- Safe havens for rebel group leaders
- Headquarters/open offices
- Training camps
- Training
- Weapons and logistics support
- Financial aid
- Transport of arms, military equipment, and supplies
- Troops

When it comes to de facto support, eight types of support are coded from these types: all of the above, excluding troop support. The underlying assumption for excluding troop support as a type of de facto support is that state troops do not fight alongside a group without the approval or sponsorship of states to which they belong.

Type 1. Safe Havens for Members

Providing safe havens for members of a rebel group is different from providing training camps or access to existing camps. "Providing safe havens for members" means that the militants of a rebel group operate and reside within a specific geographical space in the borders of a country and/or spread around the country to raise funds, recruit individuals, and organize activities to sustain the group's violent operations.

More often than not, the neighbors of a state that experiences civil war end up accepting refugees. Opening the borders to refugees does not qualify as providing safe havens to an armed rebel group, unless the refugees include militants of the armed group, who engage in violent cross-border attacks into the civil war state. There are several examples of refugees among whom militants live to escape the repression of the target state. The KNU, which has been fighting Myanmar's government for more than five decades, had their militants escape into neighboring Thailand along with the refugees. They occasionally organized armed attacks back into Myanmar. Two decisions were made in the case of the Thai government's hosting of Karen refugees: (1) whether the Karen refugees had militant members of the KNU among them, which would appear in the sources, if there are cross-border attacks from Thailand into Myanmar; (2) whether the support was intentional or de facto, which could be determined based on whether the Thai government took action to deal with the incursions from Myanmar into its territories. Indeed, though the Thai government was turning a blind eye to militants for a while, it started tightening security measures occasionally along the border with Myanmar (Horstmann 2011). Tightening of security measures came after the military regime in Myanmar pressed the Thai government to take serious action against cross-border activities, such as drug trafficking and arms smuggling.

Type 2. Safe Havens for Leaders

Providing safe havens for leaders of a rebel group is different from providing safe havens for its members. The leaders of rebel groups often end up living in other states for many reasons, such as being expelled from or no longer feeling safe in their target countries. Of the total years that leaders of rebels spent in external safe havens, 25 percent of the time, they were invited by democratic states. In contrast, 75 percent of the time, they were invited by autocratic states. Surprisingly, when it comes to rebel leaders selecting certain states as safe destinations, they end up opting for democracies 46 percent of the time.

Rebel leaders select democracies due to the institutional freedoms and liberties that make their arrest and deportation difficult. After the assassination of Indian ex-prime minister Rajiv Gandhi in 1991, the LTTE lost its support base and funding from India. As a result, they founded offices in advanced democratic countries, such as Switzerland, France, the United Kingdom, the United States, and Canada. Evidence is clear that the Sri Lankan government put pressure on these countries to stop the fund-raising activities of the group and to return the group's leaders back to Sri Lanka. Despite the pressures, these countries did not take any measures curtailing the free movement and activities of the LTTE leadership, who lived in their territories. The United States banned the group in 1997 by passing an anti-terrorism law and declaring it a terrorist organization.[10] The United Kingdom and Canada did not ban the group until 2001 (Jayamaha 2000).

Type 3. Headquarters/Open Offices

A rebel group might have a presence within the borders of a state only for peaceful purposes. In other words, it might operate offices for peaceful propaganda, recruitment, and fund-raising within the borders of another state. Several groups, such as PIJ, PKK, and PFLP, were allowed to open offices in Damascus, but they were not allowed to conduct violent operations from within Syrian borders. This is why Fatah found itself constantly searching safe havens for its militants. It had to relocate multiple times, since conducting operations into Israel from within the territories of Jordan and Lebanon had led to Israeli retaliation against these states. Aware of the risk of retaliation from Israel, and having lost territory to Israel at the end of the Six-Day War, Syria hosted very few militants within its borders (Strindberg 2000). Even if it did, these militants had to subordinate themselves to the regime in Damascus and had little autonomy in conducting operations against Israel. This was also the case with the Nasser regime in Egypt. Indeed, Arafat abandoned Gaza during the mid-1950s immediately after the Suez Crisis (Zelkovitz 2015). Nasser did not want Palestinian militants to engage in violent cross-border incursions from Gaza into Israel, since Gaza was under Egyptian control at the time.

Type 4. Training Camps

Providing rebels with training camps requires an extra effort on the part of the supporters, beyond providing safe havens. Training camps are expected to be equipped with military material and tools to provide the required training for militants. During the Syrian occupation of Lebanon from 1976 to 2005, various Palestinian groups were trained in Lebanon, with the assistance of Syria.[11] For instance, the PIJ members were trained in camps in southern Lebanon. Although its headquarters were located in Damascus since its foundation, PIJ's training camps were not in Syrian territories. In coding support of the group by Syria, providing training camps is not coded among the support types. Instead, providing safe havens to leaders is counted.

Type 5. Training

Training might occur within the borders of a state or outside of its borders. Occasionally, states will send security personnel to train militants across the borders of other states. In several cases, states end up providing training to rebels, without necessarily operating training camps for them. For instance, members of the African National Congress (ANC), fighting against the South African regime between 1981 and 1988, received training in the use of small arms obtained from the Soviet Union, Cuba, and East Germany, mostly within the borders of Angola (Albright 1985; Mitchell 1981). The GAM operated safe havens within neighboring Malaysia, but frequently sent its militants to Libya for training. This was mostly because GAM did not want to irritate the Malaysian government, which was already facing pressures from the Indonesian government to crack on GAM safe havens within its territories (Hastings 2010).

Type 6. Weapons and Logistics Support

This variable is coded if there is clear evidence that arms originated from the supporting country. The evidence for whether a state provides arms to rebels is not easily attainable; mere allegations by the target states are not enough to prove that a state provides arms to a rebel group. For instance, several South Asian rebel groups, such as KNU, God's Army, and Kachin Independence Organization (KIO) smuggled arms from Cambodia, due to the latter's inability to control its borders. Such cases qualify for de facto support. Furthermore, there were several allegations in the news during the Cold War period about Soviet weapons supplied to armed groups across the world. This kind of information has been confirmed by secondary sources, since the Cold War period witnessed extensive criticism of the Soviet regime by western media outlets. On the other hand, the IRA militants frequently were given weapons by the Libyan government, which issued false passports for them to easily smuggle these weapons into the United Kingdom (Sharrock 2007).

Type 7. Financial Aid

While in some cases, such as Iran and Hezbollah, governments provide funds to a rebel group intentionally, in many others the groups themselves raise funds within some countries, such as the IRA raising funds in the United States. When this is the case, the support is assumed to be de facto. It is possible to argue that the United States had the capacity to control the IRA's activities, in which case the support of the group would have been intentional. However, making this judgment requires a more extensive analysis of each case in the dataset, which is not an attainable goal within the timeframe spent in completing the current book. Rather, the empirical analysis allows for controlling the capacity of state to gauge its influence on de facto support.

Type 8. Transport of Military Equipment and Supplies

If a state serves as a transport point for a rebel group, it is coded separately from providing arms and military supplies. Cambodia has, for years, been a de facto transport point for arms smuggling for many armed groups in Asia (Bonner 1998). Zaire was the major transport point for the weapons sent by the UNITA, which was fighting the communist regime in Angola (Lewis 1987).

Type 9. Troop Support

Troop support should not be confused with intervening on the side of the rebels in an internal conflict or civil war. As discussed earlier, the research on external intervention in internal conflict, and the datasets constructed to study the topic, so far have focused only on overt intervention (Regan 1996, 1998, 2000; Aydin and Regan 2011). When a third-party state intervenes in an internal conflict through military means, it usually does not try hiding it or doing it covertly. Troop support is described here for cases in which outside states allowed their troops to fight on the side of the rebels against their target states. Although it is more difficult to hide troop support to rebels than other forms of support, it is easier than committing a large population of ground troops to intervene on the side of the rebels. In the former, the rebel group is still in charge of the fighting; whereas, in the latter, the intervention occurs in front of the international community, and the intervening state is in charge. A total of 6 percent of the observations (support years) involve states that provide troops to fight along rebels. This is normal, if we consider that troop support is a very risky strategy and hard to manage undercover, since it means almost directly engaging with the target of a rebel group.

3.2.2 REBEL SELECTION CASES

De facto support includes any of the above-mentioned types, except troops. It is coded for cases where there is no evidence that the state in a country purposefully create channels to accommodate the rebels seeking support. Support is an action that implies an intentional act on the part of the supporter state. Thus, it might be misleading to characterize rebel selection cases as support. Yet, states are expected to, and should, be aware of what goes on within their borders, as the sole entity with *the monopoly over the legitimate use of violent means* (Weber 1946). Since they have a choice to stop or prevent such incidents, unless they are a failed state, it is justifiable to name the rebel selection cases as support as well.

De facto support builds on the insights suggested by Byman (2005b), who seeks to distinguish between active versus passive support by states to terrorism. The idea of passive support is based on the following criteria: the state in question "does not provide assistance but knowingly allows other actors in the country," such as political parties, wealthy merchants, or others to help a terrorist group, and "has the capacity to stop such assistance or has chosen not to" do so (Byman 2005b, p.118). Byman (2005b) gives the example of al-Qaeda operating in Saudi Arabia and Pakistan, and the IRA operating in the United States. In all three cases, he argues that both governments had the capacity to control the activities of the groups, but they chose not to develop such capacity.

Building on the idea of passive support, de facto support is conceptualized to capture any act a rebel group undertakes within the borders of countries, without the government and/or its associated organs' intentionally acting to create channels to aid the group. It is based on the assertion that whether a state has the will and knowingly allows some groups to freely operate within its borders is very difficult, if not impossible, to determine in the context of the current project, which is driven by collecting data on a large number of cases. Instead of trying to figure out the intention and will of each state, the emphasis is on observable signs of whether a government or its affiliates create channels to provide assistance to an armed group. These channels are easier to identify than the intentions of states and their leaders.

Furthermore, many attributes of states, including capacity, ideational characteristics, and the type of their political systems, are treated as variables. Such treatment also advances our knowledge of the conditions under which some attributes make them more or less appealing to rebel groups, who want to bypass the cost of submitting themselves to states that intentionally support them.

Each case requires an extensive examination to determine how de facto support occurs. Lebanon and several militant Palestinian groups serve as a good example to illustrate the points discussed so far. Initial operations of the members of PLO go as far back as the late 1960s. After being expelled from Jordan, the PLO sought refuge in Lebanon. Indeed, Ahmad Shuquiri, the first chairman of the PLO lived in Lebanon until 1968, and his summerhouse there was used to train Palestinian militants. The Lebanese army also trained Palestinians during the 1967 war (Samii 1997). Initially, it seems that Lebanon provided intentional support to militant Palestinian groups. Thus, the dates between 1964 and 1968 are coded as state selection or intentional support in the case of Lebanon. Later on, though, during 1968 and 1969, the Lebanese security forces themselves waged their own operations against Palestinian militants (Maoz 2006, pp. 174–183). This provides evidence that the Palestinian groups turned Lebanon into a de facto supporter in the years following 1968. Ultimately, the start of the civil war in 1975, and the Syrian occupation in 1976, contributed to the gradual degeneration of central authority in Lebanon. Therefore, between 1968 and 1975, the support of Palestinian groups is coded as rebel selection cases resulting in de facto support. After 1976, Lebanon was not coded at all, since much of it fell under Syrian occupation and remained so until 2005. It is almost impossible to talk about an autonomous political decision-making body during these years in Lebanon.

Another case in Lebanon is Hezbollah. In an effort to curb cross-border incursions by the PLO militants into its territory, Israel invaded southern Lebanon in 1982, which contributed only to further deterioration of Lebanon as a weak state, unable to keep its territory from falling into the hands of armed groups. The foundation of Hezbollah, and its continuing presence in the political life of Lebanon, does not necessarily stem from a choice on the side of either the Lebanese government or the Shi'a militant organization. Rather, they have a territorial stronghold within southern Lebanon, which emerged as a local resistance movement against the Israeli occupation.[12] Thus, it was not coded as a case of rebel selection of Lebanon as a safe haven, since Hezbollah is native to Lebanon.

Each case has been examined in detail to make sure that the characteristics identifying a case as a rebel selection or a state selection case were present. For example, Boko Haram received training in various militant camps in Algeria, Somalia, Mali, Mauritania, and Afghanistan. None of these states was actively involved in providing training to the group. However, Boko Haram's close links with other armed groups, namely al-Shabaab and al-Qaeda in the Islamic Maghreb (AQIM), facilitated infiltration into the territory of these five countries (Onapajo et al. 2012). They entered Mauritania promising the warlords they would assist with the civil war there, after the collapse of the democratic regime in the country with the military coup of 2005. Several members of the army tried recruiting members of Boko Haram as mercenaries, promising they would be traveling across North Africa for advanced Islamic studies. Following the Nigerian military's crackdown on the group in 2009, one of its leaders, Mamman Nur, moved to Somalia and forged links with another radical Islamist outfit, al-Shabaab. Under his leadership, a branch of Boko Haram's military organization received training in al-Shabaab camps in Somalia. Another wing received training in AQIM camps in Mali and Mauritania. The group used its network of other groups to utilize the training camps of various groups, located in different parts of North Africa (BBC Monitoring Middle East 2010).

The NAGs dataset identifies approximately 355 cases of state selection and 342 cases of rebel selection. Furthermore, Table 3.1 provides information on the regional distribution of rebel groups, their supporters, and the ratio of support years to total years of support. A striking difference emerges when it comes to the number of rebel groups across regions. While the Middle East and North African (MENA) countries were targeted only by 11.65 percent of the rebel groups in the entire world, 16 percent of all supporter states, and almost 26 percent of support years, belong to the MENA. In contrast, although East and South Asia have been targeted by a higher number of rebel groups, more than double the number in the MENA region and the number of supporters, the proportion of support years are almost the same as the MENA. Sub-Saharan Africa possesses the highest number of rebel groups, and has the highest number of supporters (almost 33 percent), but with a relatively low proportion of support (15 percent). In other words, Sub-Saharan African countries

TABLE 3.1 Regional Distribution of Rebel Groups and State Supporters, 1945–2010

Region	Rebel Groups		Supporters		Support Years Proportion %
	Number	%	Number	%	
Eastern Europe and post-Soviet Union	31	6.81	9	9.09	5.38
Latin America	48	10.55	12	12.12	4.90
Middle East and North Africa	53	11.65	16	16.16	25.93
Sub-Saharan Africa	163	35.82	33	33.33	14.92
Western Europe and North America	31	6.81	12	12.12	23.11
East and South Asia	126	27.69	16	16.16	25.58
Pacific and Caribbean	3	0.66	1	1.01	0.18
Total	455	100.00	99	100.00	100.00
Cold War*					47
Rebel Group Selection					50

* This figure is calculated using the overall support without distinguishing between intentional and de facto support.

did not provide support to rebels for long periods of time, even after deciding to support them. Overall, the figures indicate that not only do some regions include a high number state supporters of rebels, but also do consist of persistent supporters.

The NAGs dataset also codes a precision level for each type of support. The precision, or confidence, level is coded as a result of the coder's assessment of the following criteria:

- The supporter outright stated its intention and/or type of support, and/or the support was officially documented by that state or another. Documents issued by government agencies, such as the U.S. Department of State or the U.S. Department of Homeland Security, are excluded unless supporting evidence from other sources was found (level 1),
- A reliable journalist, scholar, or media outlet recorded the support on the field and provides convincing evidence, and other sources confirm this information (level 2),
- Support is highly suspected by a reliable source (such as a journalist, scholar, or media outlet) but cannot be confirmed by other sources (level 3),
- One state accuses another state of supporting a group, but it cannot provide official documentation, beyond allegations (level 4).

The empirical analyses in the subsequent chapters exclude cases with the lowest precision level. Only 2 percent of the total support cases turned out to be coded with a very low precision level.

3.3 Measurement of the Key Explanatory Variables

3.3.1 EXTERNAL THREAT ENVIRONMENT

One of the main assumptions of the theoretical framework outlined in the previous chapter is that state support for rebels is endogenous to interstate relations. The nature of the interaction between a potential supporter and a target state should play a significant role in explaining why states choose to support a rebel group in the first place, and why a rebel group chooses a specific country from which to acquire resources. Scholarly work on insurgencies has shown that states support rebels in pursuit of various objectives, among which, "dealing with external adversaries" is not a trivial one (Byman et al. 2001; Bapat 2007; Salehyan 2008a, 2008b, 2010). This is also in line with the findings of research on the formation of interstate alliances. The insight from the "enemy of my enemy" argument (Maoz et al. 2007) suggests that one might expect a state to be more likely to support the rebel group that targets its external adversary, or a state from which it perceives a threat (Maoz and San-Akca 2012).

To test for the influence of external threat perception between a target and a potential supporter, I use a variable called "Strategic Reference Group (SRG)" in identifying whether two states had a previous history of conflict (Maoz 2007). The SRG of a state includes those states that are perceived to pose a security challenge to that state. This variable takes a value of "1" if a potential sponsor and a target engaged in either a militarized dispute in the last five years or a war in the last ten years, and a "0" if there are no such incidents between them.[13] The NAGs dataset reveals that almost 65 percent of the time, when states supported rebels, they did so against their adversaries. And rebels choose the external adversaries of their target states 57 percent of the time, if they make a decision to reach out to outside countries to acquire resources.

3.3.2 INTERNAL THREAT ENVIRONMENT

The selection theory of state support for rebels acknowledges that states face threats both in the internal and in the external political arenas. This does not imply that states are motivated to support rebels only when they face threats. Almost 35 percent of the time, states support rebels in the absence of a perceived threat from these rebels' targets. In an effort to refine the explanation of state support, it is hypothesized that a state is more likely to support rebels fighting its external adversaries if it is also going through a domestic turmoil, which threatens the survival of its leadership. As such, internal instability renders it vulnerable to both external and internal opponents and poses a risk for regime and leader survival.

This was the case with the regime of the shah, Mohammed Reza Pahlavi, in Iran in the early 1970s. At the time the shah was confronted with domestic opposition at home, he had to deal with a new Ba'athist external adversary in Iraq that was friendly to the Soviet Union. He chose to support the Kurdish insurgents in Iraq, in addition to confronting the Iraqi regime of Saddam Hussein directly, for a brief moment in 1969, in the Persian Gulf. Iran managed to occupy Saddam with the internal affairs of his country through Tehran's extensive support of the Kurdish insurgency between 1961 and 1970.

Furthermore, the conventional assumption in the post-9/11 period has relied heavily on state capacity as an explanation for how recent terrorist groups emerge and sustain their operations against target states. Internal instability renders states vulnerable in two ways, upsetting their capacity to govern effectively within their borders:

(1) their territories have a risk of turning into ungoverned spaces and
(2) their governments and leaders become further vulnerable to outside opponents, especially since it becomes riskier to extract resources from the domestic population and mobilize them against external adversaries.

In measuring domestic instability, or threat level, in a potential supporter, I use an instability indicator developed by the Political Instability Task Force (PITF) (Marshall et al. 2015). The task force identifies an instability event under four categories:

(1) revolutionary wars;
(2) ethnic wars;
(3) adverse regime changes;
(4) genocides and politicides. [14]

If any of these instability events were found within the borders of a country, it was used to signal a domestic threat for the government and leadership in the potential supporter. State support emerged almost 30 percent of the time within states that experienced instability incidents, either through state selection or through rebel selection.

3.3.3 TARGET AND POTENTIAL SUPPORTER IDEATIONAL AFFINITY

Commonly accepted among scholars, who do not adhere to the assumptions of realism or neorealism in interpreting world politics, state interests cannot be defined independent of states' identity. Indeed, it has long been demonstrated that whether states perceive threats from each other is also tied to their degree of affinity with respect to shared norms, ideas, and domestic political institutions. Contiguity between states is not only a matter of geographical proximity, but also driven by shared ideational characteristics and political ideology.

The liberal school of thought emphasizes shared ideas, norms, and institutions among democracies as a source of cooperation. Nonetheless, it does not go much into the details of how shared ideas are constructed and translated into preferences, which then lead to foreign policy outcomes. In comparison to liberalism' insights, constructivist school of thought does a better job of adopting identity as one of the main variables shaping international relations. It is yet to develop components of identity, ideas, and norms that can be operationalized, measured, and systematically tested by a large-N dataset in studying interstate conflict and cooperation. Indeed, the field of international security studies has lagged behind in adopting identity as a major explanatory variable for theorizing and testing its influence on foreign policy preferences of states, despite the extensive criticisms directed towards Huntington's famous article "Clash of Civilizations?" appeared in *Foreign Affairs* in 1993 (Huntington 1993).

Testing the influence of interstate ideational ties requires matching states on the basis of specific identity features. I utilize three main indicators for which states are matched: ethnic/national identity, religion, and political ideology (i.e., socialism and democracy).[15] This approach provides a greater degree of diversity when measuring ideational contiguity between states. Though recent attempts have been made to develop a more nuanced measure of civilization groups than Huntington's categories (Henderson and Tucker 2001; Chiozza 2002), they are still too broad and do not tell us much about the several ideational ties states might share, or the differences they have. For instance, both Iran and Saudi Arabia are members of Islamic civilization; however, they both adopted different interpretations of Islam, which led to the emergence of a historical rivalry between the two countries. On the other hand, while Spain and the United Kingdom adhere to different interpretations of Christianity (Roman Catholicism and Protestantism), the cultural distance between these two countries is minute in comparison to the distance between Iran and Saudi Arabia. Spain and the United Kingdom share the same worldview with respect to domestic politics, since both are democracies (Maoz and Russett 1993).

Relying on proxy measures of liberalism, socialism, and nationalism to examine ideational affinity between states is especially meaningful if one considers that all three ideologies shaped, to a great extent, the construction of the modern nation-state. The nation-state is the main constitutive actor of the current international system (Buzan and Lawson 2015, pp. 97–126). Each ideology, whether national solidarity, socialist ideals of equality, and/or liberal ideas of economic progress, was adopted with respect to both the domestic and international politics of states, so as to achieve unity around the new regimes of the 19th and 20th centuries. This unity was the primary condition for states' ability to handle domestic and international challenges. Whether a potential supporter and a target state share a common set of values and ideas that increase the affinity between them should influence how they treat one another. These three major worldviews—ethno-national characteristics, religion, and political ideology of the governing regime (that is, Marxist/Socialist versus liberal/democrat)—are used in measuring broader cultural or ideational contiguity between states.

Two main datasets exist identifying the major ethnic and religious groups in each country. The Ethnic Power Relations (EPR) dataset codes major ethnicities in each state (Cederman et al. 2010). I matched the first three groups both in target and in potential supporter states to get a sense of whether both states are populated by similar ethnicities. In other words, the variable measures whether the first major group in state A is the same as the first major group in state B; the second major group in state A is the same as the second major group in state B; and the third major group in state A is the same as the third major group in state B. To determine the major religious groups in each country, I used the World Religion Project (WRP) dataset, which has information on every country, for every five-year period (Maoz and Henderson 2013). I am interested, specifically, in whether a potential supporter has a majority group with the same religious identity as the majority group in a target. The final item in measuring ideational affinity between two states is political ideology. In addition to measurement of targets and supporters in terms of whether they are jointly democratic, I also use new data on states governed by communist/socialist regimes in the post-1945 period. [16]

In summary, four criteria have been used in determining the ideational characteristics of states:

1. Top three ethnic groups in each country, from the EPR dataset.
2. Top three religious groups in each country, from the WRP dataset.
3. Whether a state is governed by a single-party socialist regime in a given year.
4. The polity score (democracy-autocracy) from the Polity IV dataset.[17]

3.3.4 REBEL GROUP AND POTENTIAL SUPPORTER IDEATIONAL AFFINITY

The NAGs dataset codes the ethnic identity and religious affiliation of each armed group using the EPR dataset (Cederman et. al., 2010) and the WRP dataset (Maoz and

Henderson 2013).[18] In cases where a group's ethnic identity was not clear, the identity of the group's leader was used as the identity of the rebel group. For multiethnic rebel groups, whose composition included members with more than three different ethnic backgrounds, only the top three ethnicities found in their country of origin have been included. Ethnic identity is coded not only for ethno-nationalist movements, but also for all rebel groups and their potential supporters. The current dataset matches the top three identities, if more than a single ethnicity is present among the militants of a rebel group, with the identities of major ethnic groups found in potential supporters.

Furthermore, to distinguish and control for the effect of transnational ethnic kin, when a rebel group is from the same ethnic group as a minority in the potential supporter, a separate variable is coded.[19] A separate variable is built by matching the ethnicity of each rebel group with the second, third, and/or fourth ethnic group in each supporter, according to the EPR dataset. Ethnic communities might be treated like a minority within a state regardless of their size. For example, although Sunni Muslims constitute almost 75 percent of the population in Syria, the ruling elite comes from the Alawis (Shi'a), which constitutes 11 percent of the entire population. Nonetheless, such cases are not an impediment in treating Alawis as minorities. It is a separate research agenda to examine the influence of transnational minorities when they have control of and access to power.[20]

Similarly, religious identity is coded for each rebel group, regardless of whether a group has theocratic aspirations. When it was not possible to determine the specific branch of a religion that the group identifies itself with (e.g. Sunni, Shi'a, Roman Catholic, Orthodox, etc.), broad religious identities (e.g., Muslim, Christian) are used to identify a given rebel group's identity. Similar to the ethnic identity variable, for multi-religious rebel groups whose composition included members with more than three different religious backgrounds, only the top three major religions within a rebel group have been coded. In measuring the presence of religious ties between rebel groups and supporter states, religious affiliations of rebels were matched with the major religion groups within their potential supporters.

With respect to the political ideology of rebels, the NAGs dataset includes information on several indicators. To investigate various political aspirations of NAGs, the dataset codes whether an armed rebel group adopts a leftist ideology, has democratic aspirations, or endeavors to install a military, dictatorial, or theocratic regime within their targets. Almost 25 percent of rebel groups are found to adopt some form of a leftist or Marxist ideology, at some point during their existence.[21] Only 7 percent of all groups had some aspirations to establish a democratic regime in the country they were targeting. Almost 11 percent of rebel groups coded in the NAGs dataset had aspirations to found a theocratic, or religion-based, regime within the territories of their target state.

When it comes to whether a rebel group primarily identifies itself with an ethno-national or religious identity, though the two are not mutually exclusive, the NAGs dataset contains information on the primary orientation of rebel groups. Almost 23 percent of groups are identified as having no ideational affiliation. Examples include groups like Liberians United for Reconciliation and Democracy (LURD) and the Movement for Democracy in Liberia (MODEL). Both groups fought against the dictatorial regime of Charles Taylor and possessed no ethnic or religious aspirations. In contrast, they received motivation and assistance from the Liberians abroad in the forms of safe havens, training, arms, and logistics support from Côte d'Ivoire (Ivory Coast), to topple the dictatorial regime in their country.

A total of 43 percent of the rebel groups in the NAGs dataset are identified as affiliated with a specific ethno-national identity; in other words, ethno-national identity is politicized to the extent that the group has aspirations to promote the objectives of a given ethno-national group. On the other hand, 15 percent of the groups identified as religiously motivated. Finally, almost 25 percent of the rebel groups adopted a leftist or socialist ideology at some point during their existence. As mentioned previously, these are not mutually exclusive categories.

Frequently, religion can be a component of ethno-national identity. For example, although Fatah was founded as a secular, ethno-nationalist movement, with the goal of liberating Palestinian territories from the occupation of Israel, other Palestinian militant groups emphasized Islam as a component of Palestinian nationalist identity in later years. By the same token, Fatah adopted socialist teachings from its beginnings (Olson 1973). The identity and objectives of the group evolved as a result of its interaction with the target state. In other words, it is socially constructed as a result of the interaction between rebel groups and states, constructivist scholars would argue. The emphasis in this book is on an equally valuable issue: the role of ideational affinity between rebels and states, leading to the emergence of state support for rebel groups.

When it comes to coding democracy as an indicator of state-rebel group affinity, the story gets more complicated. A democratic government does not automatically end up promoting democracy abroad. So far, no scholarly consensus exists on whether a democratic state is expected to support a rebel group just because it is fighting to bring democracy to a country. The United States can be identified as a state carrying the flag of democracy, especially in the post–Cold War period. Nonetheless, it is beyond the scope of this book to examine whether democracy can guide a state's foreign policy as a political ideology (Tiller 1997).[22] Scholars have competing views on whether policymakers have used democracy as a mask, designed to hide the real intentions of the U.S. government (Ikenberry 2000; Nau 2000; Smith 2000). However, not every democracy follows the United States, promoting democracy as an idea that is perceived to guarantee global order in the long run. Therefore, though democracy can be treated as a variable in measuring ideational affinity between states, it cannot be treated the same way when it comes to rebel group-potential supporter ideational affinity. Just because a rebel group aspires to bring democracy to their target states does not mean that they really intend to do so and will establish a democratic regime once they gain access to power. Therefore, three indicators are used in capturing whether there is ideational affinity between states and rebel groups: ethnic identity, religious identity, and leftist/socialist ideology. Each rebel group is matched with potential supporter states in terms of these three indicators.

Examining state selection and rebel selection cases separately, the NAGs dataset reveals that states opted for ideationally contiguous rebels almost 48 percent of the time, when they made a decision to support a rebel group. Rebels opted for ideationally contiguous states 35 percent of the time, when they made a decision to seek support in other countries. When it comes to ideational ties between target and potential supporter states, the expectation is that states will not provide support to rebels who fight against ideationally contiguous states. The findings support this thesis, indicating that states support rebels fighting against ideationally contiguous states only 20 percent of the time, and rebels choose ideationally contiguous states to their targets only 23 percent of the time.

Several objectives have been coded for rebel groups in the NAGs dataset. Almost 50 percent of the rebel groups that existed in the post-1945 period (225 out of 455 groups) sought a change of leadership in target states. A total of 42 percent of these groups received support from states that were intentionally trying to topple leaders in the target states of the rebel groups they supported. A total of 24 percent of rebel groups acted to change the political regime type in their targets, whereas 33 percent wanted to secede from their targets and establish their own states. Out of the secessionist movements, 47 percent received backing from external states. A total of 15 percent of the rebel groups demanded some form of autonomy from the states they were targeting. A total of 39 percent of these groups received external state backing. These figures refer to the support that emerges as a result of the state selection process, and the objectives are not mutually exclusive. A rebel group might simultaneously claim "toppling an existing leadership" and "autonomy" as objectives.

3.4 Conclusion

This chapter discussed the data collection procedures, addressed the issues associated with those procedures, and clarified the measurement of dependent variables for specific cases. I discussed only the measurement of key variables here; the explanatory and control variables used to specify and predict each model—SSM and RSM—are discussed in the corresponding chapters. The chapters on each model clarify the measurement of the major explanatory and control variables, and explain the statistical methods specified to estimate the probability of support onset and the level of support.

4 States' Selection Model

BETWEEN 1945 AND 2010, India witnessed violence from a total of twenty-five rebel groups fighting to secede, topple the existing leadership, or change the governing regime type. Ten of these rebel groups received support from Pakistan, Bangladesh, Bhutan, and China. Given the troubled relations between India and the others, it is not surprising that these states ended up supporting many of the rebel groups fighting India. Neither of the states supported all of the groups fighting against India, though. Pakistan supported the ones fighting over Kashmir, with which it shares similar strategic interests and ideational ties (both ethnic and religious). [1] China supported the ones located in the northeast of India, until Mao and the communist regime consolidated their power in China in the late 1970s. After that, most Chinese support went to the socialist-oriented insurgencies.

During the same period, Pakistan was targeted by a total of nine groups, four of which were from Balochistan, the largest of Pakistan's four provinces, located in the southwestern region of the country. Despite the fact that the intense conflict in this region often went unnoticed by the international community, it consumed the lives of almost 10,000 people. [2] The Balochs led a total of five insurgencies against the Pakistani government at various times, throughout the entire post–World War II period. Since the early 2000s, three new rebel groups launched another round of violence in the area: the Balochistan Liberation Army (BLA), the Balochistan Republic Army (BRA), and the Baloch Ittihad.[3]

During the 1970s, the United States assisted the Pakistani government in repressing the insurgency, due to concerns over a weakened Pakistani government motivating the expansion of Soviet influence in the region (Khan 2009). In February 2012, a bill was proposed in the U.S. Congress to support the right of the Baloch people to self-determination, including those who live in Iran and Afghanistan (Baloch 2012).[4] Furthermore, serious allegations have been put forward blaming India, the protracted rival of Pakistan, for providing weapons and funds to the BRA (Gall 2011).[5] These cases illustrate the various motives states have when making decisions whether to support rebels fighting against other states. The rivalry between India and Pakistan is just one of many interstate rivalries that serve as an opportunity for rebel groups to acquire external resources. Not all rivals support rebels fighting their enemy, yet some do under some conditions.

The large-N statistical analysis in this chapter estimates a probabilistic model for conditions under which they are most likely to do so. Out of 193 states in the world (the entire UN members), 102 have been subject to violent acts by one or more rebel groups in the post-1945 period. The NAGs dataset codes ninety-five states[6] that intentionally chose to provide some form of support to rebels, for some period of time, according to the state selection process. The map at Figure 4.1 shows the distribution of target and supporter states across various parts of the world. Out of the total years of external state support, 72 percent belong to the states located in East and South Asia, the Middle East and North Africa, and sub-Saharan Africa.

In this chapter, I conduct a series of statistical analyses to test the hypotheses derived from the SSM, using the newly collected NAGs dataset. The primary goal is to predict the decision to support rebels and the level of support provided. I am particularly interested in the role played by material and ideational motives, when states cooperate with rebel groups targeting other states. Ideational motives are, to a great extent, shaped by the identities of major ethnic and religion groups living within states, governing political ideology, and/or regime type. Material or strategic incentives are shaped by the internal and external threat environment, and domestic extractive and mobilization capacity. While countries such as Belgium, Brazil, the Netherlands, and Azerbaijan do not seem to provide intentional support to any rebel group, it appears to be a common practice for other states, including major powers, such as the United States, Russia, and China, and states driven by ideological aspirations, such as Cuba and Iran, as is demonstrated in Figure 4.2.

Furthermore, while groups like Hezbollah and the PKK manage to appeal to multiple state supporters, others, such as ETA and the Farabundo Martí National

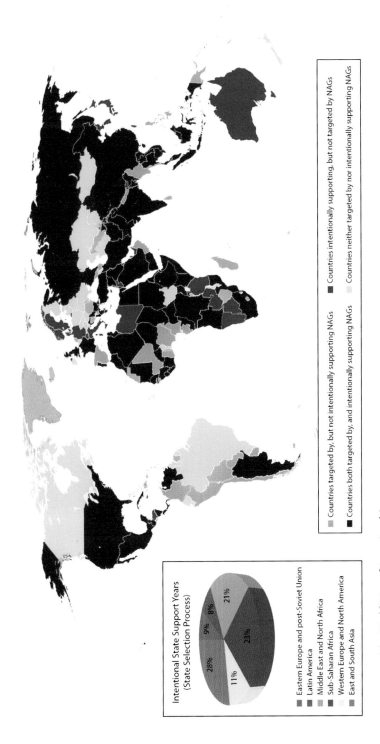

FIGURE 4.1 The World Map of Intentional Supporters, 1945–2010

Intentional State Support Years
(State Selection Process)

- Eastern Europe and post-Soviet Union
- Latin America
- Middle East and North Africa
- Sub-Saharan Africa
- Western Europe and North America
- East and South Asia

28% 9% 8%
11% 21%
23%

- Countries targeted by, but not intentionally supporting NAGs
- Countries both targeted by, and intentionally supporting NAGs
- Countries intentionally supporting, but not targeted by NAGs
- Countries neither targeted by nor intentionally supporting NAGs

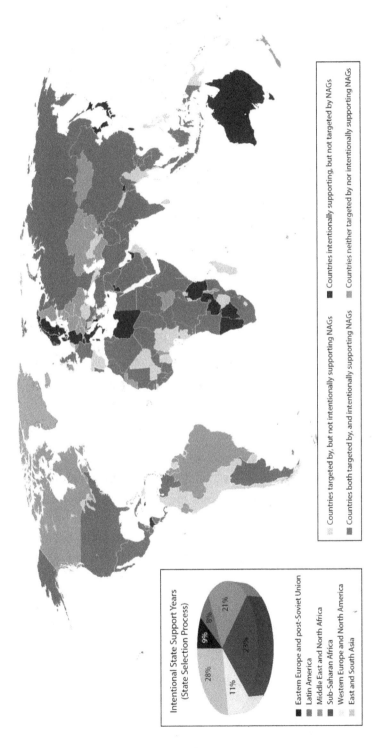

FIGURE 4.1 The World Map of Intentional Supporters, 1945–2010

Countries targeted by, but not intentionally supporting NAGs

Countries intentionally supporting, but not targeted by NAGs

Countries both targeted by, and intentionally supporting NAGs

Countries neither targeted by nor intentionally supporting NAGs

Intentional State Support Years
(State Selection Process)

21%

8%

9%

23%

28%

11%

Eastern Europe and post-Soviet Union

Latin America

Middle East and North Africa

Sub-Saharan Africa

Western Europe and North America

East and South Asia

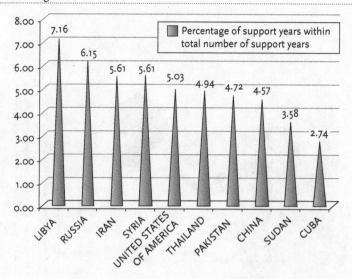

FIGURE 4.2 Top Ten Intentional Supporters, 1945–2010

Liberation Front (FMNLF), had little luck in securing long-term support from out-side states. Although the latter two groups were actively engaged in violence for at least a decade, ETA received only brief and limited support from France and Libya until the mid-1980s, and the FMNLF received some support from Nicaragua in the early 1990s. These cases illustrate that some rebels attract the interest of some states, to the extent that the latter provides support despite a possible retaliation risk from the targets of these groups.

The rest of this chapter is organized into four sections. The next section presents a brief discussion of Palestinian militant groups that have been fighting against Israel in the period between 1945 and 2010, and the external states that provide safe havens, funds, weapons, and other forms of support to them. Through a brief narrative about the interactions between Israel, Palestinian militant groups, and the groups' state supporters, such as Egypt and Syria, the theoretical foundation of intentional state support of rebel groups is highlighted. The objective of the case study of the Palestinian militant groups is not to confirm or reject hypotheses, but to point to the complex web of interactions between states and rebel groups, and show how inter-state relations further exacerbate this complexity. Subsequently, the hypotheses from the SSM are presented. The next section describes the research design, the operationalization of the rest of the explanatory variables, and the control variables included in the models. Following, that, I will specify the models for estimating the initial decision to support, and the support level, present the statistical techniques used to estimate the models, and discuss the empirical findings.

4.1 A Brief Case Study and Key Hypotheses: Which States Support Rebels?

4.1.1 PALESTINIAN MILITANT GROUPS AND EXTERNAL STATE SUPPORT

Since its foundation, Israel has been involved in several armed conflicts, with neighboring Arab states and Palestinian armed groups, frequently abetted by these countries. Most incidents of the neighboring states' support of Palestinian militant groups occurred after the Six-Day War between Israel and a united coalition of Egypt, Syria, Jordan, and Iraq in 1967, who had suffered a major defeat in the end of the war. The groups that received persistent support include Fatah, the PFLP, PFLP-GC, and the PIJ. On the other hand, the costly defeat of the Arab coalition by Israel left few options for the Palestinians, but to start engaging with the enemy directly, as their hopes faded that the Arab states would recover the Palestinian territories lost to Israel in 1948 (Perlmutter 1981; Cleveland 2004, p. 346).[7] The territorial loss suffered by Egypt, Jordan, and Syria further contributed to a loss of faith in the ability of the Arab states to defeat Israel on the battlefield.

From the perspective of the Arab states, the Palestinian militant organizations presented an opportunity to engage against their common enemy indirectly, by supporting "the enemy of their enemy." Throughout the 1950s, the 1960s, and the 1970s, Egypt and Syria also experienced domestic turmoil in trying to consolidate various forms of authoritarianism, mostly born of military coup d'états and challenged by Sunni opposition movements, such as Muslim Brotherhood. Jordan was burdened with a high number of Palestinian refugees, causing disturbances to internal stability and threatening the rule of the Hashemite dynasty.

In such an environment of simultaneous internal and external threats, accompanied by the deteriorating ability of governments to extract resources internally and mobilize the domestic population to fight for the state, Palestinian groups turned out to be convenient allies against the common enemy of Israel. Figure 4.3 presents the groups that have been fighting Israel since its foundation and their state supporters.[8] External state supporters on the graph neither continuously supported these groups, nor provided support for all militant groups. Each state chose the militant group(s) it wished to support against Israel. Indeed, in some cases, states *created* groups that would cater to their interests without asking for a great deal of operational autonomy.

Among the supporters, Jordan, Iraq, Syria, Lebanon, Sudan, Libya, Tunisia, and Algeria had some conflict history with Israel. After Israel's declaration of independence on May 14, 1948, following the end of the British mandate in the Palestinian territories, a coalition of Arab states, including Iraq, Jordan, Syria, Egypt, and Lebanon, invaded Israel. Though Lebanon contributed a lower number of troops to

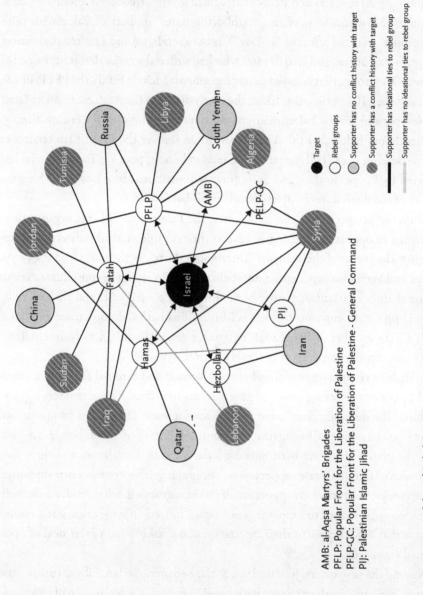

AMB: al-Aqsa Martyrs' Brigades

PFLP: Popular Front for the Liberation of Palestine

PFLP-GC: Popular Front for the Liberation of Palestine - General Command

PIJ: Palestinian Islamic Jihad

- Target
- Rebel groups
- Supporter has no conflict history with target
- Supporter has a conflict history with target
- Supporter has ideational ties to rebel group
- Supporter has no ideational ties to rebel group

FIGURE 4.3 Selected Rebel Groups against Israel and Supporters, 1945–2010

the united Arab forces, it confronted Israel in the first phase of the war and withdrew from fighting early in 1948. The case of Lebanon and Israel is considered as an interstate conflict, thus leading to a shared conflict history between the two (Cleveland 2004, p. 267). Moreover, the Lebanese army also trained Palestinians during the 1967 war (Samii 1997). Sudan sent troops to fight alongside the Egyptian army during the same war. Algeria and Libya provided aircraft to fight against Israel to support the land operations of regular Arab forces, including Egypt, Syria, Jordan, and Iraq (Oren 2002). Tunisia contributed troops to fight alongside the Egyptian army during both the Six-Day War in 1967 and the Yom Kippur War (Ramadan War) in October 1973. Although Tunisia, Libya, and Algeria did not engage as heavily as Egypt, Iraq, Syria, and Jordan, they all experienced initial conflict-ridden relations with Israel.

Among the states that suffered territorial loss at the end of the Six-Day War, Egypt was the only one that did not cooperate extensively with militant Palestinian groups. Although the PLO was founded in Cairo to represent the Palestinians, with the active leadership of Egypt, it was initially an organization composed of "Cairo-based bureaucratic notables" (Cleveland 2004, p. 359). Later, it turned into an umbrella organization that brought together several Palestinian militant groups.

It was not until 1969, in the aftermath of the Six Day War, that Yasser Arafat, the founder of Fatah, was invited to become the chairman of the organization. Indeed, the Fatah leader had long lived outside Egypt at that time, due to the Egyptian government's policy of repression against the Palestinian militant groups. Between 1959 and 1964, Fatah operated mostly underground (Zelkovitz 2015, p. 678). The Free Officers regime, which assumed power in Egypt in 1952, perceived the Muslim Brotherhood movement as the most significant internal threat to its rule. Because Palestinian militant groups appeared to emerge within the ranks of the Muslim Brotherhood, the Egyptian government maintained its distance from them.

Though Nasser allowed cross-border attacks into Israel from the Gaza Strip, which had come under Egyptian control after the 1948 war (Atzili 2010), it did not take long before he shifted strategy. The attacks were conducted by fedayeen, a group of unaffiliated militants that emerged largely within the ranks of Palestinian refugees, who migrated to the neighboring states of Jordan, Egypt, and Syria after the foundation of Israel. Indeed, fedayeen attacks were later used to justify Israel's attempted invasion of Egypt in 1956, with the help of France and Britain, otherwise known as the Suez Crisis, and the Six-Day War in 1967. In the aftermath of the 1956 Suez crisis, Nasser agreed to the expulsion of all Palestinian militants from the Gaza Strip and the Sinai Peninsula. This occurred after a decision was reached by Nasser to purchase arms from the Soviet Union through Czechoslovakia (Golani 1995).

In other words, Nasser had found conventional state allies in his struggle against Britain and Israel.

The SSM argues that facing external threats, states either engage in *internal balancing*, through extraction of material and human resources from their domestic populace, or in *external balancing*, through formation of alliances with states they have common strategic interests with. Trying to establish itself as a legitimate domestic government, the military regime in Egypt was under threat from various segments of the society, who were not happy with increasing unemployment and inflation. Since internal balancing was difficult, and Nasser and subsequent presidents did not want to ally with an armed group affiliated with the Muslim Brotherhood, Egypt had a cautious relationship with Palestinian groups after the 1970s. Adopting a socialist ideology helped Egypt to find a conventional state ally in its fight against Israel. Externally, Palestinian groups' incursions into Israel were used as an excuse by Israel to launch attacks against Egypt, both during the 1956 Suez crisis and the 1967 Six-Day War. Thus, the risk of Israeli retaliation made Egypt more selective with respect to the types of support it provided to Palestinian militant groups.

Among the other supporters of various Palestinian militant groups in Figure 4.3, China, Russia, South Yemen, and Iran were driven by their ideational affinity to several Palestinian militant groups. The most prominent of these groups was Fatah, founded in 1959 by Yasser Arafat. At the time, Fatah's ideology, though it incorporated some pan-Arabism, was a mix of Islamism, Marxism, and nationalism (Zelkovitz 2015, p. 675). Both China and Russia had ideological affinity with various leftist and/or Marxist-oriented armed movements of the time, including Fatah. Indeed, Chinese arms transfer to Fatah goes back to the period prior to the Six-Day War (New York Times 1972a, 1972b). Fatah moved away from socialism, toward Palestinian nationalism, especially in an effort to disconnect the idea of the foundation of an independent state for Palestinian Arabs from the ambitions of the strong leaders in the region (Mann 2007). While serving as the chairman, Arafat adopted a Palestinian nationalist ideology, thus disassociating the PLO from the major ideologies of the Arab states at the time, such as Pan-Arabism (Nasserism), Socialism, and Ba'athism. Thus, he managed to escape the influence of strong leaders, such as Assad and Nasser, who would have restricted the autonomy of the movement and dominate their command structure.

Ideational ties between Fatah and its two strongest potential supporters, Egypt and Syria, were already strained after the establishment of socialist oriented governments under the Ba'ath regime in Syria and the Free Officers regime in Egypt. Syria dropped its support of Fatah's autonomous activities early on, in 1968, since the latter did not ascribe to the ideology of the Ba'ath regime. Indeed, during the Lebanese civil war, Syria fought alongside Maronite militiamen against the PLO

(Cleveland 2004, p. 385). The Arab states had to interfere to broker peace between Syria and the PLO in 1976.

This confrontation with the Fatah-led PLO did not mean that these countries stopped cooperating with other PLO groups. Syria took the lead in founding and supporting groups to which it could relate ideationally, and that it could control easily. It found itself a new instrument, al-Saaiqa, which was an organization created by unifying three Palestinian organizations: the PFLP, the Pioneers of the People's War of Liberation, and the Organization for the Liberation of the Upper Galilee (Mann 2007, p. 122). Al-Saaiqa shared the Ba'athist ideology and agreed to obey the Syrian regime. A further diminution of relations between Syria and the PLO under the leadership of Arafat occurred in 1993, after the Oslo Accords. In response, Syria organized the Alliance of Palestinian Forces (APF), which consist of groups, who were not happy with the Oslo process (Strindberg 2000). Damascus became a haven for ten different Palestinian organizations, including the PFLP, Hamas, and the PIJ at this time.

Among the APF groups, the PIJ was founded during the 1970s, among Palestinian refugees in Egypt. It moved to the Gaza Strip after being blamed for the assassination of Sadat in 1981, remaining there until 1988. After the start of the first Intifada, the group was expelled and moved to Lebanon, where it established close ties with Iran and Hezbollah.[9] In 1989, the PIJ moved its headquarters to Damascus, and in the aftermath of the Oslo Accords in 1993, it became a member of the Syrian-led APF, opposed to Arafat and his moderate policy toward Israel.

The PIJ also managed to get support from Iran, which started to support Palestinian armed groups after the Islamic Revolution in 1979, first with the PFLP-GC, and later with Hamas and the PIJ. These three organizations were perceived as strategic allies of Hezbollah in the fight against Israel (Strindberg 2000, p. 63). Originally founded in 1959 and named the Palestinian Liberation Front (PLF), the PFLP-GC splintered from the PFLP in 1968, due to the latter's emphasis on Socialism. It was not difficult for the PFLP-GC to align its ideology with the new regime in Iran, thus becoming the first Palestinian organization ever to receive support from Iran (Strindberg 2000, p. 67; Gambill 2002). Though Syria did not allow any Palestinian groups to operate against Israel from the Lebanese territories it occupied, it allowed the PFLP-GC to operate alongside Hezbollah throughout the 1990s (Gambill 2002).

Jordan and Lebanon are also among the states that have a conflict history with Israel. Although initially allowing cross-border infiltrations of various Palestinian groups into Israel, and preferred by Palestinian groups as a safe haven, Jordan realized it was becoming harder to control the operations of these groups, which had rushed across the Jordanian borders after the war of 1967. The Six-Day War led to territorial loss for Jordan and turned it into one of the most preferred destinations among the neighboring states for Palestinian groups. Yet the civil war, mostly instigated by the PLO in Jordan, led the Hashemite regime to expel the Palestinians (Mutawi 2002; Oren 2002). A coup d'état attempt by a group of fedayeen, who wanted to seize Jordanian kingdom, resulted in violent repression by Jordanian army and expulsion of many Palestinians in 1970. These incidents of September 1970 came to be referred as Black September conflict, which also inspired the foundation of an armed group with the same name. Yet Jordan resumed its toleration of Palestinian militant groups after the first Intifada began. Hamas, founded in Gaza soon after the start of the first Intifada in December 1987,[10] enjoyed safe havens within Jordanian territories until the United States, Israel, and the Palestinians themselves pressured the Jordanian king to expel Hamas from its territories (Associated Press International 1999; Briggs 2006).

Although Lebanon found itself in the position of de facto safe haven for Palestinian militant groups, in 1969, it signed an agreement to transfer control of refugee camps, populated by around 300,000 Palestinian refugees, to the PLO. The condition was that the PLO consults the Lebanese government when deciding to launch operations against Israel (Cleveland 2004, p. 383). Thus, initially, it can be argued that Lebanon was providing intentional support to Palestinian militants. Though later, the Lebanese government proved reluctant to engage in war against Israel, mostly due to the Christian Maronite majority's amicable relations with Israel. However, the fact that it engaged briefly in conflict with Israel made Lebanon a friendly place to recruit militants and obtain resources, from the perspective of the PLO. In addition, Lebanon became a valuable safe haven for PLO militants, due to its geographical contiguity with Israel, its hosting a large number of Palestinian refugees who could potentially be recruited into the ranks of the PLO, and the existing arrangement of political power, based on the country's ethnic divisions.

Societal fragmentation within Lebanon curtailed the government's ability to fully mobilize the masses and extract the resources required to keep the PLO camps under control. After the Black September events, which pushed Palestinians out of Jordan, mostly into Lebanon, and following a rise in cross-border incursions into Israel from Lebanon, Israel assassinated three Palestinian leaders in Beirut in 1973. Lebanese society was divided about whether to allow Palestinian militants to conduct raids against Israeli targets from within its territory, which would provoke retaliation from Israel. The social unrest on the issue of letting cross-border attacks into Israel sparked a civil war in August 1975, between Maronite Christians and the PLO, followed by intervention by Syria and Israel into Lebanon. Though Syria interfered on the side of the Maronite Christians against the PLO, the cease-fire between Syria and the PLO only led to consolidation of PLO strongholds in southern Lebanon, which was conveniently located near Israel. Subsequent instability in Lebanon served as an invitation for Israel to invade southern Lebanon in 1982. It is not surprising that the PLO leadership next moved its headquarters to Tunisia, which had a brief show of solidarity with Egypt against Israel during the wars of 1967 and 1973.

Though it withdrew in 1983, Israel maintained a security zone across the border with Lebanon, which constituted approximately 10 percent of Lebanon's entire territory. It was also during this period that Hezbollah emerged as an armed movement within the Shi'a community residing in southern Lebanon against foreign occupation. Lebanon was under occupation by Syria until 2005 and by Israel until 2000. Thus, Lebanon is assumed not to provide any support, intentionally or de facto, between 1976 and 2005, when there was not a fully functioning independent government within its borders. After 2005, though, when the foreign occupiers left, Lebanon found itself in a de facto supporter position with no military capacity to confront Hezbollah in southern Lebanon (Harik 2004, pp. 47–48). This recent period could qualify as an intentional safe haven, since the Lebanese government has knowingly allowed its southern territory to be occupied by Hezbollah. Yet even in this case, it is a controversial coding decision, since Hezbollah is native to Lebanon; that is, it did not move into Lebanon from another state. Therefore, when it comes to Hezbollah, Lebanon is not identified as a safe haven.

Among the militant groups fighting against Israel, and the states with which they cooperate, the alliance between Iran and Hezbollah has proved the most resilient.[11] The ideational affinity Iran shares with Hezbollah, a Shi'a militant group, turned the country into the most dedicated supporter of the group (Dakroub 1995; Wilner 2012). Yet, Iran did not shy away from providing support to other fundamentalist Palestinian militant groups, such as Hamas and the al-Aqsa Martyrs' Brigades (AMB). Indeed, the Karine-A incident of 2002, when Israel captured a vessel stocked with sophisticated weaponry worth more than $2 million, revealed the relationship between Iran and other Palestinian militant groups (Levitt 2007, p. 176). It was traveling from Iran's Kish Island to Gaza and was operated by Hezbollah. Nonetheless, Iran stayed far from Fatah and the PLO, which is perceived to be a more secular and nationalist organization than Hamas and the AMB.

The theory of state-rebel group cooperation is discussed in previous chapters. Here, I reiterate the hypotheses. In general, a state's choice to support a rebel group is argued to be a function of the conflict history with the rebel group's target, as seen in the case of Israel and various Arab states, and ideational ties with both the rebel group (Iran-Hezbollah, Iran-Hamas, Syria-Hezbollah) and its target state. Furthermore, the supporter's relative strength vis-à-vis a rebel group's target, and the level of domestic instability, are claimed to determine the conditions under which conflict history and ideational ties motivate the initial decision to support rebels. Indeed, it is argued that states are most likely to provide support to rebels fighting against their enemies or rivals when they are also facing challenges domestically. Leaders or governments that experience internal threats to their rule will have a difficult time extracting resources at home and mobilizing their domestic population to fight against an external threat from another state. Under these circumstances, supporting rebel groups as proxies turns out to be an effective strategy at home in two ways. First, resources that would otherwise be expended to fight against an external threat can now be saved and directed entirely toward consolidating power at home. Second, the reaction by target states, and the international community in general, can be utilized as a scapegoating narrative, to rally support for the existing leadership and government.

This was the story of the Mohammad Reza Pahlavi regime in Iran during the 1960s and the 1970s. The end of the 1960s witnessed the transfer of power to the Ba'ath Party in Iraq, and the Pahlavi regime in Iran was worried about a similar fate. The Ba'ath government in Iraq made an alliance with the Soviets in 1972, and the Soviets agreed to provide the new regime with arms. Although the United States backed Iran, it did not provide it with arms until the mid-1970s (Gasiorowski 1988, p. 180). Actual figures indicate that while the arms delivered to Tehran by Washington amounted to about 120,000 in 1970; the figure jumped to almost a million in 1975 (Barak 2003).[12]

Internally, the Iranian government faced strong opposition from various groups, which led to increasing repression by the shah in the 1970s. The opposing groups were composed of students and intellectuals with university backgrounds, among the urban petit bourgeoisie. The period between 1970 and 1974 witnessed extensive public demonstrations of these groups against the Pahlavi regime. In January 1974, seven Iranian journalists, poets, writers, and filmmakers were sentenced to death for plotting to kidnap the shah and other members of the royal family (MERIP 1978). The regime used the army and the secret police, the Organization of Intelligence and National Security (the SAVAK)[13], to pacify the social unrest and domestic opposition (Karsh 1987–1988, p. 86). According to the report of Middle East Research and Information Project (MERIP), in 1974, the Iranian government purchased police and crowd control weapons for various security units, including the army, the SAVAK, the Imperial Guard, and the Imperial Gendarmerie (MERIP 1978). The SAVAK and the Imperial Iranian Gendarmerie employed approximately 100,000 to 130,000 people in the 1970s (Bueno de Mesquita et al. 2003, p. 344).

In this sense, the Iranian government allocated considerable resources to control both internal and external threats. The Pahlavi regime did not have sufficient military capacity to deter possible aggression from a Soviet-allied Iraq in the beginning of the 1970s. Stretched between internal and external threats, it perceived the Kurdish insurgency in northern Iraq as an opportunity to instigate internal turmoil within Iraq to divert the focus of Baghdad from engaging in an armed confrontation against Tehran (MERIP 1975). The immediate goal of the Shah's government was to force Iraq to make concessions regarding the navigation rights in the Shatt al-Arab waterway. Tehran's long-term goal was to undermine the authority of a hostile regime. Ultimately, the two states reached an agreement after a brief period of border fighting in January 1975 (MERIP 1974). Due to increasing violence by Iran-supported Kurds, and in return for a cessation of Iranian support for the Kurdish rebels, Iraq had to make concessions with regard to the Shatt al-Arab waterway.

4.1.2 STATES' SELECTION MODEL HYPOTHESES

These examples accentuate the following hypotheses proposed with respect to SSM:

Material or Strategic Motives

H_1: A state is more likely to support a rebel group that targets an adversary, rather than a group that targets a non-adversary. The level of support also tends to be higher if a rebel group targets its adversary.

H_{1a}: The likelihood of a state's support of a rebel group increases as the relative strength of the external adversary (the rebel group's target) decreases.

H_{1b}: The likelihood of supporting a rebel group against an adversary increases if leaders have to deal with internal unrest and external threat simultaneously.

$H_{1c:}$ States are more likely to support rebels against their external adversaries if they do not have conventional state allies to fight alongside with them. In the event of an attack from the adversary rebels serve as substitutes for regular state allies.

Cultural and Ideational Motives:

H_2: A state is more likely to support an ideationally contiguous rebel group than a rebel group with which it does not share any ideational ties. And, the level of support tends to be higher for these groups.

H_{2a}: The likelihood of a state's support of an ideationally contiguous rebel group increases if it is relatively strong vis-à-vis the rebel group's target.

H_{2b}: Common ideational ties between a state and a rebel group increase the likelihood of support, even if the rebel group's target is not an adversary.

H_3: The level of support increases if a state has ideational ties with a rebel group that targets its adversary (interaction effect of supporter material and ideational motives).

H_4: The likelihood of support decreases if a rebel group's supporter and target are ideationally contiguous states. In addition, the level of support also declines if two states share ideational ties.

H_{4a}: When having common ties with both rebels and their targets, supporters tend to value their ties with target states more than the ones with rebels (interstate ideational affinity).

4.2 Research Design

4.2.1 DATA

I test the hypotheses about the initial decision of states to support rebels, and the level of support, with a dataset of 455 rebel groups that targeted one or more states between 1945 and 2010, and their state supporters.[14] I define state support of rebels as any form of support that directly or indirectly contributes to rebels' capability to engage in violence against their targets. This includes providing rebels with funds, arms, transport of arms, logistics aid, safe havens, training camps, and troops, as well as allowing them to open offices and train their members.

In addition, a thorough analysis of each rebel group and its supporters has been conducted to determine whether a state intentionally created channels to support a rebel group. In other words, it is significant whether rebels are supported as a systematic policy on the part of the supporter state, or if they manage to raise funds, recruit members, find safe havens, and smuggle weapons within the borders of a state due to the latter's turning a blind eye to rebel activities, flexible policies, and/or institutional constraints that make it difficult to control the activities of such groups.[15] For example, Israel captured two Hamas members after their entry into Israel in January 1993. Both were U.S. citizens, residents of Chicago, and they were dispatched to Israel by the Hamas leadership abroad, to revitalize the local organization and headquarters of Hamas in Gaza after Israel's expulsion of 400 Hamas leaders to Lebanon in December 1992 (Mideast Mirror 1993). This is considered de facto support, where the U.S. government does not create channels to intentionally help Hamas, but Hamas leaders, like many other leaders and members of militant organizations, prefer democratic states within which to reside, organize, and recruit.

A rebel group may have both intentional and de facto supporters. A total of 9 percent of rebel groups managed to get intentional and de facto support simultaneously, according to the NAGs dataset. Around 49 percent of the observations in the dataset are characterized as support that emerged as a result of rebels' selection, and 51 percent of the observations are characterized as support that emerged as a result of states' selection. The empirical analysis in this chapter is conducted on the latter 51 percent of the cases. Chapter 5 focuses on the 49 percent of the cases that are characterized as de facto support.

4.2.2 THE UNIT OF ANALYSIS

The unit of analysis is a triad year, which includes a rebel group, a target (the state that is subject to rebel violence), and a potential supporter (the state that is likely to support a rebel group, when an opportunity to support arises). Each triad has as many observations as the number of years a rebel group is actively targeting a state. The dataset is both cross-sectional and time-series. The opportunity to support a rebel group arises with its formation and continues until the group becomes inactive, that is, it signs an agreement with its target. The time-series data allow for examining the changing nature of interactions within the same triad. For example, Fatah was a leftist-oriented group initially, mostly because it was inspired by revolutionary ideas from the Soviet Union and China. Yet, later on, it evolved into a secular nationalist movement and moved gradually away from a leftist ideology. Within the same triad, one can trace the influence of ideational ties, conflict history, and other key factors that change over time.[16]

Although the NAGs dataset includes all countries that supported rebel groups, the empirical analysis in the current and subsequent chapters is limited to countries in the PRG of each target state. Using the PRG criteria proves to be an effective way of managing the data required for empirical analysis in this book, which is not only limited to NAGs dataset, but also requires accounting for other explanatory and control variables used in the statistical models. In this respect, PRG criteria allow for identifying potential states with the opportunity to provide support to rebels, but that may or may not choose to do so. It is theoretically reasonable to expect states with a geographical proximity to rebels, in addition to those with a regional and global reach, to choose whether to support rebels fighting against other states. Since one of the distinct approaches of the book is to go beyond declaring every case of rebel support as a proxy war between major powers, relying on politically relevant group criteria does not interfere with the major theoretical and empirical objectives.

4.2.3 DEPENDENT VARIABLE: "SUPPORT ONSET AND SUPPORT LEVEL"

The dependent variable is measured as support onset and support level. The support onset variable receives a value of "1" whenever there is any type of support in a given year and "o" when there is no support. A state does not necessarily have to support a rebel group for the entire time the group is active, though long-term cooperation between groups and states is not sparse. Iran and Hezbollah, Syria and Hamas, Syria and the PKK, and Sudan and the Eritrean People's Liberation Front (EPLF) are among many examples of states offering continuous support to rebels over a long period. Considering that the majority of state support occurs only for a brief period of time, the yearly observation allows for including cases where a supporter ceases support after a while, and examining the effect of explanatory variables on the change in the supporter's decision. Both within-case and across-case analysis is possible when using cross-sectional and time-series data. Furthermore, each observation-year means an opportunity for a given potential supporter to turn into an actual supporter or for an actual supporter to terminate support. Statistical analysis with large-N data helps to uncover the conditions under which either happens.

A quick examination of the actual support years within the triads shows that there are 2,346 cases among the triad-year observations (target-rebels-potential supporter-year) in which a potential supporter turns into an actual state supporter of rebels groups. Out of overall years of support, 33 percent of the time, support emerges only as an intentional foreign policy pursued by states. In 17% of observations, rebels managed getting both intentional and de facto support from the same state. This means that 50% of the time, rebels were operating freely within the borders of other countries to acquire resources without any intentional state sponsorship. A total of 60 percent of all intentional support cases occurred during the Cold War period, in comparison to 40 percent occurring in the post-Cold War era.[17] Since the Cold War era spans almost four-and-a-half decades, one would expect a relatively lower proportion of support occurring in the post-Cold War period. But this does not seem to be the case.

Support level, the second dependent variable, is measured as an ordinal variable, ranging from 0 ("no support") to 1 ("low") to 2 ("moderate support") to 3 (high support") to 4 ("very high support). An index of support level is constructed based on the types of support a state provides to a given rebel group. Table 4.1 presents the index and the proportion of each level of support to the total number of observed support years.

When deciding to support rebels, 13.6 percent of the time, a state ends up providing high and/or very high levels of support, such as safe havens, funds, and weapons. A total of 5.9 percent of the time, a state contributes troops or training camps to rebels. When a state provides support to rebels; it is in the form of funds and safe havens for leaders and training around 44 percent of the time. In a total of 36.5 percent of observations, states choose to serve as transport points for military equipment and logistics aid and/or allow rebels to open offices. The distribution of observations in which states contribute troop support to rebels shows that 33 percent

TABLE 4.1 Support Level Index

Types	Level	Value	Percentage %
Troops or training camps and/or any of the rest of the types	Very High	4	5.9
Safe haven to members or arms and/or any of the rest of the types (excluding cases with very high level of support)	High	3	13.6
Funds, safe havens for leaders and training and/or any of the rest of the types (excluding cases with very high and high levels of support)	Moderate	2	43.9
Transport of equipment, and offices	Low	1	36.5

of troop support occurred during the post–Cold War period, in comparison to 67 percent in the Cold War period. There seems to be a pattern signaling that states are less likely to provide troop support to rebels fighting against other states, thus avoiding the risk of direct confrontation, in the post–Cold War period, by comparison to the Cold War period.

4.2.4 INDEPENDENT VARIABLES

Variables on Supporter-Target Interaction

External Threat

I use a variable developed by Maoz (2007) named the "Strategic Reference Group (SRG)" to test for the "enemy of my enemy" assumption.[18] The SRG of a state includes those states perceived as a security challenge to the focal state. This variable takes a value of "1" if a potential supporter and a target state engaged in a militarized dispute with each other in the last five years, or a war in the last ten years, and a "0" if neither happened. The presence of a conflict history between two states influences their perceptions about each other. States use rebels as substitutes to fight or weaken their enemies. Therefore, conflict history is expected to be instrumental for both the initial decision to support a rebel group and for the level of support provided. The main objective behind examining the effect of conflict history in the empirical analysis is to test the effect of other key variables after controlling for its effect. Only then, is it possible to see if ideational ties have a significant effect in motivating states and rebels to cooperate with each other.

Ideational Affinity

The measurement of ideational affinity between a rebel group and a potential supporter, and between a target and a potential supporter, has been extensively discussed in Chapter 3. Both variables are dichotomous. Whenever a potential supporter state has any ethnic, religious, or ideological ties in common with a target state, this variable takes a value of "1"; otherwise, it takes "0." In each case of ethnic and religious ideational ties, the majority group's identity is taken into consideration. The ethnic groups within potential supporters and targets are coded using the EPR Dataset (Cederman et al. 2010). EPR data include information on ethnic groups in every country. Religious ties between potential supporters and targets are coded using the Global Religion Dataset (Maoz and Henderson 2013). Whenever the major group in a target and a potential supporter are from the same ethnic background and/or religion group, the ideational affinity between a target and a potential supporter takes a value of "1" ; otherwise, it takes "0." In addition, this variable receives a value of "1" if both targets and potential supporters are governed by socialist regimes.[19]

Democracy Level

The democracy level is measured in a dyad of potential supporter-target, using the regime score adopted from the Polity IV (Marshall and Jaggers 2002) dataset. The Polity IV dataset codes each country on a scale ranging from -10 (most autocratic) to 10 (most democratic) and calculates a polity score by subtracting the autocracy score from the democracy score. As the level of democracy (calculated by taking the value of the country with the lower polity score) increases in a given dyad, I expect that the likelihood of providing intentional support to rebel groups declines. In other words, democracies are less likely to support rebels fighting against other democracies. This is also in line with the logic of democratic peace argument.

Relative Strength

The relative strength of each potential supporter vis-à-vis a target state against which it supports a rebel group is calculated using the Correlates of War (COW) database's National Capabilities dataset (Singer et al. 1972).[20] The dataset builds a composite index of national capabilities (CINC) by using six indicators for each country: energy consumption, iron and steel production, military personnel, military expenditure, total population, and urban population. The relative strength of a potential supporter is measured by the ratio of each potential supporter's CINC to the cumulative CINC of a target and a supporter in a given triad. The dataset is currently updated to 2007. To make up for missing observations in every dyad for 2008, 2009, and 2010, I calculated the average of the last five years for each dyad and included these figures in place of missing observations.

Variables for Supporter-Rebel Group Interaction

Ideational Ties

Ideational ties between rebels and potential supporter states are coded using the same datasets mentioned above. Whenever a rebel group shares a common ethnic and religious identity with the majority within a potential supporter, it receives a value of "1"; otherwise, it takes "0." In addition, whenever a rebel group has a leftist or socialist inclination, and a potential supporter is a country governed by a socialist regime, this variable takes a value of "1"; otherwise, it takes "0."

Transnational Ties

An invaluable body of research in the study of ethnic conflict and civil war suggests that civil wars are more likely to spread across the borders of neighboring states, if ethnic insurgents have kin living across the borders of these states. Among the mechanisms of contagion, ethnic kin and host country support for rebel groups are placed on the top (Saideman and Jenne 1992; Stavenhagen 1996; Saideman 1997, 2001; Gleditsch 2007; Cederman et. al 2009; Salehyan et. al 2011; Cederman et. al 2013). Transnational ethnic kin, through support of rebels inside the borders of neighboring states, frequently causes ethnic conflict to spread across the borders of these states. This argument suggests that the likelihood of support increases if a rebel group is from a similar ethnic background as a minority group in the potential supporter. To code transnational ties between rebels and potential supporters, I relied on the EPR dataset's coding of ethnic groups in each state. EPR data codes a first, second, third, etc. group, depending on representation in the entire population. *Transnational ties* match the ethnic identity of a rebel group with the second, third, and fourth ethnic group in each potential supporter. It is a binary variable, receiving a value of "1" if there are transnational ties available; otherwise, it takes "0."

Potential Supporter-Specific Variables

Internal Threat

As a proxy measure of internal threat, whether a leadership or government perceives some domestic threat to its rule, multiple variables are used. First, I use an instability indicator developed by the Political Instability Task Force (Marshall et al. 2015). This measure has also been detailed in Chapter 3. Instability events are defined as revolutionary wars, ethnic wars, adverse regime changes, and/or genocides and politicides. The political instability score is a binary measure, taking a value of "1" whenever an instability event occurs within the borders of a potential supporter.

Second, I use a variable coding whether a leader in a given potential supporter is from a minority group in his or her country. Whether a leader is from a minority group within a country is a significant indicator of the mobilization capacity of states when the time comes to mobilize the domestic populace against external and internal threats (Fearon et al. 2007). If a leader is not from the majority ethnic group in a country, (s)he might face constraints to extracting and mobilizing resources in times of need. Furthermore, high levels of extraction might provoke the majority population against the existing leadership (Lust-Okar 2005). Therefore, rebel groups that are already fighting against external enemies serve as convenient agents to delegate the fight (Byman and Kreps 2010; Salehyan 2010). Third variable is added to measure the domestic extractive capacity of a potential supporter, as the total of (1) the proportion of military personnel to the entire population and (2) the proportion of military spending to GDP.

External State Allies

Conventional wisdom suggests that when dealing with external threats, states would try balancing, that is, joining forces against a common enemy or threat. If states are motivated to join forces with other states against common enemies, a similar logic must apply when it comes to rebel groups targeting their rivals or external enemies (Byman et al. 2001; Maoz and San-Akca 2012). One implication of the theory is that states might substitute for a lack of conventional state allies by resorting to rebel groups. I use the Alliance Treaty Obligations and Provisions (ATOP) dataset to determine if a potential supporter has an offense-or-defense pact with another state (other than the target) in a given year (Leeds et al. 2002).[21] This is a dichotomous variable, taking a value of "1" if a potential supporter has an alliance with another state (than the target) or "0" if a potential sponsor has no allies in a given year.

ATOP data codes five different types of alliances: offense, defense, neutrality, nonaggression, and consultation. It further specifies whether a state has obligations toward another state or another state has obligations toward it.[22] Since states that have an offense-or-defense obligation toward each other are assumed to have a higher level of commitment toward their allies, I coded this variable as "1" only if a potential supporter had an offense-or-defense pact with another state. States that do not have conventional allies are expected to pursue a substitution strategy by resorting to rebel groups, against their adversaries, more frequently in their foreign affairs.

Major Power Supporter

This is a binary variable coding whether a potential supporter is a major power according to the COW dataset.[23]

Control Variables

Rebel Group Duration

The duration of a rebel group needs to be controlled for in order to increase the robustness of the empirical findings. Groups that remain active over a long period of time have a higher potential to appeal to state supporters, which are more willing to take the risk of retaliation and provide higher levels of support. Therefore, as the opportunity period expands, the likelihood that a rebel group will be supported by a state increases. Rebel group duration is measured as the total number of consecutive years a rebel group remains active.

Distance

Since geographical proximity is an element of PRG, used for identifying potential supporters, I use a more direct measure of distance that calculates the distance between the capital cities of two states in a given triad (target and potential supporter) (Gleditsch and Ward 2001).

Cold War

With the end of the Cold War period, the anticipation was that proxy wars would end and various dictatorial regimes and their opposing groups would lose their major power patrons. Controlling for the Cold War period is significant in fulfilling the initial promise of the book, showing that supporting rebels is neither limited to a specific era, nor to a specific group of states. Each state has the potential and motive to utilize this age-old strategy, given a particular set of conditions. Table 4.2 presents the variables used, their definition, and measurement.

4.3 Analysis

4.3.1 ESTIMATION METHODS AND SPECIFIED MODELS

Multiple methods have been used to estimate the models for both the decision to support and support level. In estimating whether a state makes a decision to support a rebel group in a given year, I use logit analysis, in conjunction with the method of Beck, Katz, and Tucker (1998), to control for temporal dependence, given the nature of the dependent variable and data (time-series and cross-sectional). Providing support in a given year also influences the probability of support in subsequent years. The method of Beck, Katz, and Tucker helps generate a variable that counts the number of years passed since the last support, and fits a number of cubic splines. In this way, it is possible to control for temporal dependence in the estimation of the onset of a decision to support a rebel group.

TABLE 4.2 Descriptive Summary of Variables for SSM (PS: Potential Supporter T: Target)

Variables	Description	Measure
Dependent Variables		
Binary Support	Any type of support	1 = yes; 0 = no
Support Level	Ordinal support	Low, moderate, high and very high
Independent Variables		
External Threat	Target & PS have conflict history	1 = yes; 0 = no
Ideational Ties	Whether a target and a potential supporter share ethnic, religious and/or ideological ties	1 = yes; 0 = no
Rebel Ideational Ties with Majority in PS	Whether a supporter and a rebel group share ethnic, religious, and/or ideological ties with the majority in PS	1 = yes; 0 = no
Transnational Ties	Whether a rebel group shares ethnic ties with minority group(s) in PS	1 = yes; 0 = no
Relative Strength	Ratio of PS capability to total capability in T-PS dyad (CINC Index)	Ranges from 0 to 1
Internal Threat	Instability variable from the State Failure Task Force Data (Version IV)	1 = yes; 0 = no
Joint Internal & External Threat	If there is concurrent internal and external threats PS needs to address	1 = yes; 0 = no
Extractive Capacity	(Military expenditure/ GDP)+(Military personnel / population)	Continuous
Democracy	Polity IV score of democracy-autocracy	Ranges from -10 to 10
Rebel Group Duration	Number of years a rebel group has been active	Continuous
Distance (log)	Distance between the capitals of PS & T (miles)	Continuous
Major Power	Whether a PS is a major power or not	1 = yes; 0 = no
Cold War	Binary measure of Cold War period	1 = CW; 0 = Post-CW

Four models have been estimated to determine the effects of the key explanatory variables on the likelihood of support: the *Global Model*, including all key variables on states' selection cases; the *Concurrent Threats Model*, examining the effect of simultaneous internal and external threats on the decision to support; the *External Threat Model*, examining the cases in which target and potential supporter have a conflict history or interstate animosity; and the *Internal Threat Model*, examining the cases in which potential supporters experience domestic threat.

The level of support is estimated by using the generalized ordered logit method, which improves the regular, ordered logit method by relaxing the proportional odds assumption (Williams 2006). Ordinal logit assumes proportional odds/parallel lines across the values of the dependent variable. In other words, it assumes that the effects of independent variables are the same across each category of the dependent variable (i.e., the coefficients of the independent variables are the same across the categories of the dependent variable) (Long and Freese 2006).[24] The benefit of generalized ordered logit (gologit) analysis over other estimation techniques, for categorical dependent variables such as multinomial logit, is that it is possible to estimate partial proportional odds models. The estimation methods, such as multinomial logit, do not impose linearity constraints on the variables. As a result, it has too many parameters, which make it complicated to interpret the coefficients.

Generalized ordered logit relaxes the linearity constraints on those variables that are most likely to break the proportional odds assumption. Since the assumption is relaxed only for some variables, it is possible to estimate a partial proportional model. The interpretation of the coefficients is discussed in the analysis of the empirical findings in detail. Two models are estimated by using generalized ordered logit: (1) the Concurrent Internal and External Threats Model and (2) the Interaction Effects Model, which tests the joint effect of rebel-potential supporter ideational affinity and target-supporter conflict history. In other words, the interaction model tests the influence on support level, when potential supporters decide whether to support ideationally contiguous rebels that also happen to target their external enemies.

4.3.2 FINDINGS

Table 4.3 presents the results for the decision to support rebels.[25] Though coefficients are not meaningful in logit estimation, odds ratios can be calculated by taking the exponentials of the coefficients. Odds ratios give us the number of times an event is more, or less, likely to occur, by comparison to nonoccurrence. In a sense, it takes the proportion of the probability of occurrence of an event to the probability of nonoccurrence of the event. In this case, odd ratios compare the probability that a potential supporter decides to intentionally support a rebel group to not support

TABLE 4.3 Logit Analysis of Support Decision, 1945–2010

	Model 1 Global Model	Model 2 Concurrent Threats	Model 3 External Threat	Model 4 Internal Threat
Supporter-Target				
External Threat	1.611***	1.551***	—	1.591***
	(0.162)	(0.169)		(0.266)
Ideational Ties	−0.601**	−0.634**	−0.427*	0.029
	(0.211)	(0.207)	(0.22)	(0.28)
Dyadic Democracy Level	−0.033*	−0.032*	—	—
	(0.015)	(0.015)		
Relative Strength	0.560***	0.562***	—	—
	(0.106)	(0.106)		
Supporter-Rebel Group				
Ideational Ties	1.109***	1.117***	1.082***	0.308
	(0.195)	(0.195)	(0.206)	(0.274)
Transnational Ties	1.238***	1.245***	0.876**	0.563
	(0.302)	(0.296)	(0.288)	(0.321)
Supporter-Specific				
Internal Threat	0.443**	0.256	0.396**	—
	(0.147)	(0.19)	(0.143)	
Major Power Supporter	−0.285	−0.266	—	—
	(0.274)	(0.275)		
External State Allies	—	—	−0.578**	−0.066
			(0.2)	(0.218)
Democracy	—	—	−0.031	−0.04
			(0.016)	(0.022)
Minority Leader	—	—	0.481*	−0.095
			(0.208)	(0.246)
Joint Internal and External Threat	—	0.46*	—	—
		(0.237)		
Control Variables				
Cold War	0.042	0.019	0.106	0.297
	(0.162)	(0.16)	(0.19)	(0.25)
Constant	−1.479***	−1.426***	−0.112	−1.065**
	(0.246)	(0.246)	(0.216)	(0.379)
R-squared	0.59	0.59	0.57	0.62
N	50523	50523	14473	9471

*** P ≤.001, ** P ≤.01, *P ≤.05

Note: In parentheses are robust standard errors that are calculated by clustering the observations by triadid, i.e., for each triad of target, rebel group, and potential supporter. Cubic splines and consecutive years of no support are not presented on the table to save space but included in the analysis.[29]

the group.[26] Another tool in presenting the findings results from a logit analysis is the percent change in the probability of occurrence of the dependent variable for the maximum change in a given independent variable, keeping all other variables constant at a certain value.[27]

The Global Model shows that potential supporters that have a conflict history with targets are more likely to end up providing intentional support to rebels targeting their enemies (H_1), as expected. Indeed, they are almost five times more likely to do so, in comparison to states that do not have a conflict history with the target, that is, do not perceive some external threat from the target state in question. One of the most significant findings is related to inter-state ideational ties. States care about their ideational ties with each other when deciding to support rebels targeting other states. This finding goes beyond the explanations suggested so far. Most systematic research is based on the logic of principle-agent dilemma, which implies that states support rebels for their own interests. Yet, we do not know much about the cases in which states do not necessarily pursue their own strategic interests when supporting rebel groups, or the conditions under which they are dissuaded from supporting them.

The findings presented in Table 4.3 show a potential supporter as less likely to support a rebel group targeting an ideationally contiguous state; that is, when the target state has similar ethnic, religious, and/or ideological identity to itself. Indeed, when a potential supporter shares ideational ties with a target state, it is 45 percent less likely to provide support to a rebel group targeting the state in question (H_4). Moreover, inter-state ideational ties have a negative effect on support of rebels even when they fight against external adversaries as is shown in Model 3. This effect cannot be explained by the endogenous effect of interstate ideational ties on interstate conflict, since the existing research did not yet find proof for such an effect.

While, from the perspective of a potential supporter, ideational ties have a discouraging effect on supporting rebels, ties with rebel groups have an encouraging effect. States whose majority populations are from the same ethnic and religious background as a rebel group are almost three times more likely to support them (H_2). This finding is especially significant within the context of the NAGs dataset, which involves several cases where multiple rebel groups end up targeting the same state. The brief case study of Palestinian militant groups and their state supporters illustrates this point. When states have an opportunity to select one from among many rebel groups targeting the same state, they opt for the one with which they share ideational ties. Syria-PIJ and Iran-Hezbollah are among such examples. By the same token, Pakistan-Kashmir insurgents are among the striking examples of states choosing to support ideationally contiguous rebels, among many that target the same external adversary.

Existing research on transnational ethnic kin and intervention in ethnic conflicts provides support for this finding as well (Saideman 1997, 2001, 2002). Yet, the empirical analysis in this book extends ideational ties beyond the ethnic ties to include religious and ideological ties. In line with the existing research, ties to minority in the borders of other states is determined to be consistently significant across three models. A state is almost three and a half times more likely to support a rebel group, if the rebel group is from the same ethnic background as the minority within its borders.

This is not surprising; given states do not want their own minorities to harbor resentment about the government for not helping their ethnic kin in other states. In providing support to the Tamil Tigers, which was fighting against the Sri Lankan government, India was motivated by its own Tamil minority (Crenshaw 2001). Although India and Sri Lanka had conventionally friendly relations, India occasionally found itself in a position to provide safe havens to the leadership and members of the LTTE. The research on transnational ethnic kin is a valuable attempt to operationalize ideational ties between states and ethnic insurgents, but a more robust test of ideational factors is presented in this book, taking into consideration various components of identity including religion and political ideology, such as socialism.[28]

The Concurrent Threats Model provides support for the hypothesized influence of joint internal and external threats. When a state faces simultaneous threats, both domestically and internationally, it is twice as likely to provide support to rebel groups fighting other states. This was the problem for the Assad and Nasser regimes during almost the entire period when they ruled through repression of opposition at home. Stretching their resources to fight against the external adversary, Israel, would make it difficult to control the opposition at home. On the one hand, when the domestic opposition assembling around the Muslim Brotherhood was relatively strong within their borders, throughout the 1970s, they were extremely cautious not to provide support to rebel groups, such as Fatah, that emerged within the ranks of the Muslim Brotherhood. On the other hand, they aided the foundation of new groups, such as PIJ, which they could use as a proxy. The hypothesis about the level of support is further tested by the means of generalized ordered logit, and the results are presented in Table 4.5.

When examining two other factors that are hypothesized to influence the decision to support rebels, the relative strength of a potential supporter has a positive effect on the likelihood of support. Across both models (Global and Concurrent Threats), the findings are robust, signaling that a potential supporter opts for a policy of supporting rebels if it is relatively strong vis-à-vis targets of rebels (H_{1a}). Furthermore, the higher the level of democracy in a dyad of potential supporter-target, the less likely a potential supporter is to provide intentional support to a rebel group fighting against another democracy, though the effect seems to be minimal, lowering the odds of support by only 3 percent.

The External Threat Model estimates the probability of support only for targets and potential supporters that share a conflict history, or when potential supporters perceive an external threat from target states. The findings indicate that ideational ties between states consistently reduce the likelihood of support. Even when a state perceives a threat from another state, it does not mean that it will automatically support the rebels targeting the enemy. It matters whether a target state shares similar ethnic, religious, and ideological ties with the potential supporter's society at large. When such ties are shared, the odds of support decline by almost 35 percent (H_4). This finding advances our knowledge about the roots of commitment problem in the relations between states and rebels. Even when they face a common enemy with rebels, states might be hesitant about supporting groups if they fight against an ideationally contiguous state. In addition, per principle-agent theory, this finding refines our understanding of the dilemma entailed within state (principle)-rebel group (agent) relations. States do not delegate their wars to rebel groups, when the latter targets ideationally contiguous states (H_{4a}).

States that are internally vulnerable, facing domestic threats, are more likely to provide support to rebels who target their external enemies. Indeed, the odds of support to rebels against external enemies increase by almost 50 percent if a state faces internal threats (H_{1b}). This finding is also a test of the "weak state" argument. In the post-2001 era, nonstate armed groups are perceived as a problem of "ungoverned spaces" or "territories." One of the main motivations for the current research is to show that weak states constitute only a small part of the explanation behind the rise and persistence of nonstate armed groups. The large-N analysis allows for controlling the key factors when investigating the motives behind external state support for rebels. Only then is it possible to empirically test arguments about the active role of states using rebels as tools of foreign policy.

Among the proxies used to measure extractive capacity of a state, the finding with respect to minority leaders shows that when facing external threats, states are more likely to support rebel groups against their adversaries if government leaders are from a minority ethnic group in their country. Figure 4.4 compares the probability of supporting rebels across internal threat and minority leadership. When governed by leaders from minority ethnic backgrounds, leaders are less likely to rely on internal mobilization and extraction to deal with external adversaries. Rather, they choose to support rebels that are the enemies of their enemies. The Assad regime's relentless support of various Palestinian militant groups is, to a great extent, a result of the dynamics of governance in a multi-ethnic society, which are dominated by leaders from ethnic minorities within a given country.

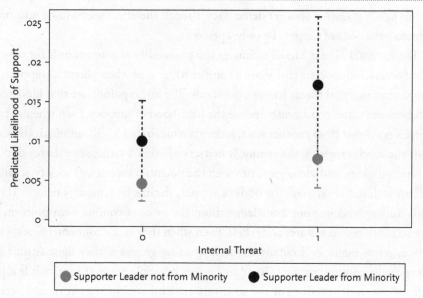

Note: Predicted values with 95% confidence intervals

FIGURE 4.4   Likelihood of Support across Internal and External Threat by Minority Leader

Ideational ties between potential supporters and rebels prove to have a robust influence on the likelihood of support. When a rebel group fighting an external adversary shares ideational ties with a potential supporter, it is three times more likely to receive support from a potential supporter state. This provides preliminary evidence for Hypothesis 3. It is further tested in the context of support level, and the results are presented in Table 4.6. Moreover, when a state has allies, it has a dampening effect on the likelihood of support. This finding is in line with the substitution thesis (H_{1c}). States that fail to establish conventional alliances with other states are more likely to seek alternative actors with which to ally against their enemies. This explains why some states, such as Iran and Sudan, are among the top supporters of rebel groups. The presence of concurrent internal and external threats, and the absence of conventional state allies on which to rely in times of emergency, lead states to look for alternative foreign policy tools. Rebel groups, which are already the "enemy of one's enemy," are easily transformed into partners against the common adversary.

The Internal Threat Model further confirms that when states have to deal with internal problems and instability, they are more likely to support rebels against external enemies. When facing internal threats, states that perceive external threat from the target state of a rebel group are almost five times more likely to support the rebel group. Perceiving an external threat from the target of a rebel group seems to be the only significant variable when estimating the decision to support rebels when states are dealing with internal threats. The r-square seems to be relatively high, given that only one variable is statistically significant. In other words, the decision of internally troubled states to provide support to rebel groups is explained, to a great extent, by whether they face a simultaneous threat from the target state(s) of the rebels in question. This finding is complementary to the findings of the External Threat Model.

When it comes to other variables, the Cold War period does not seem to have any significant effect on support. This is surprising, given that the Cold War period is conventionally perceived to be the era of the "proxy war." Yet, empirical findings indicate that states do not seem to support rebels less in the post–Cold War era.

Two additional models have been estimated to demonstrate the effects of ideational ties between states and rebel groups on the state selection process. Table 4.4 presents the findings from these two models.

States, even when they are not faced with an external threat from the target states of the rebel groups, are more likely to support rebel groups if they have common ties to them. The robust effect of state-rebel ideational ties does not change when the target state is not necessarily an external adversary of a supporter state similar to the findings of Model 1 on Table 4.4 (H_{2b}). A state is three and a half times more likely to end up selecting an ideationally contiguous rebel group, even if the latter is not targeting its external adversary. Furthermore, when a state has to make a decision whether to support an ideationally contiguous rebel group, it also takes into consideration its relative strength vis-à-vis the target state (H_{2a}). Indeed, when making such a decision, the probability of support increases by almost 200 percent, when a state is stronger than the target state.

This is not surprising, given that major powers support certain rebel groups to expand their sphere of influence, and these rebel groups are not necessarily targeting their enemies. For example, the Soviet Union supported the Democratic Party of Iranian Kurdistan (KDPI), first against the shah's regime in Iran and then against the religious revolutionary regime. Throughout the Cold War period, Soviet funds were regularly channeled to the KDPI (Gunter 2004; van Bruniessen 1986). China supported the Communist Party of Thailand (CPT) in the early 1980s. Many additional examples can be cited. The point of the empirical analysis is to show the complex mechanisms through which states choose specific rebel groups to which to provide support. The findings, so far, indicate there is more to the story than what has been offered so far.

Table 4.5 presents the findings for the support level estimations by controlling for the interactive effect of internal and external threats. I use generalized ordered logit analysis to predict the effects of the key variables on support level (Williams 2006). Since the assumption of proportional odds ratio or parallel regression does

TABLE 4.4 The Effect of State-Rebel Group Ideational Affinity on Support Decision, 1945–2010

	Model 1 No External Threat	Model 2 Ideationally Contiguous Rebels
Supporter-Target		
External Threat	—	1.800***
		(0.287)
Ideational Ties	−0.989**	−1.044***
	(0.327)	(0.280)
Dyadic Democracy	−0.046	−0.058*
	(0.027)	(0.025)
Relative Strength	0.325	0.541***
	(0.183)	(0.134)
Supporter-Rebel Group		
Ideational Ties	1.219***	—
	(0.332)	
Transnational Ties	0.103	0.896*
	(0.71)	(0.428)
Supporter-Specific		
Internal Threat	0.202	−0.07
	(0.309)	(0.280)
Major Power	0.606	0.769
	(0.444)	(0.464)
Control Variables		
Cold War	−0.072	−0.100
	(0.292)	(0.263)
Constant	−1.960***	−0.400**
	(0.405)	(0.432)
R-squared	0.41	0.66
N	35244	10035

*** P ≤.001, ** P ≤.01, *P ≤.05

Note: In parentheses are robust standard errors that are calculated by clustering the observations by triadid, i.e., for each triad of target, rebel group, and potential supporter. Cubic splines and consecutive years of no support are not presented in the table, but included in the analysis.[30]

not hold, ordered logit is not appropriate for estimating this model. The generalized order model has a feature that helps to relax the linearity constraints on variables that violate the proportional odds/parallel lines assumption. The model estimated on Table 4.5 imposes the proportional odds assumption on the following variables: ideational ties between potential supporters and targets and ties between potential supporters and rebels. Some factors push states toward a higher level of support, faster, than others.

The entries in Table 4.5 provide a comparison of the effect of each independent variable across levels of support. The first column contrasts the no support level with low, moderate, high, and very high levels of support. The second column contrasts the no support and low level with moderate, high, and very high levels of support. The third column contrasts the no, low, and high levels of support with very high level of support. The constrained variables have identical coefficients across all columns. The entries for them are interpreted the same way as the interpretation of the ordinal logit results. The positive coefficients indicate that the higher values of the independent variable make it more likely that a potential supporter responds in the current category of support rather than the other categories. For variables on which the parallel lines assumption is relaxed, the effect across three levels is just a matter of degree (Williams 2006). Negative coefficients at each column give us the influence of the independent variable for providing lower levels of support than the current, whereas positive coefficients mean higher levels of an explanatory variable, making it more likely a potential supporter is due to respond with higher levels of support than the current category.

The fact that targets of rebels pose an external threat drives potential supporters to provide higher levels of support. The highest effect is observed when a supporter moves from providing no support to providing some support, as shown in the first column. When a potential supporter faces simultaneous threats both domestically and internationally, it has a positive effect on providing support at lower levels. In other words, Model 1 indicates that a potential supporter is more likely to provide a higher level of support than no support at all. Nevertheless, when it comes to moderate and high levels of support, the sign of the coefficient seems to turn negative, signaling that a potential supporter facing internal threat wants to use rebels to delegate the business of handling the external enemy, but more cautiously. It prefers providing the current or lower level of support, rather than a higher level. Although Hypothesis 1, about the level of support, is confirmed in the bivariate models estimating the decision to support rebels or not, it seems to be partially confirmed when estimating support level. It could be attributed to the fact that

TABLE 4.5 Concurrent Threats on Intentional Support Level, 1945–2010

	Model 1 No Support vs. 1, 2, 3 & 4	Model 2 NS, 1 vs. 2, 3 & 4	Model 3 NS, 1, 2 vs. 3 & 4	Model 4 NS, 1, 2, 3 vs. 4
Supporter-Target				
External Threat	1.515***	1.189***	1.208***	1.263***
	0.066	0.068	0.072	0.114
Ideational Ties	−0.528***	−0.528***	−0.528***	−0.528***
	0.068	0.068	0.068	0.068
Dyadic Democracy	−0.029***	−0.108***	−0.099***	−0.103***
	0.005	0.007	0.007	0.009
Relative Strength	0.647***	0.042	0.002	−0.338***
	0.031	0.038	0.039	0.054
Joint External & Internal Threat	0.168*	−0.478***	−0.431***	0.14
	0.085	0.09	0.095	0.123
Supporter-Rebel Group				
Ideational Ties	0.772***	0.772***	0.772***	0.772***
	0.054	0.054	0.054	0.054
Transnational Ties	0.625***	1.362***	1.049***	0.530***
	0.094	0.099	0.108	0.127
Supporter Specific				
Internal Threat	0.166+	1.227***	1.271***	0.950***
	0.091	0.103	0.107	0.133
Major Power Supporter	−0.418***	−1.924***	−1.901***	−0.933***
	0.083	0.112	0.115	0.17
Control Variables				
Cold War	0.071	1.114***	1.014***	1.116***
	0.056	0.065	0.067	0.092
Distance (Log)	−0.447***	−0.021	−0.014	−0.414***
	0.029	0.035	0.038	0.052
Rebel Duration	−0.031***	0.100***	0.090***	0.080***
	−0.003	0.005	0.005	0.006
Constant	−0.071	−4.762***	−4.865***	−3.807***
	0.207	0.273	0.289	0.354
N		50523		
Wald test of parallel lines assumption		$\chi_2 = 4.15$		
for the final model		Prob> $\chi_2 = 0.65$		

*** P ≤.001., ** P ≤.01., *P ≤.05, P≤.10

Note: In parentheses are robust standard errors. Parallel lines/proportional odds assumption has been relaxed for domestic instability in potential supporter. The autofit process of generalized order logit yields internal threat as the variable for which parallel odds assumption holds. An insignificant likelihood ratio test comparing the constrained and unconstrained models shows that the parallel line assumption is not violated in the final estimated generalized ordered logit model using the 0.05 level of significance.

states, when making a decision to provide support to rebels, act cautiously, so as not to provoke retaliation from target states, which are already current adversaries.

Retaliation by a target state would require a potential supporter facing threats at home to stretch its limited resources to fight an external enemy. The fear of retaliation was among the most significant factors when Syria gradually abandoned Fatah, though it was the most fervent supporter of the militant group during its foundation. Although Jordan, Egypt, and Syria all fought against Israel during the 1948 war, when the opportunity arose to support various Palestinian insurgents living within their borders (referred to as fedayeen at the time in general), Syria proved to be the most dedicated state ally of fedayeen and, later, Fatah (Atzili and Pearlman 2012). Jordan and Egypt expelled them soon after they started to organize within their territories.

Throughout the early years of the Ba'ath regime, Syria allowed Fatah to use the training camps of its military and to transport arms (Shemesh 2006). Syria's support for Fatah stemmed not only from the perceived threat from Israel, or from the regime's Ba'atist ideology, rooted in leftist-oriented popular liberation ideas. But, the Syrian regime saw such support as an opportunity to consolidate its vulnerable domestic regime, and to unite the country's ethnically and religiously fragmented society, as discussed earlier. Facing concurrent threats at both the domestic and the international levels, Syria provided the highest level of support for Fatah. Later, when Fatah sought to loosen its ties to the Syrian regime and gradually move away from a leftist ideology, Syria found new partners, including the PFLP-GC and the PIJ.

Across all models, internal threat consistently estimates providing higher levels of support, even after controlling for the effect of joint threats (simultaneous domestic and external threats). Thus, even after controlling for the interaction between internal and external threats, both variables seem to have a consistently positive and significant effect on support level, signaling the autonomous effect of each variable on support level, as argued by the state-rebel selection theory.

Furthermore, ideational ties between potential supporters and target states have a negative effect on support level. When targets and potential supporters share some ideational ties, potential supporters are less likely to provide higher levels of support to groups targeting these ideationally contiguous states (H_2). On the other hand, states are more likely to provide a higher level of support to ideationally contiguous rebels. Transnational ethnic ties seem to have the largest effect on support level in shifting a state from providing lower and moderate levels of support to higher levels of support, as the findings in Model 2 indicate.

Considering joint democracy as a political regime type uniting states around similar norms, ideas, values, and worldview, the level of democracy is also included in the analysis. It is found to have a robust and negative effect across all models. Democracies are less likely to provide higher levels of support to rebels targeting other democratic states, even if they end up supporting them. Internal threat has the highest effect when it comes to shifting a potential supporter from providing a high level of support to a very high level of support. A similar pattern is observed when targets and potential supporters have a conflict history. In addition, states were more likely to provide higher levels of support to rebels during the Cold War period. Given that the Cold War was not a significant estimator of the decision to support rebels in the bivariate analysis, the finding here suggests that when they did so, it tended to be at higher levels of support. The descriptive statistics show that almost 67 percent of troop support for rebels from states occurred during the Cold War period. Considering troop support as a very high form and level of support, the finding here seems to be in line with the way major powers handled their specific foreign policy goals. During the Cold War period, the rivalry between the two superpowers was fierce, and when they supported armed groups, they did not necessarily avoid committing troops.

Table 4.6 shows the effect of external threat on support level, when rebel groups are also ideationally contiguous actors, from the perspective of potential supporters (H_3). It seems that when sharing ideational ties with rebels, supporters are more likely to opt for lower levels of support if those rebels target external enemies of supporters. This could be based on the motive of supporters to protect ethnic kin abroad. If rebels face repression, the supporter's domestic population might hold the leaders or government accountable for mobilizing rebels, causing them to incur repression from the target states.

States that have a conflict history with the target state of a rebel group are more likely to provide higher levels of support, consistently across all models. The highest effect is observed when a supporter shifts from not providing support to providing some level of support (Model1) and from providing low, moderate, and high levels of support to a very high level of support (Model 4). A supporter is five times more likely to provide a very high level of support to rebels fighting against an external enemy. The highest influence of domestic vulnerability, or internal threat, is observed when states make a decision to provide the highest level of support. A domestically vulnerable state is almost three times more likely to contribute troops or offer training camps to a rebel group. Such a state is more likely to provide moderate and higher levels of support than a lower level of support, such as allowing rebels to transport weapons, offer logistics assistance, and open offices within their borders.

The influence of ideational ties with rebels seems to be robust across various levels of support. Rebels have a higher probability of support from ideationally contiguous states, in comparison to noncontiguous ones. Such states are three times more likely

TABLE 4.6 The Effect of Ideational Ties and External Threat on Support Level, 1945–2010

	Model 1 No Support vs. 1, 2, 3 & 4	Model 2 NS, 1 vs. 2, 3 & 4	Model 3 NS, 1, 2 vs. 3 & 4	Model 4 NS, 1, 2, 3 vs. 4
Supporter-Target				
External Threat	1.684***	1.370***	1.396***	1.585***
	(0.075)	(0.077)	(0.08)	(0.118)
Ideational Ties	−0.549***	−0.549***	−0.549***	−0.549***
	(0.068)	(0.068)	(0.068)	(0.068)
Dyadic Democracy	−0.030***	−0.104***	−0.095***	−0.094***
	(0.005)	(0.006)	(0.006)	(0.008)
Relative Strength	0.637***	0.05	0.01	−0.294***
	(0.031)	(0.038)	(0.039)	(0.054)
PS-R Ties and	−0.376**	−0.376**	−0.376**	−0.376**
External Threat	(0.12)	(0.12)	(0.12)	(0.12)
Supporter-Rebel Group				
Ideational Ties	1.074***	1.074***	1.074***	1.074***
	(0.105)	(0.105)	(0.105)	(0.105)
Transnational Ties	0.813***	0.919***	0.663***	0.227
	(0.091)	(0.091)	(0.102)	(0.125)
Supporter Specific				
Internal Threat	0.292***	0.712***	0.797***	0.981***
	(0.069)	(0.072)	(0.074)	(0.089)
Major Power Supporter	−0.392***	−1.812***	−1.796***	−0.915***
	(0.082)	(0.108)	(0.112)	(0.169)
Control Variables				
Cold War	0.083	1.087***	0.988***	1.056***
	(0.056)	(0.065)	(0.067)	(0.09)
Distance (Log)	−0.458***	−0.055	−0.043	−0.405***
	(0.028)	(0.034)	(0.036)	(0.05)
Rebel Duration	−0.030***	0.096***	0.086***	0.075***
	(0.003)	(0.005)	(0.005)	(0.006)
Constant	−0.135	−4.611***	−4.743***	−3.891***
	(0.206)	(0.268)	(0.284)	(0.348)
N		50523		
Wald test of parallel lines assumption		$\chi 2 = 14.09$		
for the model		Prob> $\chi 2 = 0.119$		

*** P ≤.001. ** P ≤.01. *P ≤.05

Note: In parentheses are robust standard errors. Parallel lines/proportional odds assumption is imposed for supporter-target ideational ties, supporter-rebel group ideational ties, and interaction effect of supporter-rebel ties and external threat. An insignificant likelihood ratio test comparing the constrained and unconstrained models shows that parallel line assumption is not violated in the final estimated generalized ordered logit model using the 0.05 level of significance.

to provide higher levels of support to rebels with which they share ethnic and religious ties. Though transnational ties do not have a significant effect on the highest level of support, they have a consistently positive effect on low, moderate, and high levels of support. Ideational ties between target states and potential supporters seem to have a consistent negative effect on every level of support. States are 50 percent less likely to support rebels against other states to which they have ideational ties. A state tends to provide some level of support to a rebel group if it is relatively strong vis-à-vis the rebel group's target. The greatest effect of relative strength is observed when it pushes the potential supporter from not providing any support at all toward providing some level of support (H_{1a}).

4.4 Conclusion

The main purpose of this book is to develop and test a theory about the material and ideational context within which states and rebel groups act in seeking support from one another. Many scholars have pointed out that states have multiple motives in supporting rebel groups (Byman et al. 2001; Byman 2005a, 2005c; Salehyan 2010). However, these motives have not been empirically and systematically tested to determine how, and under what conditions, they drive support onset and level. Research on this topic remains limited, in terms of the temporal domain, focusing either on the Cold War or the post–Cold War periods, and in terms of the spatial domain, conducting case studies about proxy wars between the major powers during the Cold War period. The purpose of this chapter is to test some of these conventional thoughts in a spatially and temporally broad domain and to determine if prevalent patterns exist in the interactions between states and nonstate armed groups.

Theoretically, the current chapter advances our understanding of the conditions under which some previous insights about state and rebel groups relations, which were derived from the principle-agent approach apply. Most significantly, it offers alternative insights about the causes of state support for rebel groups. Shared identity, ideas, norms, and worldview matters in moving states to support rebel groups, even in the absence of material interests. They are especially important in dissuading states from supporting rebels that fight against other states with which they have such shared ties.

The empirical findings yield the following interesting and novel implications for the SSM and intentional support of rebel groups by states:

1. The logic of interstate balancing explains state support of rebels. States are motivated by external threats when making a decision to support a rebel

group. Almost across all estimated models, when a state perceives some threat from the targets of a rebel group, or shares a conflict history with the target state in question, it is more likely to provide support to the rebel group. In addition, external threat is robustly significant across all models when it comes to estimating the support level. This finding complies with what has been also suggested by the principle-agent approach.

2. States choose to substitute for their lack of conventional state allies by cooperating with rebels targeting their external adversaries. When making a decision to support a rebel group targeting an adversary, a state is less likely to do so if it has state allies on which it can rely. This is a novel finding and points to the significance of security communities and inter-state alliances for larger global security.

3. Ideational affinity between rebels and their supporters has a robust effect on the level of support. Yet, when it comes to ideationally contiguous rebel groups targeting external adversaries (ideational affinity and conflict history converge), no evidence appears to exist that support level increases. Though, the findings for support onset point out this effect.

4. An interesting finding concerns the influence of joint democracy on the likelihood of support onset and support level. The democratic peace mechanism seems to work in the context of state support for rebel groups. Considering supporting rebels is an act of animosity, democracies are less likely to support rebels targeting other democracies. Indeed, the support level also seems to decline if a rebel group targets a democratic state.

5. Both internal domestic (in)stability and external relative strength have implications in explaining support. The findings suggest that states are strategic decisionmakers. They consider the risk of retaliation from targets when making a decision to support a rebel group.

6. Last, ideational ties between supporter and target states prove to be another robust finding. When two states share similar ethnic and religious affiliations and political ideology, they are less likely to support rebels fighting against states with similar ties. The empirical test conducted in this book is based on one of the most extensive measure of ideational ties between two states, going beyond ethnic ties.

Analysis of the insights from the SSM shows that both the initial decision to support a rebel group, and the level of support provided, are influenced by multiple factors. States are motivated both by material and ideational factors in deciding to provide support to specific rebel groups, as well as the type and level of support. Ideational factors matter, even after controlling for conflict history between a potential supporter and a rebel group. States do provide support to ideationally contiguous rebels even when they do not perceive a threat from the rebels' target states. Furthermore, delegation to rebels is most likely to occur if rebels, who fight against external enemies, are also ideationally contiguous from the perspective of a potential supporter. In addition, interstate ideational ties and joint democracy consistently reduce the likelihood of state support for rebels.

5   Rebels' Selection Model

THE REBELS' SELECTION Model (RSM) builds on the premise that it is not only states selecting the rebel groups to support, but also the groups themselves selecting the countries within which they recruit, raise funds, and find safe havens and maintain offices.[1] The NAGs dataset reveals that out of the total years in which a rebel group receives support from an external state, 50 percent of the time, support is driven by rebel selection and 17 percent of the time, states and rebels concurrently select each other. In the aftermath of 9/11, the dominant thinking was that weak states, like Afghanistan, or ungoverned territories or spaces, like Pakistani Waziristan or insurgent-controlled areas in Colombia, constitute the main arenas for the rise of global terrorism and insurgency (Clunan and Trinkunas 2010). It is my goal in this chapter to systematically test hypotheses about the main features of states that rebel groups choose as sanctuaries, and as safe grounds for weapons and logistics aid, acquiring funds, and getting trained.

Since achieving independence, Indonesia has been targeted by seven different rebel groups, with various sectarian and ethnically driven objectives, including the foundation of an Islamic state and secession. Among them, the GAM gained international prominence after carrying out an attack on Mobil Oil in 1977 in Sumatra, the largest island of Indonesia. Driven by both political grievances and competition over the gas reserves in the region, GAM carried out an insurgency against the Indonesian government for almost three decades between 1976 and 2005. For the entire period, the leader of the group, Hasan di Tiro, managed the insurgency from Sweden with his associates (McBeth 2003; Missbach 2013). Although the top leadership of GAM did not view Malaysia as a sufficiently secure locale, many GAM sympathizers, and a significant number of Acehnese diaspora, lived in Malaysia (Missbach 2013, p. 1066).

Di Tiro managed to establish a network and offices in different countries, including Australia, the United States, Denmark, and Norway. These overseas offices were in charge of collecting compulsory donations for GAM. In no case did a government create direct channels to aid the group. Rather, the group established its de facto presence within these countries. A common feature of the countries in question is that they are either geographically contiguous states or advanced democracies. In the latter case, the governments are constrained when it comes to limiting individual liberties and freedoms, even if the goal is to fight against rebel groups, including terrorists and ethnic and religious insurgents (Byman 2005a; Chenoweth 2010; Eubank and Weinberg 2001; Eyerman 1998; San-Akca 2014). Thus, democracies serve as convenient locations for opening offices to conduct propaganda for the group, raise funds, and recruit militants.

GAM is neither the first, nor the only, group that chooses countries with certain characteristics as safe grounds of operation. Mujahedin-e Khalq (MEK) has been targeting Iran to topple the revolutionary regime from bases in Iraq, and the leadership of MEK enjoyed safe havens in France. It enjoyed a high level of autonomy, and human and material resources through its operation base. Iraq, the fervent rival of Iran, was chosen as the main operations base, whereas France was chosen as a safe haven for MEK's leadership.

The RSM begins with the assumption that the choice of certain countries by rebel groups is not coincidental. Similar to the decision-making process of states, rebels go through a selection process in deciding which states are the most helpful to reducing operational costs. Of the total years during which rebels enjoyed safe havens in other countries, almost 70 percent of the time, it was within the borders of the adversaries of their targets. A total of 37 percent of the time, when rebels acquire safe havens within the borders of other countries, they select states that have populations with common or shared ethnic, religious, and/or ideological ties. Of the years during which a rebel group chooses a state from which to acquire resources in the forms of money and weapons, 64 percent, it was the adversaries of rebel group's targets. A total of seventy-four percent of the time, weapons smuggling and transportation by rebels occurred within the borders of autocratic states, while 52 percent of the observations, in which rebels acquired funds within the borders of other states, occurred in democratic states.

Figure 5.1 shows the distribution of de facto supporters across the world. A total of 29 percent of countries that serve as de facto supporters are located in Western

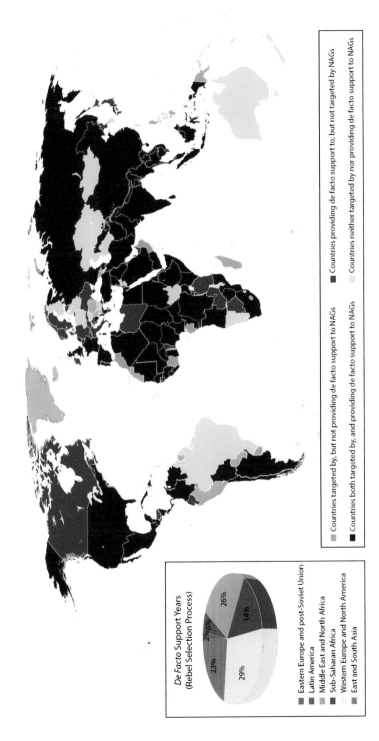

FIGURE 5.1 The World Map of De Facto Supporters, 1945–2010

De Facto Support Years
(Rebel Selection Process)

26%

14%

2% 6%

23%

29%

■ Eastern Europe and post-Soviet Union
■ Latin America
■ Middle East and North Africa
■ Sub-Saharan Africa
■ Western Europe and North America
■ East and South Asia

■ Countries targeted by, but not providing de facto support to NAGs

■ Countries both targeted by, and providing de facto support to NAGs

■ Countries providing de facto support to, but not targeted by NAGs

 Countries neither targeted by nor providing de facto support to NAGs

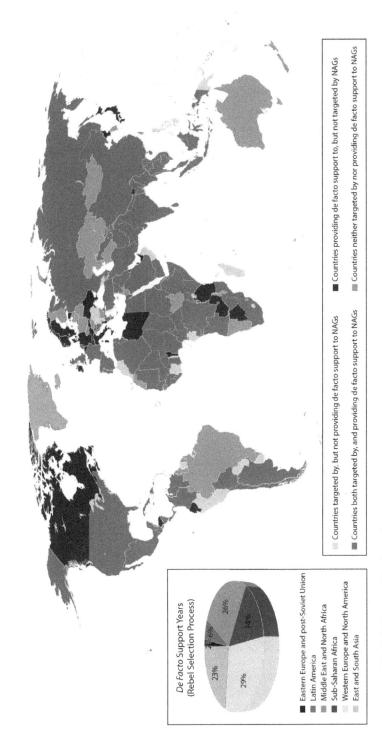

FIGURE 5.1 The World Map of De Facto Supporters, 1945–2010

Legend:

Countries targeted by, but not providing de facto support to NAGs

Countries both targeted by, and providing de facto support to NAGs

Countries providing de facto support to, but not targeted by NAGs

Countries neither targeted by nor providing de facto support to NAGs

De Facto Support Years (Rebel Selection Process)

Eastern Europe and post-Soviet Union
Latin America
Middle East and North Africa
Sub-Saharan Africa
Western Europe and North America
East and South Asia

26%
13%
29%
23%
6%
2%

Europe and North America; 26 percent are located in the Middle East and North Africa; and 23 percent are located in East and South Asia. No single region shows a particularly high score for de facto support.

In this chapter, I address the main determinants of rebels' selection of certain countries as supporters, and explain how rebels make their choices about seeking safe havens or other specific forms of support within other countries than their targets and, more specifically, turning some states into de facto supporters. I conduct a series of statistical analyses to test the hypotheses from the RSM presented in Chapter 2. My primary purpose is to explain the influence of a rebel group's calculus for autonomy and resources on their selection process, since rebels are primarily motivated by reducing the operational costs of their activities.

Figure 5.2 shows the top ten states that end up as de facto supporters of rebels. They include advanced democracies, such as the United States, France, and the United Kingdom, as well as states that have difficulty controlling their borders after opening up to rebel groups, such as Syria and Iraq.

The rest of the chapter is organized into four sections. The next section provides a brief case study of militant groups targeting Chad, and their supporters, and reiterates the hypotheses related to the RSM in light of the Chadian case study. The following section describes the research design, including the data, units of analysis, and operationalization of the key variables. The next section discusses the estimation methods, and the results of the statistical analysis, on the decision to seek support,

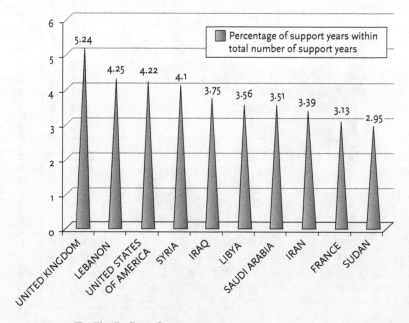

FIGURE 5.2 Top Ten De Facto Supporters, 1945–2010

and the characteristics of external supporters that seem to be the best fit for rebels. The conclusion presents a summary of the empirical findings.

5.1 A Brief Case Study and Key Hypotheses: Autonomy and Resources

5.1.1 CHADIAN REBEL GROUPS AND DE FACTO STATE SUPPORTERS

Since gaining independence in 1960, Chad has been subject to much violence by twenty-five rebel groups. All have sought to topple the existing leadership, except one group, the Chadian Armed Forces (FAT), who are of Sara ethnic origin and seek territorial secession. The post-colonial violence and conflict in Chad have, to a great extent, been shaped by tensions between the Muslim-populated North and the Christian and Animist-populated South. The rebel groups usually acquired intentional support from Libya and Sudan, external state rivals of Chad, and France and the United States, which sought to establish friendly regimes in the country—the United States during the Cold War and France since decolonization (Orobator 1984; Miles 1995). Figure 5.3 demonstrates the rebel groups targeting Chad in the post-colonization period, and the external states that acted as de facto supporters for many of these groups.

While some groups have chosen an external rival of Chad as secure ground from which to receive support, others have chosen neighboring states, such as Sudan, Niger, and Nigeria, with which they also share some ideational ties. Although rivalry exists between Sudan and Chad, it stemmed from Chad's support of rebels in Darfur and, in return, Sudan's support of rebels in northern Chad (Debos 2011). In other words, the rivalry between the two states emerged because of ongoing internal conflict in both states, and the intentional support provided by one state to rebels targeting the other.[2] This reverse causality has been the subject of recent work on how domestic conflict is internationalized (Gleditsch et al. 2008; Salehyan 2008a, 2008b). For each case, conflict history is coded for two states only if there was a rivalry or animosity between them prior to the onset of state support, to avoid reverse causality driving the relationship between external threat environment and both states and rebels selecting their partners.[3]

Rebels' selection of state supporters is based on their calculus with respect to the operational cost. It is a function of the autonomy a rebel group enjoys when organizing violence against a target state, and the level of human and material resources it is able to extract within the borders of an outside state. From the perspective of rebels, external rivals of a target state and ideationally contiguous states—that is, states with societies from similar ethnic and religious backgrounds—has a greater likelihood of yielding a high level of autonomy to a group, as well as providing the resources required to carry out attacks.

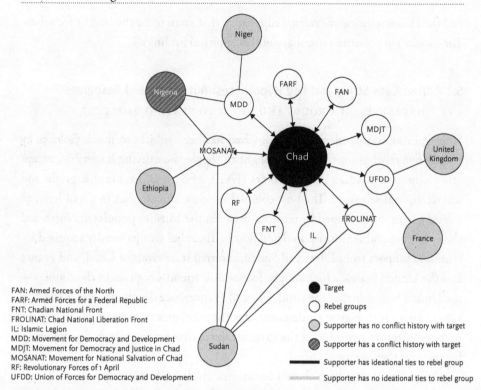

FAN: Armed Forces of the North
FARF: Armed Forces for a Federal Republic
FNT: Chadian National Front
FROLINAT: Chad National Liberation Front
IL: Islamic Legion
MDD: Movement for Democracy and Development
MDJT: Movement for Democracy and Justice in Chad
MOSANAT: Movement for National Salvation of Chad
RF: Revolutionary Forces of 1 April
UFDD: Union of Forces for Democracy and Development

● Target
○ Rebel groups
◐ Supporter has no conflict history with target
◓ Supporter has a conflict history with target
—— Supporter has ideational ties to rebel group
▭▭▭ Supporter has no ideational ties to rebel group

FIGURE 5.3 Selected Rebel Groups against Chad and Supporters, 1945–2010

Idriss Déby, the current Chadian president, a military advisor under the previous president, escaped to Sudan to organize a rebellion against the Habré regime in 1989.[4] In addition to its geographic proximity, Sudan can be seen as a preferred safe haven for Chadian rebels, due to transnational ethnic ties. Déby, who has a Zaghawa ethnic background, was able to acquire the support of Sudanese Zaghawas in western Sudan (Moghadam 2008). Ethnic kin of various Chadian groups live across the border in Sudan. Furthermore, the Sudanese government's interest in Chad is driven by its unwillingness to accept a southern-dominated North, i.e. a Christian dominated Muslim minority. For example, the National Liberation Front of Chad (FROLINAT), a group that initially sought secession of the Muslim North from Chad, was established in Sudan in 1966 (Orobator 1984).

Many rebel groups in the Muslim-dominated North prefer Sudan as a safe haven, because of their ideational affinity with Sudan. In the case of FROLINAT, no clear evidence exists of the Sudanese government's intentional support. While Sudan supported groups such as the Armed Forces of the North (FAN), the National Alliance (AN), and the Patriotic Salvation Movement (MPS) by providing weapons, logistics aid, and safe havens, it turned a blind eye to the activities of groups like FROLINAT, without, though, creating direct channels to aid them (De Waal 2006).

Groups like the National Movement for the Salvation of Chad (MOSANAT) and the Movement for Democracy and Development (MDD), that tried toppling the Habré and Déby regimes, respectively, preferred Nigeria as a safe haven. In other words, the Sudanese regime, which was supporting the religious-oriented rebels of North Chad, did not seem to be a good candidate as a supporter from the perspective of rebels who aspired to replace the Chadian regime with a democratic one. Enmity between the two countries began in the 1970s, when they competed over exploitation of the oil resources in Lake Chad (Matfess 2015). Among other states, MOSANAT chose to establish offices in Ethiopia and Sudan. MDD leaders escaped to Niger and Cameroon in 1990, after Déby established his rule. MDD's ethnic identity is Toubou, which is one of the minority groups in Niger (Dowden 1992; Huband 1992). Other than transnational ethnic ties with MDD, Niger had no history of rivalry with Chad. Cameroon was preferred by its leadership due to its geographical proximity to Chad.

The theoretical framework proposes that if a rebel group faces repression from the target state, acquiring safe havens in another state's territories increases the cost of counter-insurgency for the target state, since it now has to track the rebels across the borders of another state. Two problems are associated with acquiring safe havens in the territory of another state. One is that providing safe havens is a costly engagement on the part of the state as well, since it incurs the risk of the target's retaliation. Second, a rebel group risks autonomy, as it may face constraints from the host state (supporter).

To survive and effectively engage their targets, it is essential for rebels to attract the support of external states, and the people within their target and supporter states. A rebel group may be forced to move into another state to escape the repression of its target. It may prefer a weak state as a safe haven, since such a state does not possess the capacity to restrict its autonomy. This may be a problematic strategy, though, if the supporter is vulnerable to a point that it is unable to resist political and/or military pressures from the rebel group's target. In addition, extremely weak states do not have the infrastructure to allow for maintenance and transportation of arms and equipment. Examining piracy in Southeast Asia, Hastings (2010) finds that weak states, rather than failed or collapsed ones, are better breeding grounds for pirates, one type of armed group that is not included in this research. In contrast to conventional expectation, weak states may not be the most preferred base for rebels who decide to operate from bases in an external state.

Rebel groups occasionally choose democratic states as safe grounds of operation, as mentioned previously. The Union of Forces for Democracy and Development (UFDD) established offices in France and the United Kingdom to oppose Déby's repressive regime. It is interesting that while the French government provided extensive support to the Déby regime, UFDD called for support for the insurgency at home from their offices operating in France and the United Kingdom. They issued an online call through their website, inviting all opposition forces to unite and join them in London.[5]

A rebel group may also prefer an adversary of its target if the adversary is willing to use the rebel group as a proxy in its fight against the rebel group's target.[6] The insights offered by the principle-agent approach need to be refined, since there are several cases of rebel groups that do not automatically choose the external enemies of their target states. As with some groups in Chad, and their selection of countries like Niger, Sudan and advanced democracies—rather than Nigeria—this suggests that rebel groups try to diversify their supporter networks. The logic of selection goes beyond simply volunteering to fight the others' war or acting as a delegate of rival states.

Various rebel groups chose Libya from which to extract support. Libya interfered in the Chadian civil war on four different occasions, in 1978, 1979, 1980–1981, and 1983–1987, on the side of the rebels fighting the Chadian government. It used its involvement in the Chadian civil war as a bargaining chip to pursue claims from the Chadian government over the Aouzou strip, a narrow band of land along the Libyan border in northern Chad, known to be rich in minerals and uranium. Indeed, fighting on the side of the Chadian government, France engaged in a proxy war against Libya in Chad on several occasions. Several groups, including FROLINAT and the MPS, received Libyan backing. Eventually, Déby, the leader of MPS and the current president of Chad, came to power, ending the eight-year rule of Habré. Although the Libyan government failed to topple the Habré regime with direct confrontation from 1978 through 1987; it was able to do so through indirect confrontation by supporting MPS militants fighting the Habré regime.

5.1.2 REBELS' SELECTION MODEL HYPOTHESES

The interactions among the several Chadian rebel groups outlined above, such as FROLINAT, MOSANAT, and UFDD, and their relations with states like Sudan, Libya, Nigeria, and advanced democratic states on several occasions, illustrate prevalent trends in rebels' selection of specific states as de facto supporters. Furthermore, the two selection processes are not mutually exclusive. In other words, when investigating states' selection of certain rebels, support is not expected to emerge if the rebels in question do not agree to receive it.

The first two hypotheses are similar to those under the SSM. Rebels are inclined to select the adversaries of their target states, because they expect that such supporters are most likely to provide a higher level of autonomy in their operations, and a higher amount of resources. Ideational contiguity between rebel groups and supporter states also plays a similar role as in the SSM. Rebels choose ideationally contiguous states, since ethnic and religious kin within their domestic populace serve as a base from which to extract material and human resources. In addition, the governments in such countries are more likely to turn a blind eye to rebel group activities. The RSM is built on two key assertions: (1) Rebel groups are autonomous actors with their own agenda, independent from their state patrons, and (2) They can, and do, operate within the borders of other countries without sponsorship by the states in those countries.

The following hypotheses have been proposed with respect to the RSM.

H_5: Rebels are more likely to select the adversaries of their targets to acquire safe havens and other forms of support than the nonadversaries.

H_6: Rebels are more likely to select ideationally contiguous states as supporters than states with which they do not have common ties.

H_7: A rebel group is more likely to choose a relatively strong state vis-à-vis its target, as a safe haven than a weak one, since a strong state has the ability to repel possible retaliation from the rebel group's target. This is also true when it comes to other forms of support.

H_8: The likelihood that a rebel group will seek external safe havens is higher if it targets a domestically strong state, rather than a domestically weak one, due to the rebel group's concern for securing itself from repression by its target.

H_9 (weak state assumption): A rebel group is more likely to choose a weak state as a safe haven since it has the opportunity for a high level of autonomy in its operations against its target.

H_{10}: The level of de facto support a rebel group pursues in a country increases if the latter is the adversary of the rebel group's target and it is ideationally contiguous to the rebel group (interaction of external threat and ideational contiguity).

H_{11}: Rebel groups are more likely to seek de facto support within democratic states in comparison to autocratic states.

5.2 Research Design

5.2.1 DATA

The cases examined here include all rebel group selection cases, which I character-ize as de facto support,[7] meaning any type of support obtained by rebels without a state's deliberate act to create channels to help them. In other words, there is no observed state sponsorship, yet a rebel group's leadership or militants manage to travel freely, collect funds, purchase arms, and find sanctuary. Under this category, eight different types of support are coded: (1) safe haven for members, (2) safe haven for leaders, (3) offices for fund-raising and propaganda, (4) training camps, (5) training, (6) weapons and logistics, (7) financial support, and (8) transport of funds, arms, and logistics. For de facto support, providing troops is not coded, since sending troops to aid a rebel group must, by its nature, be an intentional act on the part of a government or its leadership.

Many states, such as Afghanistan (after 2001), Somalia, Iraq, and Cambodia, end up as breeding grounds for rebels, due to an inability to control their borders. They are selected by rebels to raise funds, smuggle arms, and get logistics aid. On the other hand, strong states, such as the United Kingdom, Germany, and the United States, serve as breeding grounds for such groups, due to established democratic norms and institutions, which make it extremely costly for such states to control and scrutinize the activities of individuals and citizens who live within their borders (Chenoweth 2010; Eubank and Weinberg 1994, 1998, 2001; Li and Schaub 2004; San-Akca 2014). An ample amount of work exists on democratic regimes and terrorism. According to the empirical findings of this well-established body of research, democracies frequently facilitate and encourage various forms of nonstate violence, including terrorism.

Two insights related to the effect of democracy on state support of rebels are further tested in the following empirical analysis. One is the external validity of the democratic peace argument; whether democratic states are less likely to be selected by rebel groups fighting other democracies. The expectation is that when targets and supporters are jointly democratic, rebels are less likely to seek support from these states. The second effect of democracy is related to the facilitation logic of democracy, specified earlier. Democracies are vulnerable due to the intrinsic values and institutions embedded in their foundation.

Figure 5.2 presents the distribution of the top ten de facto supporters of rebels in the period between 1945 and 2010. The supporters include highly democratic states, such as the United Kingdom, France, and the United States, as well as non-democratic states, such as Iraq and Libya. This is expected if we consider that rebel leaders or members frequently seek refuge in democratic regimes, which allow them to gain sanctuary or operate offices within their territories.

The LTTE had offices in London for almost two decades, from 1984 to 2001, when the United Kingdom passed an antiterrorism legislation to ban such groups.[8] Australia and Canada banned the activities of the group in 2002 (Nadarajah and Sriskandarajah 2005). Karunakaran Kandasamy, the director of the World Tamil

Coordinating Committee (one of many front organizations for LTTE), was arrested in New York in 2007 by the FBI. The charges filed against him were based on evidence gathered in his U.S.-based office, showing millions of dollars raised and sent to LTTE fighters in Sri Lanka.[9]

These examples accentuate a neglected dimension of state-rebel group relations. Rebel groups frequently operate freely in the state-governed spaces of the world, without any state sponsorship to aid their activities. Although principle-agent or patron-client approach provide a useful framework in explaining when states deliberately delegate rebel groups to fight against their enemies, we need to go beyond this approach to systematically explore how rebel groups diversify their support networks. More often than not, they do not rely on the enemies of their target states. The statistical analyses in the following section show the determinants of de facto support.

5.2.2 THE UNIT OF ANALYSIS

The unit of analysis is a triad year, which includes a rebel group, a target (the state that is the subject of nonstate violence), and a potential supporter (the state that is likely to support a rebel group when an opportunity to support arises). Potential supporters, from the perspective of a rebel group, also include states in the politically relevant group of the rebel group's target: geographically contiguous states, regional powers, and major powers (Maoz 1996; Maoz et. al. 2007). The dataset is both cross-sectional and time-series. In principle, a rebel group may start seeking external supporters as soon as it is founded, if not before its foundation. Therefore, each triad appears in the dataset as the number of years a rebel group is active. Appendix 5 lists all the rebel groups and their de facto supporters from the NAGs Dataset. When rebel groups have survived beyond 2010, the duration of rebels is calculated by taking 2010 as the cutoff point.

5.2.3 OPERATIONALIZATION OF THE VARIABLES

Most of the variables used in the estimation of the RSM have been defined in relation to the SSM earlier. Here, I discuss the operationalization of dependent variables for the RSM and review the explanatory variables in terms of their expected effect on rebel group selection.

Dependent Variable

Support resulting from a rebel group's selection has been operationalized in four different ways, reflecting the types of support and selection process by which states become supporters for rebels: (1) the rebels' decision to seek external supporters in general, (2) acquisition of safe havens by rebels, (3) acquisition of training camps, and (4) safe havens for rebel leaders and opening offices. Undoubtedly on occasion, if not frequently, rebels pick certain states as supporters out of convenience, either location or ease of access. My purpose here, though, is not to deny these natural factors, but to capture the systematic patterns in the decision to pick one country, when rebels have the opportunity to select from among many potential supporters.

The People's Liberation Army (PLA), which has been fighting the Indian government since the late 1970s for an independent state in Manipur, used training camps in Myanmar that belonged to the Kachin Independence Organization (KIO). KIO fought the Burmese government between 1961 and 1992, seeking an independent state for ethnic Kachins in northern Burma near the Chinese border. In this case, the support provided by Myanmar is de facto, since the government itself did not intentionally act to help the PLA. Yet, the PLA most likely saw an opportunity due to instability in some regions of Myanmar, where the government was unable to impose strict authority, and thus it picked the KIO camps to train its militants. Many groups, such as the LTTE, have used war-torn countries, such as Cambodia and Mozambique, for arms trafficking (Raymond 1998). This is a common pattern within rebel-state relations.

The models in Table 5.2 predict the effects of key variables on the initial decision to acquire any form of de facto support. The models in Table 5.4 present the results for three specific types of de facto support: the decision to acquire (1) safe havens, (2) training camps, and (3) safe havens for rebel leaders and maintain offices. All four dependent variables were measured as binary variables, taking the value of "1" whenever a rebel group picks a state to acquire any form of de facto support, safe havens, training camps, and safe haven for leaders and open offices and "0" otherwise. Table 5.6 and Table 5.7 show the findings about the level of de facto support. Opening offices within a country and using the same country as a safe haven for leaders often go together. Although both are coded separately in the NAGs dataset, they are aggregated in the empirical analysis as lighter forms of support in comparison to acquiring arms, training camps, and safe haven for militants.

Independent Variables

Many of the independent variables used to estimate rebels' selection cases were discussed in Chapter 4, when examining states' selection cases. Next, I will briefly talk about the ones that I also use in this chapter, explain how they help in estimating the RSM, and the additional independent variables I use to estimate the models in this chapter.

Conflict History
This variable takes a value of "1" if a potential supporter and target engaged in a militarized dispute with each other in the last five years, or a war in the last ten

years, and a "o" if there is no conflict history between two states in a given year. The presence of a conflict history between two states creates an opportunity for rebels to seek support from adversaries of their targets, which are potential safe havens. In line with the reasoning for alliance formation among states, rebels and states unite against common enemies. Situating themselves within the adversaries of their targets helps rebels secure resources and autonomy in their operations.

Ideational Affinity

Different types of ideational ties, and their operationalization, have been discussed in detail in Chapter 4. Ideational affinity within a triad measures the presence of such ties between targets and potential supporters, as well as between rebel groups and potential supporters. "Ideational ties" takes a value of "1" when at least one of the components of ideational ties (ethnic, religious, and/or ideological) is present between a target state and a potential supporter in a given triad, and a value of "o" when there are no such ties. "Rebel Ideational Ties with Majority" takes a value of "1" when a rebel group has common ethnic, religious, or ideological ties with the society of potential supporter in a given triad, and a value of "o" otherwise. For ethnic and religious ties, the majority groups' ethnicity and religious identity has been used in matching the supporter and target states, as well as supporters and rebel groups. A rebel group has an easier time recruiting from among the population of its supporter if it shares an ethnic or religious identity with the majority group in the supporter.

A more specific measure of ethnic ties is whether a rebel group shares ethnicity with one or more minority groups in the supporter state. This is a variable controlling for the effect of transnational ethnic ties on external support for rebel groups. Whether a rebel group shares ties with the second or third largest ethnic group living in a potential supporter motivates it to seek safe havens or resources from ethnic minorities ("Rebel-Supporter Common Minority"). Especially if the minorities in the potential supporter resent their government and live in poor conditions, they may help the rebel group with recruitment and safe havens.

This variable may have a negative effect on support resulting from rebels' selection, if a potential supporter is worried that helping a rebel group might lead to the spread of ethnic conflict inside its borders. In this case, rebel groups might end up facing repression from the supporter, so they act more cautiously in seeking such safe havens. The PKK militants in southeastern Turkey have found support among the Kurdish minority in Iraq. Yet, PKK militants did not start establishing safe havens and training camps in Northern Iraq until 1998, when the Saddam regime was unable to control mountainous areas by the Turkish border, due to general instability within the country. From 1984 to 1998, the major safe havens and training camps of PKK were placed in the Bekaa Valley in Lebanon, which was under the Syrian occupation at the time (Hooper 2007).

Relative Strength

The relative strength of each potential supporter, vis-à-vis the target state against which it supports a rebel group, is calculated by using the COW database, National Capabilities dataset (Singer 1972). The CINC index is used in a similar fashion to the estimation of the SSM. The relative strength of a potential supporter is measured by the ratio of each potential supporter's CINC to the cumulative CINC of a target and a supporter in a given triad.

Whether a potential supporter has the ability to resist the pressures of a rebel group's target has implications for whether a rebel group seeks higher levels of support from that state as opposed to lower level of support. More specifically, rebels' evaluation of potential supporters' relative strength plays a significant role in their decision to seek safe havens and training camps within them. A state is more likely to be chosen by rebels if they think it has the ability to resist pressures from the target state, and a motive to protect the rebels if the target state decides to chase them across its borders. A relatively strong target state makes it very costly for a state to host rebels fighting it. Considering that survival is the major goal of rebels, it stands to reason that they choose states motivated to provide protection from their target state, and with the capacity to resist demands to expel them.

Domestic Instability in Potential Supporter

As a direct measure of domestic instability, I use the PITF instability indicator developed by the (Marshall et. al. 2015), also detailed in Chapters 3 and 4. Instability events are defined as revolutionary wars, ethnic wars, adverse regime changes, and/or genocides and politicides. This variable is key for testing whether rebels select domestically troubled states as safe havens, or de facto supporters at large. The political instability score is a binary measure, taking a value of "1" whenever an instability event is ongoing.

Extractive Capacity of Potential Supporter

The total of military expenditures to total GDP ratio and military personnel to total population ratio (Singer 1972) is used to measure the domestic capacity of a potential supporter. It is essential in determining whether a state has the ability to resist the infiltration of a rebel group if it wants to. The score varies from 0 to 1 and also helps to assess whether a state is weak domestically. A weak state might provide a high level of autonomy for a rebel group that seeks safe havens and training camps within its territories, yet a low amount of resources and deficient infrastructure for transportation of human and material resources.

Extractive Capacity of Target
This variable is calculated in the same manner as the extractive capacity of a potential supporter. One may expect that rebels who target weak states do not seek safe havens in other states; rather, they focus on other resources, such as arms, funds, and logistics aid. Several groups were able to survive in Myanmar because of the inability of the government to extend its security apparatus to its entire territory.

Potential Supporter Regime Type
As mentioned earlier, democracies prove attractive due to the individual freedoms and liberties found in their political systems. As such, rebel leaders might choose a democratic state as a sanctuary. In addition, considerable support exists for rebels among diaspora groups who reside in democratic states, such as the IRA, the PKK, and Babbar Khalsa, who are at liberty to raise funds to support their movements back home (Byman et al. 2001). I use the Polity IV regime score to measure the level of democracy in potential supporters.

Target Regime Type
The same measure is used for the regime score of target countries. Rebels who target democracies and reside there may be less likely to seek outside safe havens, since democracies are less likely to repress and kill their own people (Davenport 1995, 2007a, 2007b; Davenport and Armstrong 2004).[10]

Control Variables
Mountainous Terrain (Log of Mountains)
This variable is adopted from Fearon and Laitin (2003), who examined the role of mountainous terrain in ethnic conflict onset. It shows the proportion of mountainous terrain to the entire territory of a country, using the natural logarithm of the mountainous terrain proportion in each potential supporter and target, to get robust results. States with a high proportion of mountainous terrain prove to be safe breeding grounds for the emergence of insurgency movements (Fearon and Laitin 2003). Thus, one would expect that rebels living in targets with mountainous terrain would be less likely to seek outside safe havens, since it is costly to move abroad and, in doing so, they take the risk of being expelled at some point, if it is no longer in the interest of the host state to offer sanctuary.

Major Power

Whether a state is a major power or not is controlled because major power states have global interests and can resist demands by target states.[11]

Rebel Group Duration

The duration of a rebel group needs to be controlled to increase the robustness of the empirical findings. Groups that remain active over a long period of time have a higher potential for acquiring de facto state supporters. The duration variable counts the number of consecutive years a rebel group has been active at each year.

Distance

The distance between the capitals of a potential supporter and a target helps control for specific types of support, such as safe havens and training camps. This further helps elucidate the convenience factor in acquiring safe havens, and singles out the influence of factors like regime type, conflict history, and ideational ties. Since I employ direct geographic contiguity as a mechanism of identifying potential supporters, I use the Gleditsch and Ward (2001) measure of distance between capitals, and take the natural logarithm of this variable. It ranges from 2.71 miles to 6.11 miles.

Cold War

The end of the Cold War produced a brief moment of relaxation in a long-lasting rivalry between the two superpowers. The expectation was that proxy wars would come to an end, and less internal conflict would ensue in the post–Cold War era, since nonstate armed groups could no longer have superpower patrons (Kalyvas and Balcells 2010; Hartzell et. al. 2001).

Table 5.1 presents the description and measurement of each variable.

5.3 Analysis

5.3.1 ESTIMATION METHODS

All of the dependent variables specified with respect to rebel selection and de facto support are measured as binary variables. Given the nature of the data—time-series and cross-sectional—in addition to the logistic regression analysis, I use the Beck, Katz, and Tucker method (1998) to correct for temporal dependence. Based on a hazard model, the correction includes a variable that counts the number of years since the last support in a triad and cubic spline smoothing variables. The purpose is to control for an autoregressive effect in the data. If a rebel group does not move out of its target country within several years after its formation, it might be because it neither faces repression in its target country nor has the opportunity to move to

TABLE 5.1 Descriptive Summary of Variables for RSM (PS: Potential Supporter T: Target)

Variables	Description	Measure
Dependent Variables		
Safe havens	Whether a rebel group turned a state into de facto sanctuaries	1 = yes; 0 = no
Binary de facto support	Any type of de facto support	1 = yes; 0 = no
Training camps	Obtaining training camps inside another state without the intentional support of a PS	1 = yes; 0 = no
Leader safe havens and/or offices	Whether the leader/s of a rebel group enjoys safe havens in another state and/or open offices	1 = yes; 0 = no
Independent Variables		
Conflict History	Target and PS have engaged in a war or MID	1 = yes; 0 = no
Ideational Ties	Whether a target and a potential supporter share ethnic, religious, and/or ideological ties	1 = yes; 0 = no
Rebel Ideational Ties with Majority in PS	Whether a supporter and a rebel group share ethnic, religious, and/or ideological ties with the majority in PS	1 = yes; 0 = no
Rebel-Supporter Common Minority	Whether a rebel group shares ethnic ties with minority group(s) in PS	1 = yes; 0 = no
Relative Strength	Ratio of PS capability to total capability in T-PS dyad (CINC Index)	Ranges from 0 to 1
Domestic Instability	Instability variable from the State Failure Task Force Data (Version IV)	1 = yes; 0 = no
Extractive Capacity (PS or T)	(Military expenditure/GDP) + (Military personnel /population)	Continuous
Democracy (PS or T)	Polity IV score of democracy-autocracy	Ranges from −10 to 10
Mountainous Terrain (log) (PS or T)	Log of the ratio of mountainous terrain to entire territory of PS	Continuous
Rebel Group Duration	Number of years a rebel group has been active	Continuous
Distance (log)	Distance between the capitals of PS and T (miles)	Continuous
Major Power	Whether a PS is a major power	1 = yes; 0 = no
Cold War	Binary measure of Cold War period	1 = CW; 0 = Post-CW

an external state. For example, Hezbollah preserves its largest group of militants in southern Lebanon since the Lebanese army is unable or unwilling to expel them from where they have been holding a territorial stronghold for more than three decades now.

5.3.2 RESULTS AND ANALYSIS

The GAM frequently flew recruits into Malaysia and then sent them to Libya for training. Malaysia served as a geographically convenient sanctuary for recruitment and transition of Aceh militants to Libya during the 1980s and early 1990s. Yet, in 1996, the Indonesian government convinced the Malaysian government to control the illegal employment of Acehnese refugees, which forced many of them to move abroad, particularly to European states. Furthermore, though GAM had significant financial backing from Acehnese refugees living in Malaysia, it preferred smuggling weapons into Aceh with the help of Thai mafia organizations, rather than sending them directly from cells in Thailand and Cambodia. They did so, in part, because they did not want to encounter political problems with Thailand, and sought to maintain their presence in the country. Some GAM leaders, such as Zakaria Zaman, resided in Thailand (Hastings 2010).

This is an indication of what militant groups take into consideration when deciding what types of resources to try to acquire within the borders of other states. The empirical findings in the following section will show whether some of the anecdotal evidence mentioned so far holds true in the broader context of rebels' selection cases.

De Facto Support

The RSM argues that rebels make their decisions based on a calculus of their ability to acquire as much resources as possible and autonomy in their operations against target states. Thus, it is a major goal for these groups to acquire some territorial control that will give them access to human and material resources, as well as a degree of autonomy in operations. In addition, once a group acquires territory, it gets very difficult to target and demolish their bases, since they are intertwined with civilians in the given area. This has been one of the problems associated with the international struggle against ISIS.

Obviously, not all groups have the ability to capture territory and maintain control over it. The number of groups that can do so is limited, such as Hezbollah or the FARC. Furthermore, territorial control comes at a price. The organization becomes vulnerable to outside attacks and, especially if all the members of the organization are concentrated in a given territory, target states might have an easier time repressing, even executing, members and leaders. This explains why leaders of such groups prefer living outside of their corresponding target states.

The leader of GAM, Hasan di Tiro, lived in Sweden for almost the entire time GAM fought the Indonesian government. Öcalan, founder of the PKK, lived in Syria throughout the 1990s, when the PKK was fighting against the Turkish government. Foday Sanko, the leader of the Revolutionary United Front (RUF), fighting against Sierra Leone's government during the 1990s, traveled frequently to Liberia, where he would enjoy safe havens under the friendly Taylor regime, until he was arrested in 2007 in Nigeria (Farah 2000, 2001; Rupert 2000).

It is best for rebels to maintain some presence in a geographically concentrated area, so that they can recruit, but also keep control of a dispersed network. Thus, they can guarantee survival when they are under attack from one or more states they target. GAM sought to diversify its support base in 1996, when the Indonesian government began to place pressure on the Malaysian government to expel the Acehnese diaspora and the GAM leaders Malaysia was hosting. As a result, it opened offices in Singapore and Thailand and sent GAM members to oversee activities in these countries (Schulze 2007; Byman et. al. 2001). Rebels always need states to survive and to sustain their operations. The goal of this chapter is not to test which strategy is the best for rebels to assure survival, which could be the topic of another project; rather, to systematically lay out the general characteristics of countries preferred by rebels as safe havens for training, money and arms acquisition, and/or transportation of resources.

Table 5.2 presents the results of a logit analysis of binary de facto support. Three models have been estimated, to explain patterns in the rebels' selection process. Model 1 predicts direct effects of key variables on de facto support decision. Model 2 checks for the interaction effect of the "enemy of my enemy" assumption and rebel-supporter ideational ties. Model 3 examines the effects of domestic instability in a potential supporter, and conflict history between a target and potential supporter state, in an effort to explain the influence of simultaneous threats on rebels' selection of certain states. Rebels might choose domestically troubled adversaries of their target states, if they are driven solely by a need for autonomy.

The results reveal that the "enemy of my enemy" assumption holds in cases of rebel selection as well. Rebels are more likely to select enemies of their target states as potential suppliers of safe havens for arms smuggling, fund-raising, recruitment, and training (H_5). The relative strength of a potential supporter, vis-à-vis a target state, has a positive effect on the likelihood that rebels select it to establish safe havens, smuggle arms, and raise funds (H_7). Across all models, results for the "enemy of my

TABLE 5.2 Logit Analysis of Rebels' Decision to Acquire De Facto Support, 1945–2010

	Model 1 Direct Effects	Model 2 CH*ID	Model 3 CH*Instability
Target-Supporter			
Conflict History	0.459***	0.327*	0.478***
	(0.134)	(0.153)	(0.141)
Ideational Ties	−0.353*	−0.347*	−0.349*
	(0.17)	(0.171)	(0.171)
Relative Strength	0.296**	0.292**	0.297**
	(0.094)	(0.094)	(0.094)
Rebel-Supporter			
Ideational Ties	0.411*	0.063	0.409*
	(0.165)	(0.248)	(0.165)
Transnational Ethnic Kin	0.992***	1.004***	0.995***
	(0.247)	(0.251)	(0.248)
Supporter Specific			
Domestic Instability	0.185	0.201	0.293
	(0.176)	(0.176)	(0.236)
Democracy	0.028*	0.029*	0.028*
	(0.011)	(0.011)	(0.011)
Major Power	−0.197	−0.198	−0.194
	(0.266)	(0.268)	(0.265)
Interactions			
Conflict History *PS-Rebel Ideational Ties	—	0.595*	
		(0.28)	
Conflict History *Domestic Instability in PS			−0.178
			(0.295)
Control Variables			
Cold War	−0.456**	−0.447**	−0.459**
	(0.156)	(0.155)	(0.156)
Capitals Distance (Log)	−0.487***	−0.482***	−0.488***
	(0.078)	(0.077)	(0.077)
Rebel Duration	0.375***	0.373***	0.375***
	(0.043)	(0.042)	(0.043)
Constant	1.936***	1.943***	1.933***
	(0.511)	(0.508)	(0.511)
R-squared	0.71	0.71	0.71
N	51398	51398	51398

*** p ≤ .001, ** p ≤ .01, * p ≤ .05

Note: In parentheses are robust standard errors that are calculated by clustering the observations by triadid, i.e., for each triad of target rebel group and potential supporter. Cubic splines and consecutive years of no support are not presented in the table but included in the analysis.

enemy" assumption, and relative strength, are consistent. Indeed, states that share a conflict history with rebels' targets are almost twice as likely to be selected as de facto supporters.

Overall, the analysis indicates that rebels are motivated by similar considerations in selecting their state partners as states are when selecting which rebels to support. They both have a tendency to choose the enemies of their enemies, and partners with whom they share ideational ties. An interesting finding is that across all models, rebels are dissuaded from selecting states that share ideational ties with their targets.

When it comes to ideational affinity between rebels and supporters, the highest effect is observed for rebels sharing ethnic and religious ties with minority groups in supporter states. When rebels share ethnic and religious ties with the majority group in a supporter, it has a significant, but lower, effect on the likelihood of de facto support. A state with an ideationally contiguous majority to rebels has a 51 percent higher chance of becoming a de facto supporter than a state with no such majority (H_6). This effect disappears after controlling for the interaction effect of supporter-target conflict history and supporter-rebel group ideational affinity in Model 2, indicating that rebels are mostly motivated by interstate enmities in finding de facto supporters. Table 5.3 presents odds ratios, and percent change in odds of support, for selected variables.

TABLE 5.3 Odds Ratios and Percentage Change in Odds of De Facto Support from Table 5.2

Variable	Model 1 Global Model		Model 2 CH*ID		Model 3 CH*Instability	
	Odds Ratio	%	Odds Ratio	%	Odds Ratio	%
Conflict History	1.58	—	1.39	—	1.61	—
Relative Strength	1.34	82.9	1.34	81.4	1.35	83.1
PS_R Ideational Ties	1.51	—	—	—	1.50	—
Common Minority	2.69	—	2.73	—	2.70	—
Conflict History*PS_R Ties	—	—	1.81	—	—	—
Cold War	—	-36.6	—	-36	—	-36.8

* p<.05, ** p<.01, *** p<.001   PS: Potential Supporter, T: Target, R: Rebels

Note: For the interpretation of continuous variables' effect on external support, if the effect is negative, percent change in odds of external state support per one standard deviation change in the continuous variable is used. For binary independent variables, odds ratios (or) are used if the effect is positive (i.e., or >1). If the effect is negative (i.e., or <1), percent change in odds ratios is used to interpret the effect on external support likelihood. See http://www.ats.ucla.edu/stat/stata/seminars/stata_logistic/ for the post-estimation methods using listcoefficient after logit.

When a state's major groups have common ideational ties with a rebel group, and it is also the enemy of the group's target state, it has an almost 81 percent higher chance of ending as a de facto supporter than a state that is not an enemy of a given target state, yet shares ideational ties with rebels. In other words, the effect of ideational ties between a group and a potential supporter only matters in shaping a rebel group's decision if the potential supporter is also the enemy of its target. On the other hand, rebels are almost three times more likely to choose states that have minorities with which they share common ideational ties than the ones with which they do not share such transnational ties. This is in line with existing research on transnational ethnic ties and their effect on the emergence of external state support in ethnic conflict (Carment and James 2000; Cetinyan 2002; Davis and Moore 1997). The effect of transnational ethnic ties is robust across all models in Table 5.2.

Domestic instability, by contrast to the conventional view, does not have a robust effect on the likelihood of de facto support, and this result does not change after controlling for the interaction of internal and external threats potential supporters face. This confirms previous arguments and findings that weak states or ungoverned spaces are not the best venues for rebels, who are looking for infrastructure and the ability to transport weapons and other resources along safe transportation routes (Hastings 2010). Furthermore, the results for the democracy level of potential supporters show that rebels are more likely to pick democratic states as supporters. This effect is robust across all models, though the size of the effect is very slim after calculating odds ratios and percent change in odds of external support.

This finding is not surprising, though, if we consider that democratic states, with their values of individual freedoms and liberties, may find it hard to trace individuals within their borders. Thus, after feeling threatened within the borders of Malaysia toward the end of the 1990s, even though the Malaysian government made no effort to expel the Acehnese diaspora and GAM members at the time, GAM leaders moved to Europe and continued operations from offices launched within democratic countries there, as well as the United States (Schulze 2007; Hastings 2010).

Whether or not a state is a major power does not seem to influence a rebel group's decision to select them as supporters. The reverse could be true in this case. Rebels choose to avoid major powers, since it is difficult to maintain autonomy of operations in a major power, which has an extensive capacity to expel them. Rebels are constrained when they have to rely entirely on major powers for their resources, operations, and training.

Among control variables, the Cold War period has a negative effect on the likelihood of de facto support. Across three models, rebels were about 36 percent less likely to seek support from external states during the Cold War period, indicating that de facto support seems to be a rising issue in the post–Cold War period. This could be because during the Cold War period, most support was intentional and readily available for rebels, as the major powers used rebels as proxies in their rivalries against each other. As a result, rebels did not have to seek external support from other states.

Although both works lack empirical analysis examining a large-N dataset on external supporters, Hartzell et. al. (2001) and Kalyvas and Balcells (2010) made similar arguments about the end of the Cold War and external state support for rebels. Hartzell et. al. (2001) argue that external state support is not a phenomenon limited to the Cold War period, and one should not anticipate that it will end with the Cold War. Kalyvas and Balcells (2010) state that although the Cold War ended superpower support for rebels, rebels learned to diversify their external sources of support from diaspora populations, refugees, and elements in neighboring states. The findings here provide further proof for these assertions.

Distance seems to reduce the likelihood that a rebel group will seek support from an external state. GAM members attended the training camps in Libya throughout the 1980s, yet they always came back to countries geographically contiguous to Indonesia, such as Malaysia, Thailand, and Singapore, to provide human and material resources to fighters in Aceh (Byman et. al. 2001). Geographical proximity has a consistent effect across all three models. Duration of rebels also contributes to their ability to acquire de facto support from outside states, as is predicted.

Types of De Facto Support

The theoretical framework argues that rebels seek safe havens to escape the repression of their target government, and to increase autonomy in organizing action against their target. While they may consider the adversaries of their targets as potential supporters, they also take into consideration the ability of a supporter to deal with the target's possible retaliation.

Four models have been specified to capture the effects of key explanatory variables on rebels' selection of certain states as safe havens for members, training camps, office locations, and sanctuaries for leaders. Table 5.4 presents the results for three models. The first model predicts the effects of key variables on the selection of specific states as safe havens for members of rebel groups. Rebels are two times more likely to establish de facto safe havens in the enemies of their targets (H_5). The "enemy of my enemy" assumption holds in the third model as well. Rebels are three times more likely to permit their leaders to live in enemy states of their targets and operate offices in these countries.

TABLE 5.4 Rebels' Decision to Acquire De Facto Support, 1945–2010

	Model 1 Safe Havens	Model 2 Training Camps	Model 3 Leaders SH and Offices	Model 4 Training Camps
Target-Supporter				
Conflict History	0.763***	0.347	0.943***	0.841**
	(0.195)	(0.307)	(0.205)	(0.312)
Ideational Ties	−0.187	−1.657***	−0.376	−1.463***
	(0.23)	(0.402)	(0.289)	(0.351)
Relative Strength	0.551***	0.754**	0.554**	0.908***
	(0.134)	(0.236)	(0.188)	(0.22)
Rebels-Supporter				
Ideational Ties	0.15	−0.132	0.673*	0.285
	(0.269)	(0.404)	(0.278)	(0.379)
Transnational Ties	1.514***	1.201*	1.939***	1.990***
	(0.401)	(0.562)	(0.459)	(0.478)
Supporter-Specific				
Democracy	0.02	−0.045	0.034*	−0.056
	(0.016)	(0.035)	(0.017)	(0.033)
Domestic Instability	0.446+	0.667*	0.337	0.546
	(0.239)	(0.311)	(0.253)	(0.306)
Major Power Supporter	−0.003	−5.442***	0.401	−6.656***
	(0.396)	(1.113)	(0.417)	(1.073)
Mountainous Terrain	0.018	0.306*	−0.106	0.16
	(0.104)	(0.143)	(0.126)	(0.145)
Target-Specific				
Democracy	0.024	0.105**	0	0.104**
	(0.021)	(0.04)	(0.023)	(0.039)
Extractive Capacity	0.000*	0.000***	0	0
	(0)	(0)	(0)	(0)
Mountainous Terrain	−0.226*	0.043	−0.290**	0.065
	(0.098)	(0.178)	(0.109)	(0.174)
Control Variables				
Cold War	−0.474*	−0.857**	−0.266	−0.915**
	(0.214)	(0.292)	(0.242)	(0.293)
Capitals Distance (log)	−0.670***	−0.866***	−0.555***	–
	(0.127)	(0.15)	(0.138)	

(*continued*)

TABLE 5.4 Continued

	Model 1 Safe Havens	Model 2 Training Camps	Model 3 Leaders SH and Offices	Model 4 Training Camps
Constant	4.200***	4.050***	3.174***	−1.450***
	(0.847)	(0.892)	(0.841)	(0.548)
R-squared	0.57	0.65	0.57	0.61
N	46572	46572	46572	46572

*** p ≤ .001, ** p ≤ .01, * p ≤ .05, + p ≤ .10

Note: In parentheses are robust standard errors that are calculated by clustering the observations by triadid. Cubic splines and consecutive years of no support are not presented in the table but included in the analysis.

Many rebel groups targeting Iran chose to open offices in Iraq, its protracted rival; the opposite holds true for rebels targeting Iraq, several of which opened offices in Iran. The potential supporters' relative strength seems to have a robust positive effect across all models. When they choose safe havens, training camps, leader sanctuaries, and office locations, rebels are twice as likely to choose relatively strong states, vis-à-vis their targets, than weak ones (H_7).

The presence of ideational ties between targets and potential supporters has a dissuading effect only when it comes to the selection of states as training camps. States that share ideational ties with targets are 81 percent less likely to serve as locations of training camps for rebels. When it comes to ideational ties between potential supporters and rebels, it proves influential only when rebels look for sanctuaries for leaders and office locations. This effect turned out to be much stronger when states make decisions to support certain rebels. The strongest effect of identity is observed when rebels share ethnic ties with minorities in potential supporters (H_6). The effect of transnational ethnic ties is robust across all models. States where ethnic kin of rebels reside are almost five times more likely to end up as safe havens, three times more likely to serve as training camps, and seven times more likely to end up as leaders' sanctuaries. Table 5.5 presents odds ratios and percent change in odds of various types of de facto support from Table 5.4. These findings are not surprising, given that diaspora support is significant for efforts to extract material resources and recruit members into the ranks of the insurgency.

Whether a state is a democracy does not seem to have a significant effect on the acquisition of safe havens and training camps. Though democratic states end up serving as leaders' sanctuaries, the effect is slim. Domestically unstable states are one-and-a-half times more likely to become safe havens and almost two times

TABLE 5.5 Odds Ratios and Percentage Change in Odds from Table 5.4

Variable	Model 1 Safe Haven		Model 2 Training Camps		Model 3 Leaders SH and Offices	
	Odds Ratio	% Change	Odds Ratio	% Change	Odds Ratio	% Change
Conflict History	2.14	—	—	—	2.57	—
Ideational Ties (T_PS)	—	—	—	–81	—	—
Relative Strength	1.73	195.6	2.13	341	1.74	197.4
R_S Ideational Ties	—	—	—	—	1.96	—
Transnational Ties	4.55	—	3.32	—	6.95	—
Domestic Instability	1.56	—	1.95	—	—	—
PS_Major Power	—	—	99.6	—	—	—
PS_Mountainous	—	—	1.36	—	—	—
T_Mountainous	—	–24.1	—	—	—	–25.1
Cold War	—	38	—	57.5	—	—

* p<.05, ** p<.01, *** p<.001

Note: For the interpretation of continuous variables' effect on external support, if the effect is negative, percent change in odds of external state support per one standard deviation change in the continuous variable is used. For binary independent variables, odds ratios are used if the effect is positive (i.e., or >1). If the effect is negative (i.e., or <1), percent change in odds ratios is used to interpret the effect on external support likelihood. See http://www.ats.ucla.edu/stat/stata/seminars/stata_logistic/ for the post-estimation methods using list coefficient after logit. The values are presented only for the significant variables across each model.

more likely to host training camps (H₉). The effect of internal unrest was not confirmed when estimating rebels' decisions to pursue any kind of support in Table 5.2. Yet, it is seen when investigating specific types of support, such as safe havens and training camps.

The theoretical framework hypothesized that rebels are more likely to seek external safe havens if they fight against domestically strong states. In this case, escaping the repression of the target is a primary motivation for rebels. Considering democratic targets are less repressive, the models include a measure for target states' level of democracy, as well as domestic strength. Although the findings for domestic strength of targets are statistically significant and increase the likelihood that rebels seek safe havens and training camps from external states, the coefficients are zero, that is, there is no substantial effect of targets' domestic strength on the rebels' decision (H₈).

Major powers are almost 100 percent less likely to be selected to serve as training camps. This is not surprising given that most major powers are not geographically contiguous to target states of rebels. Rebels who target states with a high proportion of mountainous terrain are 25 percent less likely to look for external safe havens for their members and leaders or open offices abroad. Furthermore, the Cold War had a dampening effect on rebels' efforts to look for external safe havens and training camps. Rebels were 38 percent less likely to look for external safe havens, and almost 58 percent less likely to look for training camps in external states, during the Cold War period, by comparison to the post–Cold War period.

Additional analyses have been conducted to refine the interpretation of the effects of key explanatory variables on the likelihood of acquisition of training camps. Considering that training camps are difficult to obtain, and rebels must travel long distances to find them, the fourth model has been predicted without controlling for distance. Many leftist rebel groups throughout the 1980s received training in Libya, since Libyan leader, Qaddafi, had almost adopted it as a lifetime mission to assist leftist rebels around the world. For example, the members of Fatah, GAM, and the IRA traveled to Libya to receive training.

When not controlling for distance between targets and supporters, adversaries of targets are almost three times more likely to be chosen by rebels as training grounds. Furthermore, states with transnational ethnic kin are almost seven-and-a-half times more likely to serve as rebel training grounds. After controlling for distance, the influence of conflict history between targets and potential supporters disappears. This means that when it comes to training camps, geographically contiguous states are preferred, regardless of whether they are adversaries of target states.

Indeed, that domestic instability turns out to be significant only in the prediction of whether a state is preferred for training by rebels after controlling for distance is a partial confirmation of the weak state assumption (H_9). Although domestic instability does not have a significant effect on rebels' choice of de facto supporters in general (Table 5.2), it emerges that weak states are perceived as an opportunity for rebels, who want to train their members free of interference from a government, when the weak state is located near their targets. In addition, weak states might be crowded with multiple rebel groups, which share their training camps in return for money.

The effect of ideational ties between targets and supporters holds in this model as well, and does not change after controlling for distance. Rebels are 77 percent less likely to choose states with ideational ties to their targets. The finding that interstate ties dissuade de facto support is robust, even after controlling for geographical distance. This demonstrates the effect of inter-state shared ideas, norms, and worldviews cutting into the networks between rebels and states. This is similar to the effect of interstate ideational ties on intentional support, which shows that states value their ideational bonds with other states more than the ones they share with rebel groups.

Support Level

Whether rebels seek support from external states is a function of several factors related to material and ideational context within which a rebel group, its target state, and a potential supporter interact. The analyses, so far, have tried capturing general patterns across any kind of support rebels choose to acquire from certain states, and specific patterns for some types, such as the rebels' preference of some states as safe havens, training grounds, and office headquarters.

When it comes to support level, two sets of analysis have been conducted by using the generalized linear model estimation technique (Williams 2006). One hypothesis associated with the RSM is that rebels get the highest level of support from states with whom their strategic and ideational motives overlap (H_{10}). Since support level is measured at an ordinal level, ranging from no support to low, moderate, and high levels of support, the ordinal logit method is suitable to predict support level. Since brant test yields that the parallel odds assumption is violated, the generalized ordinal logit (gologit) method is used to estimate support level.

The columns of coefficients can be interpreted as those from a binary logit analysis, in which the dependent variable is recoded into corresponding categories. For the first columns, coefficients are estimated for no support versus low, moderate, and high levels of support; that is, no support is recoded as "0" and low, moderate, and high levels are recoded as "1" (Williams 2006, p. 10). Positive coefficients mean that higher values on independent variables make higher levels of support more likely than the current category. Though we end up having several parameters to interpret from a generalized logit estimation, it provides an opportunity to observe whether each level of change in covariates leads to the same amount of change across different levels of support. Table 5.6 displays the direct effects on support level.

Conflict history seems to have a consistently significant effect across all levels of support. Rebels choose states that have a conflict history with their targets to receive higher forms of support. Comparing the coefficients, the greatest effect shown is that rebels are most likely to seek moderate and higher level of support, rather than lower, from their targets' enemies. Higher relative strength (of supporter in comparison to target) is associated with higher levels of support, though the difference between coefficients seems to be almost equal across each category. The higher the relative strength of a potential supporter, the more likely it is that rebels seek higher levels of support from that state rather than lower levels.

An examination of ideational ties reveals that rebels are more likely to seek a higher level of support from states with which they share ideational ties. However, this variable is significant only in the first column, not in the others.

TABLE 5.6 Direct Effects on De Facto Support Level, 1945–2010

	Model 1 NS vs. 1,2&3	Model 2 NS&1 vs. 2&3	Model 3 NS, 1&2 vs. 3
Supporter-Target			
Conflict History	0.693***	0.707***	0.533***
(External Threat)	(0.049)	(0.055)	(0.081)
Relative Strength	0.481***	0.497***	0.320***
	(0.025)	(0.028)	(0.04)
Supporter-Rebel Group			
Ideational Ties	0.266***	0.074	−0.129
	(0.053)	(0.06)	(0.087)
Transnational Ties	1.318***	1.710***	1.391***
	(0.083)	(0.085)	(0.112)
Supporter Specific			
Democracy (PS)	0.033***	0.026***	0.007
	(0.003)	(0.004)	(0.006)
Domestic Instability	0.352***	0.352***	0.352***
(Internal Threat)	(0.067)	(0.067)	(0.067)
Major Power (PS)	−0.290***	−0.397***	−5.118***
	(0.075)	(0.099)	(1.009)
Control Variables			
Democracy (T)	0.031***	0.040***	0.093***
	(0.003)	(0.004)	(0.006)
Cold War	−0.268***	0.022	0.145
	(0.046)	(0.054)	(0.076)
Capitals Distance (Log)	−0.562***	−0.629***	−0.816***
	(0.025)	(0.03)	(0.041)
Constant	1.387***	1.417***	1.480***
	(0.174)	(0.204)	(0.271)
	N = 50949		
Wald test of parallel lines		$\chi 2 = 4.90$	
assumption for the final model		Prob> $\chi 2 = 0.086$	

*** P ≤.001. ** P ≤.01. *P ≤.05

Note: In parentheses are robust standard errors. Parallel lines/proportional odds assumption has been relaxed for domestic instability in potential supporter. The autofit process of generalized order logit yields domestic instability as the variable for which parallel odds assumption holds. An insignificant likelihood ratio test comparing the constrained and unconstrained models shows that parallel line assumption is not violated in the final estimated generalized ordered logit model using the 0.05 level of significance.

Thus, it is reasonable to argue that the greatest effect of ideational ties are seen when rebels try to acquire lower, in opposition to higher, level of support. The third column shows that rebels are less likely to seek a high level of support, rather than low and moderate levels, from ideationally contiguous states, but it is not statistically significant.

Moreover, rebels are expected to seek the highest level of support from states with which they have common strategic and ideational interests (H_{10}). Table 5.7 presents the results after controlling for the interaction of conflict history and rebel-supporter ideational ties. Ideational ties consistently increase across levels of support and turn out to be negative. Rebels are less likely to seek higher levels of support from ideationally contiguous states, after controlling for the interaction of strategic and ideational ties with such states. Indeed, the greatest difference is that ideationally contiguous states are preferred less by rebels when they seek to acquire moderate and high levels of support from such states.

The coefficients for the interaction variable are consistently positive and increase across levels of support. States that share conflict history with rebels' targets, and are ideationally contiguous to rebels, are more likely to be selected by rebels, with the greatest difference being that rebels are more likely to seek higher levels of support from such states rather than low level of support. The finding that ideationally contiguous states are preferred for lower levels of support, after controlling for the interaction of strategic interest and rebel-supporter ideational ties, provides further evidence for the interaction hypothesis.

Comparing findings from both tables reveals that democratic states are more likely to be chosen as supporters by rebels, though the coefficients do not seem to be strong and significant across all support levels (H_{11}). The greatest effect is seen when states are chosen to provide low and moderate levels of support to rebels, rather than a high level of support from such states.

Domestic instability is the only variable for which the parallel odds assumption is imposed. Domestically unstable states serve as preferred grounds from which rebels seek and acquire higher levels of support. The major powers are consistently less likely to be preferred by rebels to acquire higher levels of support, with major powers least likely to be found in the moderate or high support categories.

The Cold War does not seem to have a consistent and significant effect, other than when rebels try to acquire lower levels of support. During the Cold War period, rebels were less likely to acquire higher levels of support from external states. This finding is consistent with the findings in Table 5.2, where de facto support seems to be of growing concern in the post–Cold War period. Geographical proximity has a consistent and negative effect across cutoff points. Rebels are less likely to seek higher levels of support from states located near their targets. Geographical distance

TABLE 5.7 Indirect Effects on De Facto Support Level, 1945–2010

	Model 1 NS vs. 1,2&3	*Model 2* NS&1 vs. 2&3	*Model 3* NS, 1&2 vs. 3
Supporter-Target			
Conflict History	0.571***	0.567***	0.321***
(External Threat)	(0.056)	(0.063)	(0.093)
Relative Strength	0.476***	0.486***	0.310***
	(0.025)	(0.029)	(0.041)
Supporter-Rebel Group			
Ideational Ties	−0.037	−0.298**	−0.829***
	(0.089)	(0.107)	(0.196)
Transnational Ties	1.334***	1.730***	1.441***
	(0.084)	(0.086)	(0.114)
Supporter Specific			
Democracy (PS)	0.033***	0.027***	0.01
	(0.003)	(0.004)	(0.006)
Domestic Instability	0.365***	0.365***	0.365***
(Internal Threat)	(0.067)	(0.067)	(0.067)
Major Power (PS)	−0.283***	−0.405***	−5.203***
	(0.075)	(0.1)	(1.009)
Control Variables			
Democracy (T)	0.031***	0.039***	0.091***
	(0.003)	(0.004)	(0.006)
Cold War	−0.269***	0.025	0.142
	(0.046)	(0.054)	(0.075)
Capitals Distance (Log)	−0.562***	−0.622***	−0.776***
	(0.025)	(0.03)	(0.043)
Conflict History*	0.472***	0.564***	0.982***
PS-Rebel Ideational Ties			
	(0.108)	(0.127)	(0.223)
Constant	1.438***	1.428***	1.341***
	(0.174)	(0.208)	(0.276)
		N = 50949	
Likelihood Ratio Test for Parallel		χ2 = 2.88	
Odds Assumption		Prob> χ2 = 0.24	

*** P ≤.001., ** P ≤.01.,*P ≤.05

Note: In parentheses are robust standard errors. Parallel lines/proportional odds assumption has been relaxed for domestic instability in potential supporter. The autofit process of generalized order logit yields domestic instability as the variable for which parallel odds assumption holds. An insignificant likelihood ratio test comparing the constrained and unconstrained models shows that parallel line assumption is not violated in the final estimated generalized ordered logit model using the 0.05 level of significance.

leads to a decline in the probability of acquiring higher levels of support. This is due to the fact that concentrating in nearby states makes it easy for a target state to track the insurgents and put pressure on the host states to control their borders and the activities of rebels in their territories.

5.4 Conclusion

The preceding analysis explores the conditions under which rebels select states from which to acquire resources. The results draw systematic regularities about state-rebel interactions. A comparison of the results between Table 4.3 from Chapter 4 and Table 5.2 in this chapter suggests that rebels are as motivated as their supporters to form alliances with the adversaries of their targets. Yet, the effect seems to be less significant than the findings from the estimation of the SSM, when comparing the size of the coefficients. The logic of interstate alliances holds when states select the rebels they wish to support, as well as when rebels select their supporters. Domestic threat within countries does not seem to motivate rebels in selecting them as much as it motivates states in selecting certain rebels.

Across all the models estimated in this chapter, common ties with the population of a potential supporter have proven significant to a rebel group's decision to select an external state as a safe haven, either with the latter's consent or de facto. Furthermore, rebels seem motivated more by security from the suppression of their targets, and ease of acquiring resources, than autonomy in operations against their targets. The findings on relative strength have consistent implications for a rebel group's motive in securing a supporter that can deal with a possible retaliation from its target.

The empirical results yield interesting implications for the nature of states rebels are likely to choose as supporters:

1. In contrast to the post–Cold War view, that weak states are the main source of nonstate violence, the findings here suggest that rebels are more willing to move into an external safe haven if the supporter state is able to manage possible retaliation from targets. In other words, weak states are not the best option for rebels, who are resource-dependent and need a developed infrastructure to carry out their violent conduct.
2. Domestic instability, or whether a state faces an internal threat, does not seem to have a significant effect on rebels' decision to select a state as a de facto supporter. Yet, when it comes to support level, domestically unstable states tend to provide higher levels of de facto support.
3. Rebels seek the highest levels of resources from states that are the adversaries of their targets, and also those that are ideationally contiguous to

rebels, demonstrating ethnic, religious, and ideological ties. The interactive effect seems to be more decisive in the rebel selection process than the state selection one.

4. The behaviors of nonstate actors and states are similar in terms of the way they treat the enemies of their enemies. Yet, it seems that states attribute more significance to whether a rebel group fights against an external adversary. Furthermore, rebels are motivated more by ideational ties to minority, not majority, groups in a country, when they seek support from that state.

5. Democracy seems to be a motivating factor for the decision to choose a state as a supporter, especially if a rebel group looks to maintain offices or safe haven for their leadership. Yet, when it comes to support level, rebel groups are able to acquire only a limited amount of resources from democratic states. This has significant implications for current counter-insurgency and counter-terrorism policies.

6 Conclusion
MAIN TRENDS IN STATE SUPPORT
OF NONSTATE ARMED GROUPS

ON APRIL 13, 2009, Pakistani president Asif Ali Zardari signed a bill introducing Islamic law into the Swat Valley of Pakistan's turbulent Northwest region. The bill was ratified after pressures from the Taliban, which had conducted an eighteen-month long Islamic insurgency in the valley, leading to the escape of approximately 100,000 people from the area. The provincial government party, the Awami National Party, acceded to Shari'a law because the Pakistani army was either unable or unwilling to fight the Taliban.[1] The Taliban had begun to move into the area when the U.S. offensive began in the country after the attacks of September 11, 2001. The provincial government reached an agreement with the Taliban in return for the latter's promise to stop fighting.

Between 2001 and 2009, Pakistan received approximately $10 billion in U.S. aid for its cooperative efforts in the war against terror.[2] The aid was a direct policy consequence of the shift in the U.S. threat perception with respect to weak states. The Secretary of State Condoleezza Rice argued in an interview that nations incapable of fulfilling their responsibilities as sovereign entities, both within and across their borders, constitute significant sources of international instability (Garfinkle 2005). However, the U.S. policy of giving aid to a country with a long history of supporting rebel groups proved ineffective. Pakistan's army and political leaders failed to take the necessary steps to repress the Taliban within the country's borders. The previous Pakistani president, Pervez Musharraf, had survived three assassination attempts by Islamic fundamentalist groups between January 2000 and December 2003. Despite many promises to control the tribal areas along the border with Afghanistan, he was not successful in securing the region from infiltration by Taliban militants. And the story did not change under the subsequent presidency of Zardari.

The more intriguing issue, with respect to the Taliban and Pakistan, is that during its foundation in the early 1990s, the Pakistani Intelligence Service (ISI) supported the Taliban, following the withdrawal of Soviet troops from Afghanistan. Pakistan sought to install a friendly regime in Afghanistan, in pursuit of its strategic interest in the region (Waldman 2010). This is the dilemma *States in Disguise* addressed. As the Taliban-Pakistan example shows, state and nonstate armed group relations are far more complex than weak state capacity or coincidental spillover of domestic problems into the international arena. I argue that systematic patterns exist in state-rebel group relations that could be explained by the material and ideational context, within which those interactions take place.

Furthermore, the preceding analysis highlighted that nonstate armed groups exist in parallel to sovereign states in world politics. Indeed, the examination of 355 state selection and 342 rebel selection cases indicates that rebels are not simply proxies that states rely on in times of need; rather, they appear to be in continuous search of resources in the countries they select, independent of these countries' national foreign policy objectives. Nonstate armed groups now appear to emerge as major actors alongside states, shaping and being shaped by interstate relations and states often acting in collaboration with them. The difference from interstate alliances is that the framework of collaboration is not determined officially, and does not depend on a binding written agreement. This is exactly why it has proved so appealing to support rebel groups to reach certain objectives. Walking away from the relationship between states and rebels is relatively easy for both.

While I acknowledge that, frequently, support of rebels occurs within the context of internal conflict, it also occurs independent of such a conflict. Since the emphasis in this book is on armed rebel groups, the analysis does not allow us to examine whether external support precedes internal conflict. In other words, we cannot test whether or how external states instigate violence within the borders of other states by supporting specific groups. Yet, some work exists showing that externally imposed regime change through support of rebels is rarely, if ever, successful (Owen 2010).

In addition, we now know that when multiple external actors get involved in an internal conflict between a government and a rebel group, it serves only to prolong the conflict, rather than solve it (Owen 2010; Aydin and Regan 2011; Balch-Lindsay and Enterline 2000; Cunningham 2010). Salehyan (2007) finds that external safe havens prolong civil wars. In addition, when there are multiple external states supporting different sides in a conflict, the conflict tends to last longer. The same argument is confirmed by empirical analysis of a large-N dataset on outside state intervention in internal conflict (Regan 2002). These findings are not surprising, given that states that end up supporting rebels usually do so because they have a different agenda from that of trying to resolve the conflict (Cunningham 2010). That is why it is essential to determine why states assist rebel groups fighting against other states, before trying to show whether they intend to help resolve a given conflict.

Any policy advice about dissuading state support for rebels will be deficient without addressing the underlying issues behind state support. It is the assertion of *States in Disguise* that policymakers should set their priorities more carefully when it comes to addressing the root causes of terrorism and insurgency. States and rebels frequently cooperate with each other for common goals. State support of rebels, then, is the result of a systematic selection process on both sides, much more than the convenience presented by a weak state or a geographically contiguous state. Policies designed to deal with various types of armed groups, including ethnic and religious insurgents, terrorists, and guerrilla organizations, will be misleading if they fail to take into account the fluid and flexible nature of state-rebel interactions.

Considering that the past several decades have witnessed an exceptional rise of rebel groups backed by various states, this book hopes to start a substantive discussion about international factors contributing to widespread nonstate violence, and threats posed by nonstate armed groups against humanity and against the modern state system. The findings, with respect to the role of interstate ideational affinity, are a good start for improving existing interstate networks, and building new ones, to crosscut the networks among rebel groups and states.

It is not the intent of this book to prove that weak states are not potential hotbeds for rebels. Weak and failing states can, and do, generate threats, such as transnational terrorism. They are attractive for violent groups who seek safe havens, resources, and recruitment. The most recent example of this is the ISIS, which now notoriously controls territory in various parts of Iraq and Syria. However, we can not ignore the fact that the majority of state support is provided by states that create deliberate channels to help rebels, and these states are not necessarily weak or failing. The roots of ISIS go back to the al-Qaeda organization in Iraq, which was supported by various states.

ISIS grasped the opportunity to acquire a territorial hold once a power vacuum emerged in Syria, as a result of the conflict between the forces of the Assad regime and the Free Syrian Army (FSA). The FSA was an armed militant organization supported by the United States and various Western states between August 2011 and December 2012, when it joined with other rebels to form the Supreme Military Council (SMC) to topple the Assad regime (Brown 2015; Ganley 2013).[3]

The fact that the United States defended its policy of supporting the FSA rebels, and other moderate sunni forces fighting the Assad regime, is further evidence of the complex nature of state-rebel group relations. Indeed, the United States spent about $500 million to train the rebels fighting the Syrian regime (Shear et al. 2015). The policy failed dramatically with Russia's entry into the fray, on the side of the Assad regime. *Should states support rebels who fight against repressive regimes and try to install democratic regimes? Are there good versus bad rebels?* These questions can only be answered if we first address the root causes of state support of rebel groups.

The external intervention in the Syrian civil war brought two issues to the attention of the international community. First, the rivalry between the Unites States and Russia over Syrian civil war came to be perceived as reminiscent of the Cold War proxy wars. Second, support of the anti-Assad rebels by the United States and other western states established indirect use of force as a normal and justified foreign policy instrument for states, especially democracies. Since democratic states are directly accountable to the public, their war-making capacity depends on whether their public supports war (Caverley 2014). Therefore, indirect use of force seems to gradually become an appealing foreign policy instrument for democratic states. Though the nature of this support is not covert, it definitely has the potential to inspire and justify covert support for states that are relatively weak in comparison to major states.

The current unipolar power in the international arena, namely the United States, is a democracy and often uses indirect force to topple unwanted regimes, most recently, the Assad regime in Syria. Especially with respect to international norms, the existing research shows that great powers have a significant role to play (Ikenberry 2006; Ramos 2013). Frequently, other states emulate major powers in their foreign policy behavior. The NAGs dataset shows that approximately 30 percent of total observations of intentional support are provided by democracies.

The dataset includes thirty-four rebel groups with aspirations to establish democracy in the countries they have targeted. The targeted countries include states such as Chad, Burundi, Cuba, Ethiopia, Djibouti, Guatemala, Iran, Pakistan, and Tajikistan. Although thirteen of these democracy-leaning rebels received support from outside states, little progress appears to have been made with respect to regime change and the transition to democracy in the countries they target. The difficulty associated with such groups and their supporters is that it is hard to know whether these groups will establish democratic regimes once they come to power. In addition, it is hard to determine the motives of external interveners: to promote democracy or to pursue their own interests in these countries? And, such a differentiation matters, especially if we count on external state actors, and the international community in general, to promote democracy in authoritarian settings. Only actors committed to the promotion of democracy will provide the long-term support needed by rebel groups fighting for democracy. So far, few such examples exist.

The theoretical framework is built on two models of selection, SSM and RSM, to explain the instrumental factors in the calculations of states and rebel groups. In this chapter, I present the common findings across both models and discuss the primary trends in state-rebel relations, without distinguishing between the two selection processes. In other words, in this section, the analysis is built on cases of cooperation between states and rebels, when they mutually select each other as partners. I continue my discussion, revisiting the insights offered by state-rebel group selection theory in light of the empirical findings. In addition, I discuss the policy implications and conclude with a discussion of future avenues of research on this topic.

6.1 Determinants of Support Onset

The initial decision to support a rebel group, and to seek support from a state, is based on a number of factors that vary from the perspective of states and rebels. One of the main assumptions of the theoretical framework is that cooperation between states and rebels is endogenous to interstate relations. The nature of the interactions between a supporter and a target should play a significant role in explaining why a state chooses to support a rebel group in the first place, and why a rebel group seeks resources within some countries.

If a supporter and a target of a given group have a conflict history, it is expected that both the supporter and a rebel group perceive each other as potential allies. If a supporter and a rebel group share ideational ties, it is expected they may collaborate even outside the context of interstate enmity. Furthermore, relative strength of a potential supporter matters both from the perspective of a rebel group and its supporter.

Table 6.1 presents four models for decision making by both states and rebels in selecting each other as partners. The first is an overall model examining major trends in state-rebel relations in the triadic context of targets-rebels-supporters. The second model examines state support when there is no conflict history between targets and supporters. The third model examines conditions under which ideationally contiguous states and rebels collaborate. The fourth model estimates state-rebel relations when potential supporters experience domestic instability.

TABLE 6.1 Main Trends in State-Rebel Group Relations, 1945–2010

	Model 1 Global Model	Model 2 No External Threat	Model 3 Ideationally Contiguous Rebels	Model 4 Internal Threat	Model 5 External Threat
Supporter-Target					
External Threat	0.776***	—	1.001***	0.625**	—
	(0.11)	—	(0.21)	(0.235)	—
Ideational Ties	−0.337*	−0.376	−0.264	−0.152	−0.256
	(0.141)	(0.196)	(0.232)	(0.278)	(0.176)
Dyadic Democracy	0.017	0.03	0.021	0.001	0.013
	(0.009)	(0.015)	(0.017)	(0.023)	(0.01)
Relative Strength	1.513***	1.063**	1.893***	1.766***	1.774***
	(0.211)	(0.343)	(0.383)	(0.43)	(0.239)
Supporter-Rebel Group					
Ideational Ties	0.465***	0.447*	—	0.589*	0.506**
	(0.136)	(0.204)	—	(0.265)	(0.156)
Transnational Ties	1.099***	0.825	0.980**	0.322	1.177***
	(0.198)	(0.456)	(0.331)	(0.443)	(0.211)
Supporter-Specific					
Internal Threat	0.396*	0.683**	0.477	—	0.269
	(0.155)	(0.231)	(0.293)	—	(0.184)
Major Power	−0.187	0.425	−0.444	−3.097**	−0.661**
	(0.191)	(0.308)	(0.357)	(1.137)	(0.237)
Control Variables					
Rebel Duration	0.313***	0.386***	0.263***	0.254***	0.259***
	(0.028)	(0.053)	(0.041)	(0.047)	(0.029)
Cold War	−0.197	−0.430*	−0.073	−0.06	0.053
	(0.117)	(0.175)	(0.222)	(0.257)	(0.134)
Distance	−0.549***	−0.740***	−0.434***	−0.655***	−0.429***
	(0.058)	(0.081)	(0.11)	(0.158)	(0.070)
Constant	1.316	2.678***	0.689	2.437*	1.213*
	(0.482)	(0.674)	(0.863)	(1.176)	(0.526)
R-squared	0.70	0.66	0.74	0.74	0.69
N	50523	35244	10035	4438	15279

*** P ≤.001, ** P ≤.01, *P ≤.05

Note: In parentheses are robust standard errors, calculated by clustering observations by triadid, that is, for each triad of target, rebel group, and potential supporter. Cubic splines and consecutive years of no support are not presented in the table, but included in the analysis. Extractive capacity also turned out to be statistically significant in the fourth model, with a coefficient of almost "0," so it is not displayed in the table.

Table 6.1 presents the findings based on a binary logit analysis of the entire population of cases included in the state and rebel selection models. The dependent variables is coded as (1) a dichotomous variable taking a value of "1" if either intentional or de facto support occurs. I control for the effect of the consecutive nonsupport years by using the Beck, Katz, and Tucker method (1998). I specify four models by controlling for time-dependence in the dataset.

6.1.1 SUPPORTER-TARGET INTERACTION

Both states and rebels seem to follow the logic of interstate alliance formation. A state is more likely to support a rebel group if they share a common adversary. By the same token, a rebel group has an easier time acquiring resources from adversaries of its target. The effect of conflict history between a potential supporter and a target is positive and significant, even when we do not distinguish between the two selection processes.

The interstate environment is conducive for both state and rebel selection processes. When the opportunity rises, states do not hesitate to resort to rebel groups to take revenge on their adversaries. By the same token, interstate enmity creates an environment easily manipulated by rebel groups seeking resources to sustain operations against their targets. From the perspective of rebels, the adversaries of their targets are potential supporters. Multiple examples can be cited of states using rebels against their adversaries: Armenia's support of the Armenian Separatist Movement in the Nagorno-Karabakh region in southwestern Azerbaijan; Libya's support of various groups against Chad; Eritrea's support of various groups against Ethiopia; and Pakistan's support of Islamic Kashmiri insurgents against India. And we know this effect increases if they are also troubled domestically. If states experience domestic instability, this makes it easier for rebels to enter these states in case they need safe havens or seek other forms of support. Across the first and second models, domestic instability increases the likelihood that states and rebels will select each other.

External adversaries of a rebel group's target are also among the most preferred states, even if a rebel group is picking from among ideationally contiguous potential supporters (Model 3). This was the case of Fatah and the PLO. When there were multiple states with which Fatah shared common ties, it chose the ones harboring animosity against Israel. For example, it did not seek extensive resources from Tunisia and Algeria, though both states are ideationally contiguous to Fatah. Rather, it sought support from Egypt, Jordan, and Lebanon. This finding is valid even after controlling for distance between targets and supporters. Model 4 presents the results for potential supporters that face internal threat. These states choose to support rebels targeting their adversaries, and the same finding is valid for rebels. They select internally destabilized states if the latter is an adversary of their target.

Ideational ties between supporters and targets seem to have a dampening effect on cooperation between states and rebels in the global model. Though much attention has been given to geographical proximity, or physical contiguity, between states, not much attention is paid to ideational contiguity among them. This book attempts operationalize such interstate ideational contiguity. By the same token, rebels are less likely to seek support from states with common ties to their targets. For instance, in conjunction with ongoing animosity within Nagorno–Karabakh, the Armenian Separatist Movement did not seek support from Turkey against Azerbaijan, since Turkey and Azerbaijan harbor majority groups in their societies from the same ethnic and religious background. When it comes to ideational affinity between a potential supporter and a target in other models, it does not seem to have a significant effect on the likelihood of support. Relative strength has a robust effect on supporting rebels fighting against relatively weaker targets. And rebels seem to acquire resources from relatively stronger states, vis-à-vis their targets, even in the absence of animosity between supporters and targets (Model 2).

6.1.2 SUPPORTER-REBEL GROUP INTERACTION

Ideational ties between a rebel group and a potential supporter consistently prove significant across all models. In cases in which more than one rebel group targets the same adversary, ideationally contiguous rebels are potential allies for supporters. This is also in line with real-world examples, such as Iran's support of Hezbollah among the many groups that target Israel; Rwanda's support of Palipehutu, a Hutu-based ethnic insurgency in Burundi sharing ties with Rwanda's ruling Hutu elite; and Nepal's support of various Maoist/communist groups that target India. Most significantly, ideational ties drive support even in the absence of enmity between supporters and targets (Model 2). When a rebel group seeks to acquire resources from other states, it prefers states with which it shares common ties. Among states that are not adversaries of a given rebel group's target, rebels opt for those with which they share ethnic, religious, and ideological ties.

Furthermore, if a rebel group shares common ties with a minority ethnic group in a potential supporter, support onset is more likely to occur (Model 1). Outside the context of interstate animosity between targets and supporters, transnational ties do not seem to play a significant role in motivating either states or rebels to seek support from each other (Model 2). Yet, it is significant if the supporter shares common ties with rebels. When it comes to selecting from among ideationally contiguous states, states and rebels choose each other if transborder ethnic kin of rebels live within the borders of a given supporter. This supports previous research on ethnic ties and intervention in ethnic wars by neighboring states (Saideman 2001, 2002). When supporters are domestically troubled, they seem to be selected by rebels if they are ideationally contiguous to rebels and/or have conflict history with the rebels' targets (Model 4).

When rebels have to choose among the adversaries of their targets, ideational factors, rather than domestic instability, seem to be most influential in their decision (Model 5). Even in the presence of external animosity, Fatah did not choose Syria from which to acquire resources, since Arafat was concerned about the autonomy of Fatah operations against Israel. When rebel groups have the opportunity to choose one from many potential supporters, their choice is determined by their ideational ties to the supporters. Internal threat does not seem to influence cooperation among states and rebel groups when they face a common adversary. Yet, when limiting analysis only to cases where supporters face internal threats, external threat seems to drive states and rebels toward each other. This finding is line with the diversionary theory of war as well as the concurrent threats hypothesis.

Facing an internal threat, indirect use of force appears to be the most viable option for states, which also face threat at the international front. Furthermore, in these cases, ideational ties between states and rebel groups are also significant. This could be because when states face internal and external threat simultaneously, it is easier to justify support in the presence of ideational ties with rebels, to secure the support of the public. The current crises between Russia and Ukraine and Georgia and Ukraine are examples of such a mechanism. It is easier for Russia to hide behind the shield of protecting ethnic kin while pursuing strategic interests in both countries.

6.1.3 SUPPORTER-SPECIFIC FACTORS

Domestic instability increases the likelihood of support onset, both in the model that includes all cases, and in the absence of a conflict history between a target and a supporter (Model 2). These findings confirm the estimates of the States' Selection Model in Chapter 4. Domestically troubled states are more likely to ally with rebels when they have to manage external adversaries simultaneously. Domestic instability is not significant in the ideational model, as revealed in Model 3. Rather, the relative strength of a supporter is significant. This might be because when states and rebels join out of ideational concerns, both make sure they have the resources to repel possible retaliation by the target.

In general, while cooperating to pursue strategic interest is driven by the relative external strength of the potential supporter and ideational ties between a rebel group and a potential supporter (Model 5), ideationally contiguous rebels and states are driven by the presence of animosity between states when collaborating with each other (Model 3). This might be because states support ideationally contiguous rebels more if they are the enemies of their enemy. In other words, when an opportunity arises to provide support to rebels who are ideationally contiguous, states and rebels select each other if supporter states harbor animosity against the targets of rebels (Model 3).

Across all models, relative strength proves to be robust and significant. Both supporter states and rebels are driven by their ability to deal with a possible retaliation from rebels' targets. Next, I will examine the influence of the key variables on support level. The methods used to estimate the effect of key variables on support level are discussed in detail in earlier chapters.

6.2 Determinants of Support Level

The level of support is expected to be a function of the interplay among several factors: the relative strength of a potential supporter, domestic capacity to protect the borders from infiltration by certain groups, conflict history between a potential supporter and a rebel group, and ideational ties between a rebel group and a potential supporter. I use the generalized ordered logistic regression to estimate the influence of key variables on the level of support. The generalized ordered logit model, and the reason for its use to predict support level, have been extensively discussed in earlier chapters. The estimated partial proportional odds model relaxes the parallel lines assumption for conflict history between targets and supporters.

Table 6.2 presents the findings of the generalized ordered logit analysis on the support level. The first column contrasts the no-support level with low, moderate, high, and very high levels of support. The second column contrasts the no-support and low level with moderate, high, and very high levels of support. The third column contrasts the no, low, and moderate levels of support with high and very high levels of support. The fourth column contrasts the no, low, moderate, and high levels of support with very high levels of support. The support level index is measured on a five-point scale: "0" for no support to "4" for highest level of support in the form of providing safe havens and training camps to the members of a group and/or troops to fight alongside the rebels.

6.2.1 SUPPORT-TARGET INTERACTION

Conflict history between a supporter and a target has a positive effect on support level. Positive coefficients in each model in Table 6.2 suggest that higher values on the explanatory variable make it more likely that both states and rebels will reach

TABLE 6.2 Determinants of Global Support Level, 1945–2010

	Model 1 NS vs. 1, 2, 3 & 4	Model 2 NS, 1 vs. 2, 3 & 4	Model 3 NS, 1 & 2 vs. 3, 4	Model 4 NS, 1, 2 & 3 vs. 4
Supporter-Target				
External Threat	0.996***	0.996***	0.996***	0.996***
	(0.041)	(0.041)	(0.041)	(0.041)
Ideational Ties	−0.464***	−0.433***	−0.331***	−0.919***
	(0.055)	(0.056)	(0.057)	(0.079)
Joint Democracy Level	−0.001	−0.012***	−0.011**	−0.015**
	(0.003)	(0.003)	(0.004)	(0.005)
Relative Strength	1.999***	1.856***	1.460***	1.255***
	(0.06)	(0.062)	(0.075)	(0.105)
Supporter-Rebel Group				
Ideational Ties	0.532***	0.476***	0.156**	0.396***
	(0.043)	(0.045)	(0.053)	(0.064)
Transnational Ties	1.263***	1.265***	1.474***	1.110***
	(0.084)	(0.084)	(0.085)	(0.096)
Supporter-Specific				
Domestic Instability	0.463***	0.484***	0.590***	0.643***
(Internal Threat)	(0.056)	(0.058)	(0.061)	(0.073)
State Allies	−0.022	−0.051	0.001	−0.465***
	(0.045)	(0.047)	(0.05)	(0.065)
Control Variables				
Capitals Distance (Log)	−0.757***	−0.726***	−0.846***	−1.095***
	(0.019)	(0.02)	(0.024)	(0.031)
Cold War	−0.138***	−0.112**	0.011	−0.034
	(0.041)	(0.042)	(0.045)	(0.063)
Political Party	0.238***	0.441***	0.496***	0.573***
	(0.045)	(0.047)	(0.053)	(0.069)
Rebel Group Duration	0.012***	0.021***	0.024***	0.016***
	(0.002)	(0.002)	(0.003)	(0.004)
Constant	1.457***	1.054***	1.658***	2.918***
	(0.147)	(0.155)	(0.172)	(0.218)
N			44991	
Wald test of parallel lines			$\chi^2 = 4.15$	
assumption for the final model			Prob> $\chi^2 = 0.25$	

*** $P \leq .001$., ** $P \leq .01$., *$P \leq .05$.

Note: In parentheses are robust standard errors. Parallel lines/proportional odds assumption has been relaxed for conflict history between supporter and target states. The autofit process of generalized order logit yields conflict history as the variable for which parallel odds assumption holds. An insignificant likelihood ratio test, comparing the constrained and unconstrained models, shows that parallel line assumption is not violated in the final estimated generalized ordered logit model, using the 0.05 level of significance.

a greater degree of cooperation than the current category. This means that a state with the opportunity to support a rebel group is more likely to provide a higher level of support if the rebel group targets its adversary. The finding with respect to the relative strength of a potential supporter indicates that high relative strength encourages states and rebels to seek a higher level of cooperation from each other. However, the highest effect of relative strength of potential supporters is observed in pushing them from providing no support at all to providing some support, either at low, moderate, high, or very high levels.

A striking finding, when it comes to the determinants of support level, concerns the effect of joint democracy on support level. It seems to have a consistent negative effect on support across all levels. Democratic states are less likely to provide higher levels of support to rebels targeting other democracies, when they decide to provide support at all. Rebels, by the same token, are less likely to seek higher levels of support from democratic states if their targets are also democracies.

This effect was not significant in Table 6.1, which presents findings on the initial decision to support a group, and to seek support from a state. Both intentional and de facto support levels decline if, in a given triad, a target state and a potential supporter state are jointly democratic. This finding highlights the democratic peace theory in a different context. Democratic states are less likely to provide higher level of support to rebel groups fighting against other democracies, though there is not a significant effect of democracy on the initial decision of states and rebel groups when cooperating with each other. Ideational ties between states also seem to have a robust and negative effect on support level. States are less likely to provide higher levels of support to rebels targeting states with which they share some ideational ties. The highest effect of supporter-target ideational contiguity is observed when it comes to moving states away from providing the highest levels of support, as seen in the fourth column.

6.2.2 SUPPORTER-REBEL GROUP INTERACTION

Supporter-rebel group ideational ties, and transnational ethnic ties, seem to have a positive effect on the level of support across all levels. When states and rebels share ideational ties, they are more likely to seek a higher level of partnership from each other. The highest effect of ideational affinity is observed when it leads supporter states from providing no support at all to providing some level of support. Furthermore, transnational ethnic ties seem to matter more than ties with the major groups in a country. This could be attributed to the fact that rebels frequently find refuge among their ethnic kin, who live across the border from their target states.

6.2.3 SUPPORTER-SPECIFIC VARIABLES

Higher levels of domestic instability are associated with higher levels of support. Indeed, the highest effect of domestic threat is observed when a supporter is led from providing lower levels of support to providing the highest level of support, as seen in the fourth column. Furthermore, states seem to provide lesser amounts of support to rebels when they have conventional state allies to call upon for help in times of need. The results, with respect to substitution of alliances, seem to be mixed, since it is only significant at the highest level of support.

In addition to the key factors, the analysis controlled for the effect of the Cold War period. It seems that the Cold War has a negative effect on support level, but the results are not robust across different levels of support. States were less likely to provide higher levels of support to rebels during the Cold War period, but the finding is significant only when states move from providing low and moderate levels of support to no support at all.

Another variable included in this analysis is the ability of rebel groups to participate in the daily politics of the target countries. If rebels have political parties, which would help them express themselves through regular political channels, they are expected to be less likely to seek higher levels of support from outside states. Yet, the finding indicates the reverse. This could be attributed to the fact that rebels with political parties are also the most enduring and ambituous ones. Thus, it is normal for them to be also ambitious about seeking outside support. Such groups also appeal to states in search of alternative partners, since they are seen as more determined to continue their fight against the target states.

6.3 Revisiting the Selection Theory of State-Rebel Relations

Five general arguments were laid out at the end of Chapter 2, concerning the theory of state-rebel group selection. Here, I reiterate the arguments and discuss the implications of the empirical findings for each. *What factors are instrumental to states' and rebels' selection of one another as partners?*

Several studies have already shown that states support rebels, insurgents, and terrorists fighting their enemies or rivals (Byman et al. 2001; Saideman 2001; Salehyan 2010; Salehyan et al. 2011; Bapat 2012; Maoz and San-Akca 2012). Yet, we do not know the conditions under which they do so, or the factors driving states to support one rebel group rather than the other, when fighting against the same enemy.

States provide intentional support to rebels that target their adversaries, especially if they are troubled domestically and face constraints to extraction and mobilization of resources to deal with their adversaries through conventional means, and they do not have conventional state allies to call on for help in times of need (Table 4.3). The findings reveal that conflict history and domestic instability are consistently less important after controlling for the interaction effect. Indeed, domestic instability is no longer significant after controlling for simultaneous internal and external threats. States tend to delegate their external wars to rebels if they have to deal with domestic threats at the same time as external adversaries. Doing so helps leaders allocate more resources to control internal troubles than if they had to stretch them across internal and external fronts.

This trend does not hold true in the selection process of rebels. Rebels seem to be less motivated by exploiting domestic instability within their targets. The calculation of rebels for selecting supporters seems to be consistently driven by ideational ties to potential supporters, and the level of democracy in the potential supporters (Table 5.2). This makes sense, if one considers that priority of rebels is to continue their violent actions as long as possible, which can be realized only if they are able to recruit from a specific pool of people with whom they share ideational ties. These trends are also revealed on de facto support level (Table 5.6 and Table 5.7). The level of democracy among potential supporters motivates rebels to seek de facto support from them. Furthermore, conflict history between targets and supporters motivates rebels to seek higher levels of support from external adversaries of their targets, if they also have common ties with them.

States form alliances with ideationally contiguous rebels, whether or not the latter targets an adversary. However, ideational factors reinforce a state's decision, if a state has to choose one rebel group to support among many that target its adversary. An interesting finding of this book is that both material and ideational ties—equally— drive states to the rebels they support. States occasionally end up supporting rebels even if the latter does not fight against its enemy. This confirms the earliest arguments of the book: strategic and ideational factors are complementary explanations of state-rebel group interactions, rather than competing ones. The assumptions of both realism and constructivism offer significant insights in explaining various layers of interaction among states and rebels.

The substitution effect is confirmed in the findings of Model 4 in Table 6.2. *States are less likely to support rebels against their adversaries if they have conventional state allies they can trust in times of emergency.* In other words, when making a decision to provide support to a rebel group fighting against its adversary, a state is less likely to provide higher levels of support to the rebel groups in question if they have state allies. They seem to substitute state allies with rebels, in the absence of such allies. This makes sense, if one considers that supporting rebels is a highly risky strategy for two reasons. One, a state might be hesitant to provoke retaliation from the target state, and to accept blame for supporting rebels, which can serve as a justifiable cause for the target state to retaliate. Second, when conventional state allies are in place, states rely on their allies rather than rebels, who are not always credible partners and can create problems for their supporters.

States are less likely to provide support to rebels that target ideationally contiguous states. This finding is consistent across all models specified in the empirical analyses. In an attempt to operationalize and test the influence of factors like culture, ideas, and identity, this book develops an extensive measure to capture not just the institutional similarity among states—that is, joint democracy—but also cultural or ideational similarity among them. Thus it goes beyond the normative explanation of democratic peace. The similarity between two states should also be measured at the societal level. By matching the ethnic and religious identities of major groups in each state with each other, *States in Disguise* takes a significant step toward measuring ideational contiguity between states.

The highest level of support occurs when a state and a rebel group have a common adversary (i.e., a rebel group targets a state's adversary) and/or share ideational ties, and a state is relatively strong, vis-à-vis the rebel group. The theoretical framework also suggests that from the perspectives of both supporters and rebels, the ability to handle possible retaliation from the target is instrumental in the selection of one another. Whatever the motive of a state, it tends to support rebels that target relatively weak states, and rebels tend to choose states that are relatively strong, vis-à-vis their adversaries. This is confirmed when rebels seek both safe havens and other forms of de facto support from states.

Rebels do not necessarily choose weak states as supporters. States that experience domestic disturbances, thus a potential power vacuum, do not seem to be the only option for rebels, who want to move outside. Although states resort to rebels when they experience domestic turbulence, it is not necessarily because they lack the capacity to control their borders from incursion. It is a deliberate choice on their part, and they remain concerned about possible target retaliation. In other words, it seems that a domestically unstable, but externally stronger, state (vis-à-vis the target of a rebel group) seems more likely to support rebels. This suggests that supporting rebels is a diversionary strategy states resort to when they experience domestic troubles.

Finally, rebels are more likely to choose democratic states to acquire specific sorts of support, such as maintain offices and safe havens for leaders. The institutional structure of democracies, and individual freedoms and liberties embedded in their foundation, make them vulnerable to exploitation by rebel groups. Indeed, rebel groups freely recruit, raise funds, benefit from logistics support, and operate offices within these countries, without the sponsorship of their governments. The freedom-versus-security dilemma will cast a shadow on democracies for decades to come in their fight against terrorism in this respect.

6.4 Policy Implications

The empirical tests on 455 rebel groups active between 1945 and 2010 show that states and rebels have convergent and divergent motives in selecting each other as allies. The assumption that "terrorism is the weapon of the weak" is dubious, in light of the general patterns found in state support of rebels in this project. Indeed, nonstate armed groups, including terrorists, manage acquiring resources from states frequently due to various motives.

The resurgence of armed rebel groups around the world in the years following World War II provides proof that interstate competition, as seen during the Cold War and in the post–Cold War era, paves the way for the rise of rebel groups. In recent decades, they emerged as a major security threat for states, and they have not hesitated to emulate states in terms of organizational structure, attempts to achieve territorial control, and efforts to interact with the larger society. Thus, it is necessary to test the long-standing paradigms of international relations in this new context. The purpose of this book is not to refute the teachings of these paradigms, but to build on them, by demonstrating that violence in world politics should not be consigned solely to the study of interstate relations, nor should the direct use of force be identified as the only display of enmity in world politics. The way states interact with each other should provide some clues for how they do cooperate with or fight against the new actors of international arena. Or, does it?

It seems that rebels are driven by ideational ties to certain states. Therefore, policies intended to break ideational networks between states and rebels, or build counter-networks, might prove effective for minimizing state support. Furthermore, interstate ideational ties might be reinforced as a counterterrorism or counterinsurgency strategy, in minimizing state support for rebels. An example of this is the success of the United States in encouraging Libya to terminate its support for various Islamist fundamentalist groups, shortly after the end of the Cold War (Collins 2004; Schweitzer 2004).

By interstate ideational networks, I do not mean that every state has to become a democracy. The effort to promote democracy militarily in the world has, to date, met with little success. Rather, I mean that states can unite under a common denominator in, at minimum, agreeing to respect basic human rights and not treat armed groups as potential allies in foreign policy. The findings with respect to the alliance substitution show that states support rebels against their adversaries if they do not have conventional states allies to trust in times of emergency. Interstate alliances or security communities should help to dissuade states from supporting rebel groups.

An analysis of the historical records on piracy in the Mediterranean also confirms that it requires mutual consent by the major states to prevent further escalation of violence by rebel groups in world politics. From the 16th to the 18th centuries, the maritime trade of European states was threatened by the Barbary corsairs, who formed pirate states in Algiers, Tunisia, and Tripoli. Britain, Spain, and the United States had to pay ransoms—passage fees—to these pirates to ensure safe passage of their merchant ships through waters of the North African Mediterranean coasts. Only after the formation of a coalition of states to fight the corsairs, and enactment of an agreement to cease support for them, did the threat from the pirates gradually decline (Thomson 1994). It was not until the European powers themselves stopped benefiting from piracy, as part of their rivalry with each other in the sea trade, and after they succeeded in mounting a collective effort of sovereign states, that piracy entirely disappeared.

Although the current engagement of major powers, such as the United States, Russia, the United Kingdom, and France, in the Middle East might work to contain the violence in the region temporarily, it will eventually require more decisive action by these states, in a coordinated manner. It is not safe for world society to have significant Iraqi and Syrian territories ungoverned. This is the time for the international community to act together to contain violent extremism and impose a common strategy with respect to the treatment of armed rebel groups. It is no longer about individual material interests of states; rather, it is in the interest of the global community if we want to continue organizing world affairs around the entity of "state" as the main legitimate and constitutive element of the current global order.

6.5. Future Venues of Research

Future research on this topic might focus on four main areas. First, the relationship between regime type and state support of rebels should be closely investigated, to reveal whether the assumption of democratic peace holds when it comes to state support of rebels. Despite some early findings here, whether democracies are less likely to support rebels that target other democracies should be investigated further.

The second topic that calls for additional research is the conflict history between targets and supporters. More nuanced measures of conflict history, such as the number of military encounters, the duration of these disputes, and the level of violence in each instance of military aggression, might be incorporated into the analysis, to develop more informed implications about the role of interstate rivalries on the likelihood of support.

The third issue entails a more systematic testing of the substitution effect of interstate alliances. The findings of the SSM provide preliminary evidence that states are less likely to support rebels against their adversaries if they have conventional state allies on which to rely. In other words, states use rebels as substitutes for their lack of state allies. Confirmation of this finding requires further analysis that incorporates event history and the timing of alliance formation.

Last, but not least, future research might separate out ideational ties into ethnic, religious, and ideological movements, and examine the types of rebels who prove most appealing for state supporters. Such an analysis would also allow for investigating the conditions under which state support help rebel groups to realize their objectives. In addition, one should examine how state support influences the way rebel groups interact with their target states and whether target states repress or accommodate them.

Although the analysis in this book does not cover the cases in which some rebel groups should be supported by the international community, especially if they fight against repressive and autocratic regimes, future research should clarify the conditions under which democracy promotion through nonstate armed groups is a viable strategy in the long run. And, most significantly, the scholarly research should investigate the conditions under which such regime transformation from autocracy to democracy is successful and whether the international community can play a constructive role.

Sample Data Table

Year	Target	Rebel Group[1]	Potential Supporter	State Selection	Rebel Selection
1989	Somalia	SPM	United States of America	0	0
1990	Somalia	SPM	United States of America	0	0
1991	Somalia	SPM	United States of America	0	0
1989	Somalia	SPM	United Kingdom	0	0
1990	Somalia	SPM	United Kingdom	0	0
1991	Somalia	SPM	United Kingdom	0	0
1989	Somalia	SPM	France	0	0
1990	Somalia	SPM	France	0	0
1991	Somalia	SPM	France	0	0
1991	Somalia	SPM	Germany	0	0
1989	Somalia	SPM	Russia	0	0
1990	Somalia	SPM	Russia	0	0
1991	Somalia	SPM	Russia	0	0
1989	Somalia	SPM	Kenya	1	0
1990	Somalia	SPM	Kenya	1	0
1991	Somalia	SPM	Kenya	1	0
1989	Somalia	SPM	Djibouti	0	0
1990	Somalia	SPM	Djibouti	0	0
1991	Somalia	SPM	Djibouti	0	0

Year	Target	Rebel Group[1]	Potential Supporter	State Selection	Rebel Selection
1989	Somalia	SPM	Ethiopia	o	o
1990	Somalia	SPM	Ethiopia	o	o
1991	Somalia	SPM	Ethiopia	o	o
1989	Somalia	SPM	China	o	o
1990	Somalia	SPM	China	o	o
1991	Somalia	SPM	China	o	o
1991	Somalia	SPM	Japan	o	o

[1] The Somali Patriotic Movement (SPM) fought the Somali government between 1989 and 1991 in the Ogaden region of Somalia. Its objective was to topple the existing leadership in the country. The government of Kenya provided a safe haven to the leaders of the SPM for the entire period. The selection of a short-lived group such as SPM is due to space considerations.

Dangerous Companions

Cooperation Between States And Nonstate Armed Groups (NAGs)

A Triadic Level Time-Series Dataset on Support for NAGs by States

CODEBOOK
v. April 2015

Belgin San-Akca
bakca@ku.edu.tr

Department of International Relations
Koç University
Istanbul, Turkey

This research is funded by Marie Curie International Reintegration Grant (Proposal Ref. No. FP7-268486 and Grant ID No. REA.P3(2010)D/3202).

Research Team

Coders	Data Portal and Website
Gizem Türkarslan (Research Assistant)	Burak Demir (Research Assistant)
	Ferit Demircioğlu
Barış Arı	Özge Nur Kamcı
Efe Çoban	Suat Alper Orhan
Aytaç Denk	Halit Sezgin
Melissa Meek	Irena Atnaguzina
Ilayda Bilge Önder	Elif Burcu Gundoğdu
Burcu Sağıroğlu	
Paulina Schenk	
Burcu Yiğiter	

WHEN USING OR REFERRING TO THE DATA, CITE:

San-Akca, Belgin. "Dangerous Companions: Cooperation between States and Nonstate Armed Groups (NAGs)," ver. April/2015. nonstatearmedgroups.ku.edu.tr.

San-Akca, Belgin. *States in Disguise: Causes of External State Support for Rebel Groups.* New York: Oxford University Press. 2016.

WHEN REFERRING TO THE CONCEPT OF NAGs, CITE:

San-Akca, Belgin. "Supporting Non-state Armed Groups: A Resort to Illegality?" *Journal of Strategic Studies* 32 (4) (August 2009): 589–613.

A2.1 INTRODUCTION

The Dangerous Companions Project (DCP) aims to realize two objectives with respect to the interactions between states and nonstate armed groups (NAGs). Building on a novel conceptualization of state and armed rebel group relations, it (1) collects data on state-rebel relations and (2) builds a continuously maintained data portal, which is accessible by the public and includes information on individual profiles of NAGs and their state supporters including the sources used for coding each case. The DCP operates on the understanding that NAGs are not mere agents of states, simply serving to realize the objectives of states, which support them. Obviously, when trying to provide support to an armed opposition group, a state engages in a decision-making process since it is a risky experiment. Nonetheless, states have historically used these alternative actors in international politics to pursue certain foreign policy goals, regardless of whether it proved to be a successful strategy. Similarly, the leaders and members of NAGs go through a decision-making process in deciding whether to receive external support from other states and in deciding which states are likely to provide the most effective grounds for extracting human and material recourses. In other words, the current conceptualization of state-NAGs relations goes beyond a simple treatment of these actors as a part of proxy wars between two major states. When it comes to the motives of actors—states and NAGs—the theoretical framework is further developed in *States in Disguise* so as to capture the varieties of state-NAGs relations.

Each of these decision-making processes are referred to as States' Selection Model and Rebels' Selection Model, respectively, with the understanding that states might select the NAGs to which to provide support, but it does not tell us the entire story about the ways that NAGs select and extract resources from external states. For examples, Hamas received support from several countries, including Jordan, Syria, and Iraq, states that, since 1993, provided, on occasion, safe haven to its leaders and/or members. On the other hand, Hamas counted on supporters in the United States and the United Kingdom, who raised funds for the organization and transferred them to Hamas, despite the lack of observable evidence related to state sponsorhip from these countries. These are two distinct processes referenced by the framework developed in the current project. In the former, states choose intentionally to support Hamas. In the latter, states do not create channels with the goal of supporting the organization; rather, are exploited due to the individual freedom and liberties intrinsically found in democracies. Though in either case Hamas was able to acquire resources, they are not necessarily the same, thus they should be treated and coded separately.

NAGs refer to any armed opposition group that uses violent means to pursue certain political objectives. It is an overarching concept used to refer to ethnic and religious insurgents, revolutionary movements, and terrorists. Insurgency, terrorism, and revolution are various forms of violence that NAGs resort to in realizing their objectives. Therefore, it is not useful for the purposes of the current project to refer to these groups by politically loaded terms, such as revolutionaries or terrorists. It is commonly accepted now that NAGs acquire resources through various channels, such as support from elements in the diaspora, fund-raising by charity organizations, smuggling of drugs and weapons, and engaging in illicit trade, among others. The purpose of the current project is to examine general patterns concerning the nature of states in which NAGs most frequently conduct such activities to acquire these resources. Therefore, the current project stands in direct challenge to the post-9/11 assumption that the major source abetting terrorism and armed rebels, in general, is ungoverned territories or weak states. Designated borders between states divide the vast majority of the world's territory. So it must be the case that more than 90 percent of the time, armed groups are operating within the borders of states, which claim a monopoly over the legitimate use of violent means. *What kind of domestic and international environment attracts armed groups to certain states when it comes to acquiring resources within their territories?*

The State-NAGs Cooperation dataset (NAGs dataset) is an attempt to operationalize external state support for NAGs that are engaged in violent conflict against one or more governments within or outside the state(s) in which they live. The groups and the states they target are borrowed from the UCDP/PRIO Armed Conflict database (ver. 4-2014a) (Gleditsch et al. 2002; Pettersson and Wallensteen 2014). In total, information is available on 455 NAGs in existence during the post-1945 period. The first version of the dataset (ver.4/2015) covers the period between 1945 and 2010. Each case in the dataset is a triad that involves a NAG, a target (the country subject to violence by the NAG), and a supporter (the country that has provided one or more types of support, such as training camps, safe havens, arms and equipment, funds, and troops to the NAG). A detailed description of each variable is given in the table below. Next, case selection, each variable, and corresponding coding rule have been explained in detail. A triad is listed for the entire period of a NAG's activity if a state ends up supporting it for at least one year during the period it is active.

The other contribution of this project is the public data portal site with information on each rebel group and states from which they acquire resources. Given that it is a challenging task to find and code information about state support, whether it is an intentional act on the part of a state or a case of rebels selecting a country from which to extract resources, the best one could do is to transparently share the sources used to collect and code such information. The DCP data portal presents profiles of each NAG, listing thousands of sources used to gather the required information. In addition, it provides data visualization by using maps and profiles for each group.

A2.1.1 How Is the NAGs Dataset Placed Next to Other Existing Datasets on the Issue of External State Support?

There are several other existing datasets on nonstate armed groups and third-party interventions. Cunningham, Gleditsch and Salehyan's Non-state Actor dataset (NSA) (2009) is a dyadic dataset with information on each NSA's military strength and capacity, leadership characteristic, popular support, and political linkages as well as external sponsorship. However, external state support is not broken into diverse types. We only know if explicit or implicit support is given by external states. Similarly, UCDP's External Support Data is another dyadic dataset, which also codes external state supporters that give support to a NAG in a given year from 1975 to 2010 (Hogbladh et al. 2011). These data are limited in their temporal domain, not going beyond 1975 and not distinguishing between state selection and rebel selection processes as described in detail later. Finally Regan and Aydin's data on external interventions into civil conflicts look particularly at military, economic, and diplomatic third-party interventions (2006). This dataset takes intrastate conflicts as one single unit and does not distinguish between rebel groups when multiple groups are involved in a given intrastate conflict (Regan et al. 2009). The NAGs dataset lists each rebel group and contains information on its ideational characteristics, detailed objectives, and whether support emerges as a result of state or rebel selection processes.

A2.1.2 What Is New about the DCP and NAGs Dataset?

The NAGs dataset differentiates between state and NAGs selection cases. Though it might be misleading to refer to interactions emerging at the end of both processes as state support or cooperation, to some extent it is justified since states turn out to be de facto supporters of rebels at the end of the rebel selection process. We do not have a way of understanding the intentions of each state about whether its politicians really want to support or curb support for a given NAG, if they found themselves selected by them. As a result, the healthiest way to go about coding such information relies on observed behavior. In the case of NAGs selection, some countries turn into facilitators of violent operations of NAGs despite the absence of state sponsorship in these countries. Therefore, it is not wrong to refer to both cases as state support, which emerges either from a state's intended or unintended acts. In addition, the NAGs dataset starts coding a NAG as soon as it declares a name regardless of whether, at the onset, it conducts violent operations, while the ACD takes the start of a NAG as the year in which at least one battle-related death occurs for the first time. This is despite the fact that sometimes NAGs might have existed long before they resort to violence. Another contribution of this project is the detailed coding of group objectives and ideational characteristics.

Byman (2005b) took the initiative in classifying several paths by which armed opposition movements, specifically terrorists, acquire resources from states. He refers to passive support of terrorists by states under three conditions: "(1) the regime in question itself does not provide assistance but knowingly allows other actors in the country to aid a terrorist group, (2) the regime has the capacity to stop this assistance or has chosen not to develop this capacity, and (3) often passive support is given by political parties, wealthy merchants, or other actors in society that have no formal affiliation with the government" (Byman 2005a, 118). Except for the last criterion, the first two are very difficult to determine in each case even if given extensive time and resources to do so. It is very difficult to determine whether "a government chooses not to develop capacity" to curb support of rebels within its territories. And it is very difficult to know whether a regime or government "knowingly allows other actors in the country to aid" rebel groups.

Though the way to conceptualize passive support of terrorism is to be commended, the ambitious data collection and coding project specified under DCP requires developing a standardized set of criteria that will make coding a large number of cases possible. Such criteria can be developed if we rely on what is observed rather than what is intended, since the intentions do not always lead to observable outcomes. Rather than treating capacity as a selection criterion when coding cases, it is better to treat it as a variable. This way it is possible to detect whether NAGs or armed rebels select states with weak or low capacity to organize their activities. Each variable is defined and explained in the following sections.

A2.2 LIST OF VARIABLES

Variable Short Name	Variable Long Name & Measurement
TriadID	Triad identifier—Unique Triad Id Number for a given NAG, its target, and supporter
DyadID	Dyad identifier—UCDP/PRIO Dyad Code
ConflictID	Conflict identifier—UCDP PRIO Conflict ID
Year	Year of observation
Yr_Active (not coded)	1—the year the group was formed, 2—the year in which at least one BRD (battle-related death) is observed (Startdate1 in UCDP/PRIO), 3—the year in which at least 25 BRDs are observed (Startdate2 in UCDP/PRIO), 4—formation date and one BRD year are the same, 5—formation date, one BRD, and 25 BRD year are the same year, 6—one BRD and 25 BRD year are the same.
Foundyr	Foundation year
Startdate1	Year in which at least one BRD is observed in UCDP/PRIO

Variable Short Name	Variable Long Name & Measurement
Startdate2	Year in which at least 25 BRDs are observed in UCDP/PRIO
Target	Target country name—abbreviation
TarNum_GW	Numeric Gleditsch and Ward ID of target country
TarNum_COW	Numeric COW ID of target country
NAG_name	Full name of the NAG
NAGcode_1	Numeric code of the nonstate armed group
NAGcode_2	Numeric UCDP/PRIO Actor code of the NAG
Incomp	Incompatibility—UCDP/PRIO
Terr	Name of territory
NAGID 1-5	Identity of NAG (Numeric): 1: NOID, 2: Ethno-nationalist, 3: religious, 4: leftist, 5: other
NAGEth	Ethnic identity of the NAG (Name)
NAGRel	Religion the nonstate actor belongs to (Name)
NAGLeft	Whether a NAG is a leftist revolutionary group (Binary)
NAGRight	Whether a NAG is a right-wing group (Binary)—fascist or conservative or other (specify)
NAGDem	Whether a NAG has democratic aspirations (Binary)
NAGAuth	Whether a NAG aspires to establish an authoritarian regime (Binary)
NAGDict	Whether a NAG is supporting a dictatorial regime (Binary)
NAGMil	Whether a NAG is supporting a military regime (Binary)
NAGTheo	Whether a NAG aspires to establish a theocratic regime (Binary)
NAGObj 1-6	Objective of the NAG (Numerical): 1: toppling an existing leadership, 2: change of regime type (transition from autocracy to democracy or the reverse regime change), 3: demands for autonomy, 4: secession/territorial demand, 5: demands for policy change, 6: Other—specify. Each category is coded as separate binary variables. A group may have more than a single objective.
PolParDummy	Political party dummy—whether the group has a party wing
PartyName	Political party name
Supporter	Country providing support to a NAG—abbreviation
SupNum_GW	Gleditsch and Ward country code of the supporter
SupNum_COW	COW country code of the supporter
StateSup (State Selection)	Binary variable of state selection cases of support
S_Precision 1-4	Support precision 1: supporter state clear intention, 2: reliable sources document support, 3: support is highly suspected by reliable source, 4: target state accuses supporter state without documentation

(*continued*)

Variable Short Name	Variable Long Name & Measurement
S_SafeMem	Safe haven to members
S_SafeLead	Safe haven to leadership
S_Headquar	Headquarters
S_TrainCamp	Training camp
S_Training	Training
S_WeaponLog	Weapons and logistics aid
S_FinAid	Financial aid
S_Transport	Transport of the military equipment, military advice
S_Troop	Troops
S_Other	Any other kind of intentional support
De facto Support (NAGs Selection)	Binary variable of de facto Support (NAGs Selection Cases)
DS_Precision 1-4	De facto support precision 1: supporter state clear intention, 2: reliable sources document support, 3: support is highly suspected by reliable source, 4: target state accuses supporter state without documentation
DS_SafeMem	Safe haven to members
DS_SafeLead	Safe haven to leadership
DS_Headquar	Headquarters
DS_TrainCamp	Training camp
DS_Training	Training
DS_WeaponLog	Weapons and logistics aid
DS_FinAid	Financial aid
DS_Transport	Transport of military equipment, military advice
DS_Other	Any other kind of de facto support
DomSup	Domestic support dummy
DomSup_P	1—not much confident, 2—somehow confident, 3—confident
SupTermDummy	Support termination dummy
TargetPressure	Target country pressure
IntlComPressure	International community pressure
RegChTar	Regime change in the target country
RegChSup	Regime change in the supporting country
LeadChangeSup	Leadership change in the supporting country
GroupCeaseAct	Group ceased activity
GroupCeasefire	Group signed a cease-fire
GroupPol	Group turned into a political movement
Other_term	Other termination—explain

A2.3 CASES

A2.3.1 Identifying the Targets

To identify the states that have been targets of nonstate violence in the post–World War II period, I rely on the UCDP/PRIO Armed Conflict dataset ver. 4-2014a, 1946–2014 (Gleditsch et al. 2002; Themnér and Wallensteen 2014).

A2.3.2 Identifying the Groups

The groups included in the dataset have to meet the criterion of "25-battle related deaths" according to the UCDP/PRIO Armed Conflict dataset (ACD). I use the same groups as in UCDP/PRIO Armed Conflict dataset ver.4-2014a, 1946–2014 (Gleditsch et al. 2002; Pettersson and Wallensteen 2014). The ACD identifies an opposition organization as following: "Any non-governmental group of people having announced a name for their group and using armed force to influence the outcome of the stated incompatibility." Two types of incompatibility are identified by the ACD: (1) "incompatibility concerning government: type of political system, the replacement of the central government, or the change of its composition," (2) "incompatibility concerning territory:Incompatibility concerning the status of a territory, e.g. the change of the state in control of a certain territory (interstate conflict), secession or autonomy (internal conflict)" (Gleditsch et al. 2002; Pettersson and Wallensteen 2015). As described below, the NAGs dataset has a further detailed coding of group objectives.

A2.3.3 Identifying the Period

The temporal domain in the dataset is identified as the "opportunity period," that is, the period during which a state has the opportunity to support it. This basically stems from the fact that a group has to be active in order for a state to have an opportunity to support a group. Therefore, the year variable specifies the years during which a group is active. In some cases, a group ceases activity for a while and then reinstates violence. As long as the group and the government it targets do not sign an aggrement and the dispute is not entirely resolved, these brief cease-fires are treated as activity years. In other words, once a group is caught to declare a name, whether or not it resorts to violence initially, the opportunity to support the group emerges. Concerning the information about conflict termination, this dataset draws upon the UCDP Conflict Termination dataset (ver. 201-1) (Kreutz 2010). The UCDP Conflict Termination dataset identifies seven types of termination: Peace agreement, cease-fire agreement with conflict regulation, cease-fire agreement, victory, low activity, other, and joining alliance. As long as the conflict does not end with the first four types of outcome, it is not considered that a NAG terminated.

UCDP/PRIO Armed Conflict Dataset codes two different start years for a group. The first year (Startdate1) is coded when there is at least one battle-related death in a conflict. And a second start date (startdate2) is coded when there are at least twenty-five battle-related deaths in a conflict. The second start date is considered as the onset of a conflict within a given government-opposition group conflict. And there might be multiple conflicts within a given government-opposition organization conflict. The current data code the first year when a group is formed as the beginning of the activity period regardless whether violence is observed. This way it is also possible to observe whether receiving external support prompts groups to resort to violence. Of course, this is attainable when the formation year is before the first year in which a minimum of one battle-related death is observed. See description of Yr_Active variable below for a more detailed coding.

A2.3.4 DEFINITION OF VARIABLES:

> **TriadID:** Each row in the dataset represents a triad year. A triad consists of a target, a supporter, and a NAG that resorts to violent means against a country (target) to achieve its political objectives. This number is constituted in the following way: target COW ID*1,000,000 + NAGcode*1,000 + potential supporter COWID. For example, in calculating the triad ID number for Algeria (target), Armed Islamic Group (NAG), and France (supporter);
> COW ID for Algeria: 615
> NAGcode for the Armed Islamic Group: 2
> COWID for France: 220
> Triadid = $[(615 * 1000000) + (2 * 1000) + 220] = 615002220$
>
> **DyadID:** A unique identifier generated by UCD/PRIO Armed Conflict Dataset Dyadic Codebook to identify each dyad of a rebel group and its target state (Gleditsch et al. 2002; Pettersson and Wallensteen 2015).
>
> **ConflictID:** Conflict identifier from the UCDP/PRIO dataset.
>
> **Year:** The year of observation. Each triad is listed for the period during which a NAG is active, beginning from its formation year regardless whether there is violence in that year.
>
> **Yr_Active:** 1: the year groups was formed, 2: the year in which at least one BRD (battle-related death) is observed (Startdate1 in UCDP/PRIO), 3: the year in which at least 25 BRDs are observed (Startdate2 in UCDP/PRIO), 4: formation date and one BRD are the same year, 5: formation date, one BRD, and 25 BRDs are the same year, 6: One BRD and 25 BRDs are the same year.

When coding the activity periods of some NAGs, one issue concerns the groups that capture control of the government for a brief period during their insurgency. For example, the Armed Forces Revolutionary Council (AFRC) staged a coup against the government of Sierra Leone in 1997 and controlled the capital of Freetown until forces of the Economic Community of Western African States Monitoring Group (ECOMOK) drove them out in 1998. In other words, they did not secure acknowledgment by the international community. In such cases, the rebel group is not considered as representing the government. Rather, its activity is considered as continuing in these periods even though the group controlled the government. Another case is the Khmer Rouge in Cambodia. Although the Khmer Rouge began as a rebel group, it won control of the Cambodian government between 1975 and 1979. It allied with the North Vietnamese government and no regional and/or international efforts were launched to remove them from power. In such cases, the rebel group is not considered as continuing its activity in the period it is in charge of the government.

> **Foundyr:** The UCDP/PRIO dataset starts coding a group after at least one BRD death is observed. However, some groups existed long before a battle-related death occurred. Therefore, this variable is coded separately.
>
> **Startdate1:** Adopted directly from UCDP/PRIO dataset.
>
> **Startdate2:** Adopted from UCDP/PRIO dataset.
>
> **Target:** The country facing a threat from a NAG.
>
> **TarNum_GW:** Numeric Gleditsch and Ward ID of target country.
>
> **TarNum_COW:** COW country code for target.
>
> **NAG_name:** Full name of the group.
>
> **NAGcode_1:** The numeric code of the NAG (ranges from 1 to 455). In the end, a list of groups, their codes in the dataset, and the period of activity are listed. As long as the group did not sign an agreement with the government, it is not considered terminated.
>
> **NAGcode_2:** Numeric UCDP/PRIO code of the NAG.
>
> **Incomp:** Incompatibility as coded by UCDP/PRIO ACD.
>
> **Terr:** Name of territory under dispute (from UCDP/PRIO).
>
> **NAGID:** Identity of the NAG (Numeric):
> > 1: NOID
> > 2: Ethno-nationalist
> > 3: Religious
> > 4: Leftist
> > 5: Other (specify)

These categories are not mutually exclusive. In many cases, it is possible to associate a NAG with multiple identities. Groups such as the Palestinian Islamic Jihad and Hamas can be identified both as an ethnic and as a religious-oriented group. The ideational identity of these groups has been recorded for both variables of ethnic and religious identity. If a group does not associate itself with any identity and/or ideology, such as the Cocoyes in the Democratic Republic of Congo, then it is coded as not having any ideational identity. Although the group has aspirations to change the leadership, it does not carry out propaganda for a specific ethnic or religious group and/or political ideology. Rather it aspires to be inclusive by bringing together multiple ethnic groups in the southern Congo.

Determining the ethnic, religious, or ideological aspirations of each group requires extensive analysis of the components of the ideational spectrum with which they identify. For example, the Moro National Liberation Front (in contrast to the Moro Islamic Liberation Front) does not aspire to found an Islamic state in the southern Philippines. Rather it seeks autonomy for areas populated by Moro Muslims. This group is coded as an ethno-nationalist group. Although Islam is a part of their identity, it is not the main driving force. In cases in which there are multiple identities, the one that is overwhelmingly emphasized is coded in addition to recording each component of a group's identity under the corresponding variables below. To attract international attention and support from major powers such as the ex-Soviet Union,

China, and the United States, some NAGs have claimed to follow a "communist" or a "democratic" ideology despite the fact that their actions clearly do not conform to either of these. For example, the National Liberation Front in Algeria has been given different ideological labels over the course of its history, including calling it an anti-colonial, nationalist, and communist movement. In such cases, their discourse has been disregarded and their actions have been taken as a basis for coding.

NAGeth: Ethnic identity of the group. Ethnic identity is not only coded for ethno-nationalist movements, but for all movements. The Ethnic Power Relations dataset (EPR) was used to code the ethnic identity of each group (Cederman et al. 2010). The EPR dataset is hosted by the GROWup portal (http://growup.ethz.ch/), which matches each UCDP/PRIO Armed Conflict data rebel group with corresponding ethnic groups in each target state (Girardin et al. 2015). However, at the time of the coding of the NAG dataset, ethnic identities of groups were not yet available. Therefore, each NAG's ethnic identity was coded according to EPR identities by the Dangerous Companions Project team. In cases in which a group's ethnic identity was not clear, the identity of the group's leader was coded instead. For multiethnic NAGs whose composition included members with more than three different ethnic backgrounds, only the top three ethnicities found in their country of origin have been used in matching them with supporter major groups.

NAGrel: Religious identity of the group. It does not necessarily mean that the group seeks to establish a religious regime or identifies itself openly with a religious affiliation. For example, the Kurdistan Workers' Party (PKK) never cites religion as part of its identity, yet it is coded in accordance with the religious identity to which group members overwhelmingly belong. The religion categories are coded according to the indicators of the World Religion Project (Maoz and Henderson 2013). If the specific religion with which the group identifies itself is readily found (e.g. Sunni, Shia, Catholic, Orthodox, etc.), such labels are used in coding. Otherwise, this variable is coded as broad religious identities (e.g. Muslim, Christian). The categories coded for religion can be found in the list below. Similar to the NAG ethnic identity variable, for multireligious NAGs, whose composition included members with more than three different religious backgrounds, only the top three religious identities found in their country of origin have been included.

NAGleft: Dummy variable for whether a NAG is a leftist revolutionary group or not.

NAGright: If the NAG has fascist or conservative or other aspirations that we may relate to right-wing views.

NAGdemoc: If a group claims that it has democratic aspirations, this variable is coded as "1," and "0" otherwise. There is a problem that any group may argue that it will bring democracy. Usually any ethnic group that has aspirations for secession or partial autonomy has demands about reforms advancing individual political rights and liberties. Indeed, such groups usually claim to represent ethnic minorities, such as the Basque people who live in Spain (ETA) or the Kurdish people who live in Turkey (PKK). They claim to seek further rights for the minorities they claim to represent. When we code this variable, we do not take into consideration such demands. Both PKK and ETA do not seek primarily to bring democracy to the country in which they live. Rather, they prioratize other aspirations for their own ethnic communities. An example of a group that aims to bring democracy to a country is the All Burma Students' Democratic Front (ABSDF). The primary motivation of ABSDF has been to overthrow the military regime in Burma and establish a democratic regime.

NAGauth: If a group is fighting for a form of autocratic regime other than theocracy, dictatorship, and military government, this variable is coded "1," "0" otherwise.

NAGdict: If a group is fighting for a dictatorial regime, this variable is coded as "1," otherwise "0."

NAGmil: If a group is fighting for a military regime, this variable is coded as "1," "0" otherwise. Most NAGs that carry out military coups fall under this category.

NAGtheo: If a group is fighting for a form of theocracy, this variable is coded "1," "0" otherwise. Most fundamentalist Islamist groups fall under this category.

NAGobj: Goals pursued by a NAG might be various and can change over time. The UCDP/PRIO dataset codes the demands for government change and autonomy as main forms of incompatibility over government and territory, respectively. The objective of the group is recoded in a more detailed manner in the NAGs Dataset. A demand for a change of leadership is different from a demand for a change of regime. By the same token, the ACD take the stated incompatibility in the beginning of the conflict as if it continues until the end. It is known that various groups can change their objectives throughout the conflict and this in itself is a very important variable that is captured in the NAGs Dataset.

   1: toppling an existing leadership

   2: change of regime type (transition from autocracy to democracy or the reverse regime change)

   3: demands for autonomy

   4: secession/territorial demand

   5: demands for policy change

   6: Other—specify

TABLE A2.1 World Religion Project Religion Categories Coded for NAGs

Variable Label	Variable
chrstprot	Christianity—Protestants—No. of Adherents
chrstcat	Christianity—Roman Catholics—No. of Adherents
chrstorth	Christianity—Eastern Orthodox—No. of Adherents
chrstang	Christianity—Anglican—No. of Adherents
chrstothr	Christianity—Others—No. of Adherents
chrstgen	Christianity—Total No. of Adherents
judorth	Judaism—Orthodox—No. of Adherents

(continued)

Variable Label	Variable
jdcons	Judaism—Conservatives—No. of Adherents
judref	Judaism—Reform—No. of Adherents
judothr	Judaism—Others—No. of Adherents
judgen	Judaism—Total No. of Adherents
islmsun	Islam—Sunni—No. of Adherents
islmshi	Islam—Shi'a—No. of Adherents
islmibd	Islam—Ibadhi—No. of Adherents
islmnat	Islam—Nation of Islam—No. of Adherents
islmalw	Islam—Alawite—No. of Adherents
islmahm	Islam—Ahmadiyya—No. of Adherents
islmothr	Islam—Other—No. of Adherents
islmgen	Islam—Total No. of Adherents
budmah	Buddhism—Mahayana—No. of Adherents
budthr	Buddhism—Theravada—No. of Adherents
budothr	Buddhism—Other—No. of Adherents
budgen	Buddhism—Total No. of Adherents
zorogen	Zoroastrian—Total No. of Adherents
hindgen	Hindu—Total No. of Adherents
sikhgen	Sikh—Total No. of Adherents
shntgen	Shinto—Total No. of Adherents
bahgen	Baha'i—Total No. of Adherents
taogen	Taoism—Total No. of Adherents
jaingen	Confucianism—Total No. of Adherents
confgen	Jain—Total No. of Adherents
syncgen	Syncretic Religions- Total No. of Adherents
anmgen	Animist Religions—Total No. of Adherents
nonrelig	Non-Religious—Total No. of Adherents
othrgen	Other Religions—Total No. of Adherents

PolParDummy: Binary variable indicating whether there is a political party affiliated with the group in a given year. Affiliation is described as whether the party shares similar aspirations as the group and there is evidence that the party leaders communicate with militants.

PartyName: Name of the political party affiliated with a NAG.

Supporter: The state that supports the NAG in a given year.

SupNum_GW: Numeric Gleditsch and Ward ID of supporter country.

SupNum_COW: The COW country code of the supporter.

A2.3.5 Intentional versus De Facto Support

Support is an action that implies an intentional act on the part of an external actor. The post-9/11 debate about terrorism has focused on weak states and how they have become safe havens for various terrorist organizations. Yet the fact that weak states may turn into safe havens for terrorists or other NAGs does not qualify for "support of nonstate violence." State capacity should not be used as a coding criterion when deciding whether or not a form of support is provided. It should be treated as an independent variable in explaining the ability of a government to control its borders in determining whether they become as safe havens or sources of other forms of support for NAGs. As previously argued, the best way to code whether a NAG is able to acquire resources from other states is to focus on the observable outcomes rather than intentions, since the latter can be hard to determine. Therefore, the current coding protocol treats cases in which evidence is clear that states create channels to abet certain groups as intentional support emerging through state selection process. Furthermore, multiple reliable sources are used to confirm information for each case of support. On the other hand, when a rebel group is able to operate within the borders of a country without a clear evidence of sponsorship of that country's state, it is treated as an incident of NAGs selection, or de facto support. In that case, two criteria have been used to code state support of NAGs:

(1) Whether there was an observable indication that a given NAG was operating within the borders of a country; i.e. leaders finding safe havens, a source for raising funds, weapon smuggling, etc.

(2) Whether the government or leadership in a given country knowingly creates channels to support a given NAG. For example, Egypt knowingly let the fedayeen operate within its borders until the Suez Crisis, after which the Egyptian government expelled them from the country.

(3) In the absence of confirmable information that the government or leadership in a given country provides support to a given NAG or creates channels to facilitate its activities, it is assumed to be de facto support, i.e. NAGs selecting the countries in which to acquire resources to sustain their operations against their targets.

The following set of sources are used in confirming intentional state support and de facto support incidents:

(1) News wires and press releases from credible sources, such as Agence France-Presse (AFP), the United Press International (UPI), Xinhua News Agency, Reuters, Aljazeera, CNN, BBC Monitoring, etc.

(2) Major newspapers, such as the *New York Times*, the *Washington Post*, the *Guardian*, the *Financial Times*, the *Globe and Mail*, etc.

(3) Scholarly research articles, books, book chapters, and research notes published in academic and peer-reviewed journals.

In coding state selection cases, *the emphasis was on whether a government directly provides assistance to facilitate violent conduct of a NAG*. In other words, when making a decision about coding a case of support, some evidence was required with respect to the government or a political actor or organization formally affiliated with the government providing support. The Revolutionary United Front (RUF) targeted Sierra Leone between 1991 and 2001. It received intentional, direct support from Liberia, Burkina Faso, and Libya in the form of safe haven for members and leaders, funds, arms, logistics, and troops. In coding state support for RUF, the following is an exemplary statement adopted from a news source:

> Nine years ago, the state's collapse, the poverty of its people and the eternal tussle for Sierra Leone's diamonds led to war. A cashiered army corporal named Foday Sankoh joined his vague notions of revolution with money and guns from Libya and Liberian warlord--now president--Charles Taylor to form the Revolutionary United Front. The RUF seized diamond fields, smuggled gemstones and became one of Africa's most thuggish militias. (Rupert 2000)
>
> In 1991, while still fighting in Liberia, Taylor helped launch the civil war in Sierra Leone by providing troops, training and supplies to Foday Sankoh, leader of the Revolutionary United Front. Richie was assigned to Sankoh's forces for their first incursion into Sierra Leone and has been fighting here ever since. (Douglas 2001)

Another task when coding support is determining the time and duration of support. In some cases it is easy to find out from the sources used for collecting data on a particular NAG. Yet it can sometimes prove challenging to code the time and duration of support. When an external support is mentioned in the sources but the period of support is not clear, the release date of the sources is used as an approximate date of support. The All Tripura Tiger Force (ATTF) was an ethno-nationalist group fighting the Indian state between 1992 and 2010 in seeking an independent state for the Tripuri people. The sources, dated mostly in 2002, 2008, and 2010, pointed out that ATTF received support from Bangladesh and Pakistan. Thus the support is coded as continuing from 2002 to 2010 given that we confirm this information with some scholarly case studies.

Furthermore, for each type of support coded, a precision level is determined. For the ATTF and Indian conflict, the above-stated sources mentioned the accusations or allegations of the Indian government. Therefore, when coding, the lowest precision level was assigned to this particular group. Another example is the Nicaraguan Democratic Force (FDN), which fought against the Sandinista regime between 1981 and 1990. Between 1981 and 1984, support for the FDN was authorized by the U.S. Congress (Cody 1984; Woodward et al. 1984). Once Congress stopped overt support channels from the U.S. government, the administration of President Reagan approved covert efforts to support the FDN, which resulted in the notorious Iran-Contra affair. It is a clear case of state support with a very high precision level. Indeed, congressional reports indicate clearly that support was given during the specified period.

Precision (S_Precision & DS_Precision): To specify how confident the coder is that there is evidence of active support, the variable receives the following rating:

1: The supporter stated its intention and/or type of support, and/or the support was officially documented by that state or another.
2: A journalist on the field, a scholar, or a media outlet records the support and provides convincing evidence and there are other sources that confirm this information.

3: Support is highly suspected by a reliable source (such as a journalist, scholar, or media outlet) but cannot be confirmed by other sources.

4: One state accuses another state of supporting a group, but it cannot provide official documentation beyond allegations.

SUPPORT TYPES: States selection cases are denoted by "S" and NAGs selection cases are denoted by "DS" (De facto support).

For each rebel group, a table of direct citations, including stories and news from reliable sources, has been created by using the Lexis-Nexis academic web program, Keesing's Archives, and published secondary sources, including political science journals, journals focusing on particular regions of the world, books, and book chapters. Each coder received training and was given a sample NAG with which to code. After inter-coder reliability is confirmed at the end of the sample group coding, they were assigned groups on a weekly basis. Regular meetings were held with the coders to respond to questions and concerns. In Lexis-Nexis Academic, a keyword search was done for each group for all available dates. Each coder was given a questionnaire, which is available on the DCP website, with directions and guidance about how to conduct research in online databases and sources to find and collect the required data. To determine the supporters and the type of support provided, the following keywords have been searched in the Lexis-Nexis categories "Major U.S. and World Publications," "News Wire Services," and "TV and Radio Broadcast Transcripts" with each group's name: support, assistance, sponsor, safe haven, sanctuary, training camps, camps arms, weapons, funds, troops.

A2.3.6 Coding Rules for State Support

After a preliminary analysis and coding of 20 percent of all the rebel groups and their supporters, the following rules were applied with respect to some ambiguous forms of support referenced in the sources used for data coding:

1. If a state provides health services to a group's members or leaders, it qualifies as providing safe haven for members or leaders.
2. In some instances, states become hosts to negotiations and meetings between a group's leaders and the target government. This does not qualify as a form of support.
3. Some states host the headquarters of rebel groups. These headquarters organize propaganda and fund-raising activities of a group and provide communication with the militants at home. This is coded as a form of support under the name of "headquarters or opening offices."
4. Some states host TV channels and radio stations operated by rebels that are used to disseminate information about the group. This does not qualify as a form of support for the purposes of this project but can be the subject matter of another research project.
5. A state may provide one or more of the specified support types.
6. Some specific cases proved to be particularly complex. One such case was Palestinian militant groups finding safe havens in Lebanon. Lebanon was under the occupation of Syria and Israel between 1979 and 2005 and between 1982 and 2000, respectively. Prior

to the civil war and Syrian occupation, Lebanon served as a host territory for several Palestinian militant groups as well as Palestinian refugees, primarily in the southern part of the country. It is not clear the degree to which the Lebanese government might have resisted the pressures of strong Arab states, such as Egypt and Syria; yet, under the Cairo agreement, the country was designated a safe haven for several groups. Initially, it is coded as a state support case. Yet later after foreign occupation, no support was coded for Lebanon and for several groups, such as the Palestinian Islamic Jihad, PFLP, and Fatah. Furthermore, Hezbollah emerged in southern Lebanon in response to the Israeli occupation. So Hezbollah did not choose to reside in southern Lebanon. In other words, it could not have emerged in Jordan or Egypt. Yet if Hezbollah sought support from external states, such as Iran and Syria, then it is coded as a clear case of state support by Iran and Syria.

7. In some cases, NAGs establish a presence in a foreign country with the assistance of another rebel group targeting that foreign country. The Maoist Communist Center of India (MCC) operated safe havens and training camps in Nepal. The Nepalese government was not involved in this assistance; Maoist insurgents fighting against Nepal helped the MCC to establish facilities inside Nepal. This is a choice on the part of the MCC, thus it is coded as de facto support from Nepal to the MCC against India.

SafeMem: Providing safe havens to members. A certain number of militants are present within the territories of a state or they establish some bases. Safe havens are defined as "geographical spaces where non-state armed groups members are able to establish organizational and operational base that allows them to engage in financing activities, developing a communications network for command and control, achieving access to weapons and developing logistics network to enable travel, the movement of money and weapons" (Kittner 2007, p. 308). Geographical spaces in which militants acquire operational space for training are coded separately as "training camps." This does not annul the fact that training camps are also operational spaces. Mere refugee camps do not qualify as safe havens. There needs to be some proof that militants are found in these camps and operate from these places.

Providing safe havens to members of a rebel group is different from providing training camps or access to existing camps. More often than not, the neighbors of a state that experiences civil war or ethnic conflict end up accepting refugees within their own borders. Opening the borders to refugees does not qualify for providing safe havens to an armed group that is fighting its target government unless the group is engaging in violent cross-border attacks. The members of the Karen National Union, which has been fighting Myanmar's government for more than five decades, frequently escape into neighboring Thailand. They occasionally organize armed attacks back into Myanmar. The following statement illustrates the type of evidence used to determine whether a state provides safe havens to a group:

Thai television reported that Burma was preparing to attack Karen refugee camps inside Thailand. Mortars reportedly were fired at one camp across the border in the Teakaplaw region, forcing thousands of refugees to flee. The fighting comes two weeks after a Karen splinter group supported by government launched cross-border raids against three camps of refugees loyal to the Karen National Union inside Thailand. Two camps were burned to the ground and 8,000 refugees fled into the Thai jungle. ("Burmese Army Launches. . . ." 1997)

This statement indicates that the KNU had safe havens in Thailand. Whether the support is provided intentionally by the state is discussed more generally in the beginning of this section in explaining intentional versus de facto support. In addition, multiple sources were used to determine whether the KNU members were engaging in cross-border attacks into Myanmar.

SafeLead: Providing sanctuary to leadership. Providing safe havens to leaders of a group is different from providing safe havens to its members. Group leaders live in other states due to reasons such as being expelled from their target countries or no longer feeling safe in the target countries. Of the total years that leaders of rebels spent in external safe havens, 35 percent were in democratic states, in contrast to the 65 percent spent in autocratic states. Despite that fact, democratic states might be preferred by leaders due to the individual freedoms and liberties enjoyed there that make their arrest difficult. After the assassination of Indian president Rajiv Gandhi, the Liberation Tigers of Tamil Eelam (LTTE) lost its support base and funding from India. As a result, it set up offices in western European countries, such as Switzerland, France, and the United Kingdom, as well as in the United States and Canada. Evidence is clear that the Sri Lankan government put pressure on these countries to stop the fund-raising activities of the group and to return the group's leaders back to Sri Lanka. The United States banned the group and its fund-raising activities in 1997 in passing an anti-terrorism law and declaring LTTE a terrorist organization ("Tamil Tigers, from a Rag-Tag Band. . . ." 1997). The United Kingdom and Canada did not ban fund-raising activities of the group until 2001 (Jayamaha 2000).

Headquarters/Open Offices: The group has a physical office that does not oversee the violent activities of the organization or is used to spread propaganda and raise funds, not necessarily directed toward violence. Usually if a supporter country provides headquarters for a NAG or allows it to open offices within its territories, there is a high probability that the country provides a safe haven to its leadership.

TrainCamp: Providing training camps. Providing rebels with training camps requires extra effort on the part of the supporters than providing safe havens. Training camps are expected to be furnished with military equipment to help the members of a group in organizing and implementing violent attacks against their targets. During the Syrian occupation of Lebanon from 1976 to 2005, various Palestinian groups were trained in Lebanese territories with the assistance of Syria ("Qom Meeting of Fundamentalist Groups. . . ." 1996). For instance, Palestinian Islamic Jihad members trained in the camps in Lebanon. Although the headquarters of the group had been in Damascus since its foundation, the training camps were not in Syrian territories. In coding the support of PIJ by Syria, providing training camps is not coded among the support types but providing safe havens to leaders is coded among the types of support.

Training: In addition to training camps, some states provide training not necessarily within their own borders. This refers to the temporary assignment of a state's security forces to train the militants.

WeaponLog: Providing weapons and logistics aid. This variable is coded if there is clear evidence that the arms originated from the supporting country. The evidence for whether a state provides arms to rebels is not easily attainable. Mere allegations by the target states are not enough to prove that a state provides arms to a rebel group. In the following narration directly cited from the source, it is clear that the giving of arms by the Libyan government to the Irish Republic Army (IRA) was not a mere allegation by the United Kingdom:

Histories of the IRA have identified Mr Murphy as an IRA weapons smuggler who helped to procure supplies by travelling to Libya using false passports. In the 1980s, Libya supplied the Provisional IRA with more than 100 tonnes of weaponry. (Sharrock 2007)

FinAid: Fund-raising is different from receiving money from the supporter state's government. While in some cases, such as Iran and Hezbollah, governments provide funds to a rebel group, in many others the groups themselves manage to raise funds within the borders of another state, such as the IRA raising funds in the United States. When this is the case, the support is assumed to be *de facto*, i.e. rebels select certain states as supporters without necessarily any intentional effort on the part of the supporter. It is possible to argue that the United States had the capacity to control the IRA's activities, in which case the support of the group would have been intentional. However, making this judgment requires a more extensive analysis of each case in the dataset, which is not an attainable goal within the time frame of the current project. The specific type of support the IRA obtained in the United States is called "passive support" by Byman (2005a). It is coded as *de facto* support in the NAGs Dataset.

Transport: Providing transport of the military equipment and military advice. If a state serves as a transport point for a rebel group, it is coded separately from providing arms and military supplies. Cambodia has for years become a de facto transport point for arms smuggling for many NAGs in Asia. (Bonner 1998). Zaire (now the Democratic Republic of Congo) was the major transport point for the weapons sent by the United States to the National Union for the Total Independence of Angola (UNITA), which was fighting the communist regime in Angola (Lewis 1987).

Troop: In some cases, states allow their troops to fight on the side of the rebels against their targets. When civil wars or ethnic conflicts cross the borders of other states, there is a risk that the latter will act to protect its borders. This variable is not coded for de facto support since it is impossible for a state to send its troops to help a NAG and do this without the sponsorship of the state in question. This leads to the accusation of providing troop support to rebels. Myanmar accused the Thai army multiple times of providing the KNU with troops during the cross-border operations of Myanmar's government into the Karen National Union camps in Thailand. The following illustrates the type of statements and narratives used to code troop support:

Angola, allied to Sassou Nguesso's Cobra militia, staged a weekend attack along the border between its oil-producing Cabinda enclave and southwestern Congo, sending some 1,000 troops into Congo, according to diplomats. ("Angolan Tanks and Troops Enter. . .." 1997)

Following the 1979 establishment of the Islamic Republic and as a response to Israel's invasion of Lebanon in 1982, Iran organized, equipped, and trained Hezbollah. Tehran deployed 1,500 personnel from its IslamicRevolutionaryGuardCorp (IRGC)—a semi-autonomous vanguard of Iran's military used to foment regional disorder and support terrorist organizations—to Lebanon. (Wilner 2012, pp. 19–20)

Only a total of 6 percent of the binary support years involves states that provide troops to rebels. This is normal if we consider that troop support is a very risky strategy, since it means directly engaging with the target of a rebel group. The primary purpose of supporting a group is to avoid direct confrontation with the adversary, besides trying to undermine the power of an adversary.

Other: Any other kind of support not listed above.

DomSup: Whether there is a support basis from within the target or the supporter country.

DomSup_P: The confidence by which we can claim domestic support from a NAG's target or supporter. The domestic support refers to support from among the people rather than the political leadership. 1: not very confident, 2: somewhat confident, 3: confident.

SupTerm: Why did the support end?
1. Pressures from the target of a given NAG
2. Pressures from the international community in general: other states (other than the target)
3. Regime change in the target country
4. Regime change in the supporting country
5. Leadership change in supporting country
6. Group ceased activity
7. Group signed a cease-fire
8. Group turned into a political movement
9. Other: describe

Support termination is coded as missing when there is no external state support for a NAG in a given year.

REFERENCES

___. 1997. "Angolan Tanks and Troops Enter Congo's Oil Town Pointe Noir." *Deutsche Presse-Agentur*. (October 15). Accessed on August 17, 2007.

___. 1997. "Burmese Army Launches Offensive against Karen Rebels." *International News section*. (February 13). Accessed on August 21, 2008.

___. 1997. "Tamil Tigers, from a Rag-Tag Band to a Fighting Force." *Associated Press Worldstream*. (October 15). Accessed on August 20, 2008.

___ "UCDP/PRIO Armed Conflict Dataset Codebook, ver.4. 2014a." Available at http://new.prio.no/CSCW-Datasets/Data-on-Armed-Conflict/. Accessed on June 10, 2015.

Bonner, Raymond. 1998. "Tamil Guerrillas in Sri Lanka: Deadly and Armed to the Teeth." *New York Times*. (March 7). Available at www.nytimes.com. Accessed on August 15, 2008.

Byman, Daniel. 2005a. "Passive Sponsors of Terrorism." *Survival* 47(4): 117–144.

Byman, Daniel L. 2005b. *Deadly Connections: States That Sponsor Terrorism*. Cambridge, UK: Cambridge University Press.

Cederman, Lars-Erik, Brian Min, and Andreas Wimmer. 2010. "Ethnic Power Relations Dataset." http://hdl.handle.net/1902.1/11796. Harvard Dataverse, Version1. Accessed on June 20, 2015.

Cody, Edward. 1984. "Contras Say Supplies Sufficient Until June". *The Washington Post*. (April 24).

Cunningham, David E., Kristian Skrede Gleditsch, and Idean Salehyan. 2009. "It Takes Two: A Dyadic Analysis of Civil War Duration and Outcome." *Journal of Conflict Resolution* 53(4): 570–597.

Douglas, Farah. 2001. "'Commander Poison' Sheds Name, and Hits Taste for War." *The Washington Post*. (June 4).

Girardin, Luc, Philipp Hunziker, Lars-Erik Cederman, Nils-Christian Bormann, and Manuel Vogt. 2015. "GROWup: Geographical Research On War, Unified Platform." ETH Zurich. Available at http://growup.ethz.ch/.

Gleditsch, Nils Peter, Peter Wallensteen, Mikael Eriksson, Margareta Sollenberg, and Havard Strand. 2002. "Armed Conflict, 1946–2001: A New Dataset." *Journal of Peace Research* 39(5): 615–637.

Högbladh, Stina, Therése Pettersson, and Lotta Themnér. 2011. "External Support in Armed Conflict, 1975–2009: Presenting New Data." Paper presented at the 52nd Annual International Studies Association Convention, Montreal, Canada, March 16–19, 2011.

Jayamaha, Dilshika. 2000. "AP Photos COL101-102." Associated Press Worldstream. (December 11). Accessed on August 20, 2008.

Kittner, Cristina C. Braffman. 2007. "The Role of Terrorist Safe Havens in Islamist Terrorism." *Terrorism and Political Violence* 19(3): 307–329.

Kreutz, Joakim. 2010. "How and When Armed Conflicts End: Introducing the UCDP Conflict Termination Dataset." *Journal of Peace Research* 47(2): 243–250.

Lewis, Neil A. 1987. "Washington Talk: Working Profile; Chester Croker: Inside, Making Policy on Africa." (June 9). Accessed on August 28, 2007.

Pettersson, Therése, and Peter Wallensteen. 2015. "Armed Conflicts, 1946–2014." *Journal of Peace Research* 52(4): 536–550.

Regan, Patrick M., and Aysegul Aydin. 2006. "Diplomacy and Other Forms of Intervention in Civil War." *Journal of Conflict Resolution* 50 (5): 736–756.

Regan, P., R. Frank, and A. Aydin. 2009. "Diplomatic Interventions and Civil War: A New Dataset" *Journal of Peace Research* 46(1): 135–146.

Rupert, James. 2000. "Africa Journal." *The Wahington Post*. Available https://www.washingtonpost.com/archive/politics/2000/07/10/africa-journal/fbed9a6f-f0ee-4e81-87ed-abf81b82eb7b/. Accessed on April 20, 2015.

Sharrock, David. 2007. "IRA Baron Charged: On Tax." (November 10). Weekend Australian. Accessed on July 24, 2008.

Themne'r, Lotta, and Peter Wallensteen. 2014. "Armed Conflict, 1946-2013." Journal of Peace Research 51:541–54.

Wilner, Alex S. 2012. "Apocalypse Soon? Deterring Nuclear Iran and Its Terrorist Proxies." *Comparative Strategy* 31: 18–40.

Woodward, Bob & Shapiro, Margaret & Feinman, Barbara. 1984. "CIA Sought 3rd-Country Contra Aid". *The Washington Post*. (May 19).

Zeev Maoz, and Errol A. Henderson. 2013. "The World Religion Dataset, 1945–2010: Logic, Estimates, and Trends." *International Interactions* 39: 265–291.

States with a Single-Party Communist Regime (Up to 2010)

State	Period of Communist Regime
Cuba	1959–2010
German Democratic Republic	1949–1990
Poland	1947–1988
Hungary	1948–1988
Czechoslovakia	1948–1989
Albania	1944–1989
Yugoslavia	1945–1990
Bulgaria	1946–1989
Romania	1947–1990
Russia	1917–1921
USSR	1922–1990
Benin	1977–1989
Congo	1963–1992
Somalia	1969–1991
Ethiopia	1975–1990
Angola	1975–1990
Mozambique	1975–1990
Yemen People's Republic	1967–1990
Afghanistan	1979–1990

State	Period of Communist Regime
China	1949–2010
Mongolia	1924–1989
North Korea	1948–2010
Cambodia	1976–1978
Laos	1975–2010
Vietnam	1954–2010

The Entire Cases of Intentional Support, 1945–2010

Target	Nonstate Armed Group	Period Active	Supporters	Type of Support	Period of Support
Afghanistan	Harakat-i Inqilab-i Islami-yi Afghanistan	1980–1988	Pakistan	Safe havens to members	1980–1988
				Open offices	1981–1988
				Financial aid	1980–1987
			USA	Transport of military equipment, military advice	1980–1988
				Weapons and logistics aid	1980–1988
				Financial aid	1980–1987
			Saudi Arabia	Weapons and logistics aid	1980
				Financial aid	1980–1987
			China	Weapons and logistics aid	1980
Afghanistan	Harakat-i Islami-yi Afghanistan	1984	Iran	Open offices	1984
Afghanistan	Hizb-i Islami-yi Afghanistan	1980–1991	Pakistan	Safe havens to members	1980–1989
				Safe havens to leadership	1987–1989
				Open offices	1989
				Training camp	1980–1991
			USA	Weapons and logistics aid	1980–1991
				Financial aid	1980–1991
				Weapons and logistics aid	1980–1991
				Financial aid	1980–1989
			Saudi Arabia	Financial aid	1980–1991
Afghanistan	Hizb-i Islami-yi Afghanistan-Khalis faction	1980–1989	Pakistan	Safe havens to members	1985–1987
				Safe havens to leadership	1981–1989
				Open offices	1982–1989
			USA	Weapons and logistics aid	1985–1989

Country	Group	Years	Supporter	Support	Years
Afghanistan	Hizb-i Wahdat	1989–1990	Iran	Safe havens to leadership	1989–1990
				Training	1989–1990
				Weapons and logistics aid	1989–1990
				Financial aid	1989–1990
Afghanistan	Ittihad-i Islami Bara-yi Azadi-yi Afghanistan	1981–1988	Pakistan	Safe havens to leadership	1981–1988
				Open offices	1981–1989
Afghanistan	Jabha-yi Nijat-i Milli-yi Afghanistan	1980–1988	Pakistan	Safe havens to leadership	1988
				Open offices	1980–1988
Afghanistan	Jam'iyyat-i Islami-yi Afghanistan	1979–1989	Pakistan	Safe havens to leadership	1980–1989
				Open offices	1979–1989
				Transport of military equipment, military advice	1987
			Iran	Safe havens to leadership	1981–1987
				Open offices	1981–1985
Afghanistan	Mahaz-i Milli-yi Islami-yi Afghanistan	1980–1989	Pakistan	Safe havens to members	1986–1989
				Safe havens to leadership	1980–1989
				Open offices	1980–1990
Afghanistan	Military faction (forces of Shahnawaz Tanay)	1990	Pakistan	Safe havens to leadership	1990
Afghanistan	Taliban	1995–2012	Pakistan	Open offices	1996–2001
				Training camp	1998–2001
				Training	1995–2001
				Weapons and logistics aid	1995–2001
				Financial aid	1995–2000

(continued)

Target	Nonstate Armed Group	Period Active	Supporters	Type of Support	Period of Support
Afghanistan	Taliban	1995–2012	Saudi Arabia	Financial aid	1995–2001
			United Arab Emirates	Financial aid	1995–2002
Afghanistan	United Islamic Front for Salvation of Afghanistan (UIFSA)	1996–2001	Russia (Soviet Union)	Weapons and logistics aid	1997–2001
				Financial aid	1997–2001
			Iran	Weapons and logistics aid	1996–2000
				Financial aid	1997–2001
			Tajikistan	Weapons and logistics aid	1998
Algeria	Armed Islamic Group of Algeria (GIA)	1993–2003	Afghanistan	Training	1992–2001
Angola	Front for the Liberation of the Enclave of Cabinda–Armed Forces of Cabinda (FLEC-FAC)	1994–present	Democratic Republic of Congo (Zaire)	Training camp	1994–2010
			Congo	Training camp	1994–2011
Angola	National Front for the Liberation of Angola (FNLA)	1961–1974	Democratic Republic of Congo (Zaire)	Safe havens to members	1962–1974
				Training camp	1962–1974
				Troops	1962–1974
			China	Training	1962–1974
				Weapons and logistics aid	1962–1974
Angola	National Union for the Total Independence of Angola (UNITA)	1975–2002	South Africa	Safe havens to members	1975–2002
				Training camp	1975–2002
				Weapons and logistics aid	1975–2002

			Côte d'Ivoire (Ivory Coast)	Safe havens to members	1975–2002
			Portugal	Open offices	1975–2002
			USA	Training	1975–2002
				Weapons and logistics aid	1975–2002
Argentina	Montoneros / Movimiento Peronista Montonero (MPM)	1975–1977	Mexico	Safe havens to members	1975–1977
				Safe havens to leadership	1975–1977
			Cuba	Financial aid	1975–1977
Azerbaijan	Republic of Nagorno-Karabakh	1994–2005	Armenia	Safe havens to members	1994–2005
				Safe havens to leadership	1994–2005
				Open offices	1994–2005
				Training camp	1994–2005
				Training	1994–2005
				Weapons and logistics aid	1994–2005
				Financial aid	1994–2005
				Transport of military equipment, military advice	1994–2005
				Troops	1994–2005
Bangladesh	Jana Samhati Samiti/Shanti Bahini (JSS/SB)	1975–1991	India	Safe havens to members	1979–1989
Bosnia-Herzegovina	Autonomous Province of Western Bosnia	1993–1995	Croatia	Transport of military equipment, military advice	1993–1994
				Troops	1993–1994

(continued)

Target	Nonstate Armed Group	Period Active	Supporters	Type of Support	Period of Support
Burundi	Palipehutu	1991–2000	Rwanda	Training camp	1991–1992
Cambodia (Kampuchea)	Kampuchean United Front for National Salvation (KNUFNS)	1978–1979	Vietnam	Weapons and logistics aid	1978–1979
Cambodia (Kampuchea)	Khmer People's National Liberation Front (KPNLF)	1979–1991	China	Weapons and logistics aid	1979–1991
			Thailand	Transport of military equipment, military advice	1981–1991
Cambodia (Kampuchea)	Khmer Rouge (KR)	1967–1989	Thailand	Safe havens to members	1967–1989
				Training camp	1967–1989
				Transport of military equipment, military advice	1967–1989
			China	Safe havens to leadership	1987–1989
				Weapons and logistics aid	1987–1989
				Financial aid	1987–1989
Chad	Armed Forces of the North (FAN)	1976–1981	Egypt	Weapons and logistics aid	1981
			Sudan	Weapons and logistics aid	1981
Chad	National Liberation Front of Chad (FROLINAT)	1966–1970	Libya	Safe havens to leadership	1968–1970
				Open offices	1968–1970
Chad	Islamic Legion	1989–1990	Libya	Training	1989–1990
				Weapons and logistics aid	1989–1990
Chad	Movement for Democracy and Development (MDD)	1991–1999	Niger	Safe havens to leadership	1991–1997
			Senegal	Safe havens to leadership	1991–1997
Chad	Movement for Democracy and Justice in Chad (MDJT)	1999–2005	Italy	Open offices	1999–2005
			Libya	Financial aid	2000–2004

Country	Organization	Years	Sponsor	Support	Year
Chad	National Alliance (AN)	2008	Sudan	Safe havens to members	2008
				Safe havens to leadership	2008
				Weapons and logistics aid	2008
Chad	National Council of Chadian Recovery (CNR)	1992–1994	Libya	Safe havens to leadership	1993–1994
Chad	Patriotic Salvation Movement (MPS)	1990	Sudan	Safe havens to members	1990
				Safe havens to leadership	1990
			Libya	Weapons and logistics aid	1990
Chad	Popular Front for National Resistance (PFNR)	2010	France	Safe havens to leadership	2010
Chad	Rally of Democratic Forces (RAFD)	2006	Sudan	Safe havens to members	2006
Chad	Transitional Government of National Union (GUNT)	1983–1986	Libya	Weapons and logistics aid	1983–1986
				Troops	1983–1986
Chad	Union of Forces for Democracy and Development (UFDD)	2006–2007	Sudan	Safe havens to members	2006–2007
				Safe havens to leadership	2006–2007
				Open offices	2006–2007
				Weapons and logistics aid	2006–2007
Chad	Union of Resistance Forces (UFR)	2009	Sudan	Safe havens to members	2009
				Safe havens to leadership	2009
				Weapons and logistics aid	2009
Chad	United Front for Democratic Change (FUCD)	2005–2006	Sudan	Safe havens to members	2005–2006

(continued)

Target	Nonstate Armed Group	Period Active	Supporters	Type of Support	Period of Support
China	East Turkestan Islamic Movement (ETIM)	1990–present	Afghanistan	Safe havens to members	1997–2001
				Safe havens to leadership	1997–2001
				Open offices	1997–2001
				Training camp	1997–2001
Colombia	19th of April Movement (M-19)	1978–1988	Libya	Training	1980–1988
				Weapons and logistics aid	1980–1988
				Financial aid	1980–1988
			Cuba	Training	1982–1986
				Weapons and logistics aid	1982–1986
				Financial aid	1982–1986
			Nicaragua	Training	1979–1988
				Weapons and logistics aid	1979–1988
				Financial aid	1979–1988
Colombia	Revolutionary Armed Forces of Colombia (FARC)	1964–present	Cuba	Safe havens to members	2001–2010
				Training	2001–2010
			Vietnam	Training	1970–1999
			Soviet Union	Training	1970–1979
Colombia	The National Liberation Army (ELN)	1966–2008	Venezuela	Safe havens to members	1998–2008
				Safe havens to leadership	2001–2008
				Open offices	2008
				Training camp	2002–2008
			Cuba	Safe havens to leadership	2000–2001
Congo	Cocoyes	1997–1999	Israel	Training	1997–1999
			South Africa	Training	1997–1999

Country	Group	Years	State supporter	Type of support	Years
Cuba	26th of July Movement (M-26-7)	1953–1958	Mexico	Safe havens to leadership	1953–1958
Cuba	Cuban Revolutionary Council (CRC)	1961	USA	Safe havens to leadership	1961
				Training	1961
				Weapons and logistics aid	1961
				Troops	1961
Djibouti	Front for Restoration of Unity and Democracy - Ahmed Dini (FRUD-AD)	1999	France	Safe havens to members	1999
				Safe havens to leadership	1999
				Open offices	1999
Djibouti	Front for Restoration of Unity and Democracy (FRUD)	1991–1994	France	Safe havens to members	1993–1994
				Open offices	1991–1994
			Yemen	Open offices	1991–1994
DR Congo (Zaire)	Alliance of Democratic Forces for the Liberation of Congo (AFDL)	1996–1997	Rwanda	Safe havens to members	1996–1997
				Safe havens to leadership	1996–1997
				Training camp	1996–1997
				Training	1996–1997
				Weapons and logistics aid	1996–1997
				Transport of military equipment, military advice	1996–1997
				Troops	1996–1997
			Uganda	Safe havens to members	1996–1997
				Safe havens to leadership	1996–1997
				Training camp	1996–1997
				Training	1996–1997
				Weapons and logistics aid	1996–1997

(continued)

Target	Nonstate Armed Group	Period Active	Supporters	Type of Support	Period of Support
DR Congo (Zaire)	Alliance of the Democratic Forces for the Liberation of Congo (AFDL)	1996–1997	Uganda	Transport of military equipment, military advice	1996–1997
				Troops	1996–1997
			Angola	Transport of military equipment, military advice	1996–1997
				Troops	1996–1997
DR Congo (Zaire)	Front for the National Liberation of the Congo (FNLC)	1977–1978	Angola	Safe havens to members	1977–1978
				Safe havens to leadership	1977–1978
				Open offices	1977–1978
				Training camp	1977–1978
				Training	1977–1978
				Weapons and logistics aid	1977–1978
				Financial aid	1977–1978
				Transport of military equipment, military advice	1977–1978
				Troops	1977–1978
DR Congo (Zaire)	Movement for the Liberation of Congo (MLC)	1998–2000	Uganda	Safe havens to members	1998–2000
				Safe havens to leadership	1998–2000
				Open offices	1998–2000
				Training camp	1998–2000
				Training	1998–2000
				Weapons and logistics aid	1998–2000
				Financial aid	1998–2000

Country	Organization	Dates	Supporter	Support type	Years
DR Congo (Zaire)	National Congress for the Defence of the People (CNDP)	2006–2009	Rwanda	Transport of military equipment, military advice	1998–2000
				Troops	1998–2000
				Safe havens to members	2006–2008
				Safe havens to leadership	2006–2008
				Open offices	2006–2008
				Training camp	2006–2008
				Training	2006–2008
				Weapons and logistics aid	2006–2008
				Financial aid	2006–2008
				Transport of military equipment, military advice	2006–2008
				Troops	2006–2008
DR Congo (Zaire)	Rally for Congolese Democracy (RCD)	1998–2000	Uganda	Troops	1998–2000
				Safe havens to members	1998–2000
				Safe havens to leadership	1998–2000
				Open offices	1998–2000
				Training camp	1998–2000
				Transport of military equipment, military advice	1998–2000
			Rwanda	Troops	1998–2000
				Safe havens to members	1998–2000
				Safe havens to leadership	1998–2000
				Open offices	1998–2000
				Training camp	1998–2000

(continued)

Target	Nonstate Armed Group	Period Active	Supporters	Type of Support	Period of Support
DR Congo (Zaire)	Rally for the Congolese Democracy (RCD)	1998–2000	Rwanda	Transport of military equipment, military advice	1998–2000
				Troops	1998–2000
Egypt	Al-Gama'a al-Islamiyya (Islamic Group)	1993–1998	Sudan	Safe havens to members	1993–1998
				Safe havens to leadership	1993–1998
				Weapons and logistics aid	1993–1998
El Salvador	Ejército Revolucionario del Pueblo (ERP)	1979	Cuba	Safe havens to members	1979
				Training camp	1979
				Weapons and logistics aid	1979
			Nicaragua	Open offices	1979
				Weapons and logistics aid	1979
				Transport of military equipment, military advice	1979
El Salvador	Farabundo Marti National Liberation Front (FMLN)	1980–1991	Cuba	Safe havens to members	1980–1991
				Training	1980–1991
				Weapons and logistics aid	1980–1991
				Financial aid	1980–1991
				Transport of military equipment, military advice	1980–1991
			Nicaragua	Safe havens to leadership	1985–1991
				Open offices	1985–1991
				Training	1985–1991
				Weapons and logistics aid	1985–1991

Country	Group	Year	Supporter	Support type	Dates
El Salvador	Popular Liberation Forces (FPL)	1979		Financial aid	1985–1991
				Transport of military equipment, military advice	1985–1991
			Soviet Union	Weapons and logistics aid	1980–1990
				Financial aid	1980–1990
				Transport of military equipment, military advice	1980–1990
			Nicaragua	Safe havens to members	1979
			Cuba	Safe havens to members	1979
				Training camp	1979
				Training	1979
Eritrea	Eritrean Islamic Jihad Movement - Abu Suhai (IEIJM - AS)	1997–2003	Sudan	Safe havens to members	1997–2003
Ethiopia	Afar Liberation Front (ALF)	1975–1976	Saudi Arabia	Safe havens to leadership	1975–1976
			Somalia	Training	1975–1976
Ethiopia	Afar Revolutionary Democratic Union Front (ARDUF)	1996	Eritrea	Training camp	1996
Ethiopia	Al-Itihaad al-Islamiya (AIAI)	1993–1999	Sudan	Training camp	1993–1999
				Weapons and logistics aid	1993–1999
			Iran	Training	1993–1999
				Weapons and logistics aid	1993–1999
				Financial aid	1993–1999
Ethiopia	Al-Shabaab	2008–present	Eritrea	Weapons and logistics aid	2008–2010
				Financial aid	2009–2010

(continued)

Target	Nonstate Armed Group	Period Active	Supporters	Type of Support	Period of Support
Ethiopia	Al-Shabaab	2008–present	Iran	Weapons and logistics aid	2010
				Financial aid	2010
Ethiopia	Eritrean Liberation Front (ELF)	1964–1980	Syria	Training camp	1964–1980
				Training	1964–1980
				Weapons and logistics aid	1964–1980
				Financial aid	1964–1980
Ethiopia	Eritrean People's Liberation Front (EPLF)	1973–1991	Sudan	Safe havens to members	1973–1991
				Weapons and logistics aid	1973–1991
				Financial aid	1973–1991
				Transport of military equipment, military advice	1973–1991
				Troops	1973–1991
Ethiopia	Ethiopian Democratic Union (EDU)	1977–1978	Sudan	Safe havens to members	1977–1978
				Open offices	1977–1978
				Training camp	1977–1978
Ethiopia	Ethiopian People's Revolutionary Party (EPRP)	1976–1987	Sudan	Safe havens to members	1978–1987
				Safe havens to leadership	1978–1987
				Open offices	1978–1987
			Saudi Arabia	Financial aid	1976–1987
Ethiopia	Ogaden National Liberation Front (ONLF)	1994–2009	Eritrea	Training	1994–2009
				Weapons and logistics aid	1994–2009
			Libya	Training	1994–2009
				Weapons and logistics aid	1994–2009

Country	Organization	Duration	Supporter	Type of aid	Period
Ethiopia	Oromo Liberation Front (OLF)	1977–present	Sudan	Open offices	1977–1990
				Training camp	1977–1990
Ethiopia	Somali Abo Liberation Front (SALF)	1977–1980	Somalia	Training	1977–1979
				Weapons and logistics aid	1977–1979
Ethiopia	Western Somali Liberation Front (WSLF)	1976–1983	Somalia	Weapons and logistics aid	1976
				Troops	1976
France	Khmer Issarak	1946–1953	Thailand	Safe havens to members	1946–1947
				Open offices	1946–1947
				Training camp	1946–1947
France	League for the Independence of Vietnam (Viet minh)	1946–1954	USA	Training	1946–1949
				Weapons and logistics aid	1946–1949
			China	Training	1946–1954
				Weapons and logistics aid	1946–1954
France	National Liberation Army (NLA)–Mauritania	1957–1960	Morocco	Safe havens to leadership	1957–1958
France	National Liberation Front (FLN)	1954–1962	Egypt	Training camp, training, weapons and Logistic aid, financial aid, transport of military equipment, military advice	1954–1962
			Tunisia	Safe havens to members	1954–1962
				Transport of military equipment, military advice	1954–1962
			Morocco	Safe havens to members	1954–1962
				Transport of military equipment, military advice	1954–1962
			China	Weapons and logistics aid	1954–1962

(continued)

Target	Nonstate Armed Group	Period Active	Supporters	Type of Support	Period of Support
Georgia	Republic of South Ossetia	1992–2008	Russia (Soviet Union)	Safe havens to members	1992–2008
				Safe havens to leadership	1992–2008
				Weapons and logistics aid	1992–2008
				Financial aid	1992–2008
				Transport of military equipment, military advice	1992–2008
				Troops	1992–2008
Greece	Democratic Army of Greece (DSE)	1946–1949	Bulgaria	Weapons and logistics aid	1946–1949
			Yugoslavia	Weapons and logistics aid	1946–1949
Guatemala	Forces of Carlos Castillo Armas	1954	Honduras	Transport of military equipment, military advice	1954
			USA	Weapons and logistics aid	1954
Guatemala	Guatemalan National Revolutionary Unity (URNG)	1982–1995	Mexico	Safe havens to leadership	1993–1995
			Cuba	Training	1982–1994
				Weapons and logistics aid	1982–1993
				Transport of military equipment, military advice	1986–1989
Guatemala	Guerrilla Army of the Poor (EGP)	1975–1981	Nicaragua	Open Offices	1981
				Training	1981
				Weapons and logistics aid	1981
			Cuba	Training	1981
				Weapons and logistics aid	1981
			Mexico	Transport of military equipment, military advice	1980–1981

Country	Group	Years	Supporter	Type of aid	Years
Guatemala	Revolutionary Armed Forces (FAR I)	1963–1981	Cuba	Training	1979–1981
Guatemala	Revolutionary Organization of Armed People (ORPA)	1979–1981	Cuba	Training	1979–1981
				Weapons and logistics aid	1979–1981
			Nicaragua	Training	1979–1981
			Mexico	Financial aid	1979–1981
Guinea	Rally of Democratic Forces of Guinea (RFDG)	2000–2001	Sierra Leone	Safe havens to members	2000–2001
Haiti	OP Lavalas (Chimères)	2004	Central African Republic	Safe havens to leadership	2004
			Jamaica	Safe havens to leadership	2004
				Transport of military equipment, military advice	2004
			South Africa	Safe havens to leadership	2004
				Weapons and logistics aid	2004
India	Kashmir Insurgents	1989–2012	Pakistan	Safe havens to members	1989–2010
				Training camp	1989–2010
				Training	1989–2010
				Weapons and logistics aid	1989–2010
				Financial aid	1989–2010
India	Maoist Communist Centre of India (MCC)	1992–2004	Pakistan	Training	2000–2004
				Weapons and logistics aid	2000–2004
India	Mizo National Front (MNF)	1966–1968	Pakistan	Safe havens to members	1966–1968
				Safe havens to leadership	1966–1968
				Training camp	1966–1968

(continued)

Target	Nonstate Armed Group	Period Active	Supporters	Type of Support	Period of Support
India	Mizo National Front (MNF)	1966–1968	Pakistan	Training	1966–1968
				Weapons and logistics aid	1966–1968
India	Naga National Council (NNC)	1956–1968	Pakistan	Safe havens to leadership	1956–1960
				Training camp	1957–1968
				Training	1957–1968
				Weapons and logistics aid	1957–1968
			China	Training	1967–1968
				Weapons and logistics aid	1967–1968
India	National Socialist Council of Nagaland - Isak-Muivah (NSCN - IM)	1992–2000	Pakistan	Training camp	1993–1999
				Financial aid	1993–2000
India	People's Liberation Army (PLA)	1982–present	China	Training	1990–2010
India	People's War Group (PWG)	1990–2004	Pakistan	Weapons and logistics aid	2000–2004
				Financial aid	2000–2004
India	Sikh insurgents	1983–1993	Pakistan	Safe havens to members	1987–1993
				Weapons and logistics aid	1987–1991
India	National Liberation Front of Tripura (NLFT)	1995–present	Bangladesh	Safe havens to members	1995–2010
				Safe havens to leadership	1995–2010
				Open offices	1995–2010
				Training camp	1995–2010
India	United Liberation Front of Assam (ULFA)	1990–2010	Bhutan	Safe havens to members	1990–2003
				Safe havens to leadership	1990–2003
				Open offices	1990–2003
				Training camp	1990–2003

Indonesia	Free Aceh Movement (GAM)	1990–2005	Bangladesh	Training	1990–2003
				Transport of military equipment, military advice	1997–1999
				Safe havens to members	1990–2009
				Safe havens to leadership	1997–2009
				Training camp	1990–2009
				Transport of military equipment, military advice	1990–2009
			China	Weapons and logistics aid	1995 and 2008
			Sweden	Safe havens to members	1990–2005
				Safe havens to leadership	1990–2005
				Open offices	1990–2005
			Denmark	Safe havens to members	2000–2005
				Safe havens to leadership	2000–2005
				Open offices	2005
			Norway	Safe havens to members	1999–2005
				Safe havens to leadership	1999–2005
				Open offices	1999–2005
			Libya	Training camps	1980–1990
Indonesia	Permesta movement	1958–1961	USA	Training	1958–1959
				Weapons and logistics aid	1958–1959
				Financial aid	1958–1959

(continued)

Target	Nonstate Armed Group	Period Active	Supporters	Type of Support	Period of Support
Indonesia	Permesta Movement	1958–1961	USA	Transport of military equipment, military advice	1958–1959
				Troops	1958–1959
			Australia	Weapons and logistics aid	1958
Indonesia	Revolutionary Government of the Republic of Indonesia (PRRI)	1958–1961	USA	Training	1958–1959
				Weapons and logistics aid	1958–1959
				Financial aid	1958–1959
				Transport of military equipment, military advice	1958–1959
				Troops	1958–1959
			Australia	Weapons and logistics aid	1958–1959
					1958
Iran	Kurdistan Democratic Party of Iran (KDPI)	1946–1996	Russia (Soviet Union)	Safe haven to leaders	1947–1958
				Financial aid	1946–1996
Iran	Party of Free Life of Kurdistan (PJAK)	2004–present	Sweden	Safe havens to members	2005–2008
			Germany	Safe havens to leadership	2004–2010
				Training	2005–2007
			Israel	Weapons and logistics aid	2005–2007
Iran	Mujahedin-e Khalq (MEK)	1979–2001	United Kingdom	Open offices	1991–1998
Iraq	Kurdistan Democratic Party (KDP)	1961–1991	Iran	Safe havens to members	1961–1979
				Safe havens to leadership	1961–1979
				Open offices	1961–1979
				Training camp	1961–1979
				Training	1961–1979

Country	Group		Sponsor	Type of support	Years
				Weapons and logistics aid	1961–1979
				Financial aid	1961–1979
			USA	Transport of military equipment, military advice	1961–1979
				Troops	1961–1979
				Safe havens to members	1961–1991
				Safe havens to leadership	1961–1991
				Financial aid	1961–1991
			Israel	Training	1961–1991
				Weapons and logistics aid	1961–1991
				Weapons and logistics aid	1961–1991
			Iran	Weapons and logistics aid	1977–1978
				Financial aid	1977–1978
				Transport of military equipment, military advice	1977–1978
Iraq	Kurdistan Democratic Party-Provisional Command (KDP-QM)	1977–1978			
			Syria	Safe havens to members	1976–1996
				Safe havens to leadership	1976–1996
				Open offices	1976–1996
Iraq	Patriotic Union of Kurdistan (PUK)	1976–1996	Iran	Safe havens to members	1976–1983
				Safe havens to leadership	1976–1983
				Open offices	1976–1983
				Troops	1976–1983

Target	Nonstate Armed Group	Period Active	Supporters	Type of Support	Period of Support
Iraq	Supreme Council for the Islamic Revolution in Iraq (SCIRI)	1982–1996	Syria	Safe havens to members	1982–1996
				Safe havens to leadership	1982–1996
				Open offices	1982–1996
			Iran	Safe havens to members	1982–1996
				Safe havens to leadership	1982–1996
				Open offices	1982–1996
Israel	Fatah	1959–2010	Tunisia	Safe havens to members	1982–1993
				Safe havens to leadership	1982–1993
				Open offices	1982–1993
				Training camp	1982–1993
			Jordan	Safe havens to members	1959–1970
				Safe havens to leadership	1959–1970
				Training camp	1959–1970
			Syria	Safe havens to members	1965–1973
				Safe havens to leadership	1965–1973
				Open offices	1967–1973
				Training camp	1967–1973
				Training	1967–1973
				Transport of military equipment, military advice	1967–1973
			Lebanon	Safe havens to members	1970–1975
				Safe havens to leadership	1970–1975
				Open offices	1970–1975
				Training camp	1970–1975

Group	Target	Period	Supporter	Type of aid	Years
			Sudan	Safe havens to leadership	1967–1973
				Open offices	1967–1973
			China	Weapons and logistics aid	1965–1975
			Iraq	Transport of military equipment, military advice	1967–1989
			Soviet Union (Russia)	Weapons and logistics aid	1972 and 1976
Hamas	Israel	1993–present	Jordan	Safe havens to members	1993–1999
				Safe havens to leadership	1993–1999
				Open offices	1993–1999
			Qatar	Safe havens to leadership	2000–2010
			Syria	Safe havens to leadership	2000–2010
				Open offices	2000–2010
			Iraq	Financial aid	1993–2001
			Iran	Training	1993–2010
				Financial aid	1993–2010
Hezbollah	Israel	1990–present	Iran	Weapons and logistics aid	1990–2010
				Financial aid	1990–2010
			Syria	Transport of military equipment, military advice	1996–2010
Palestinian Islamic Jihad (PIJ)	Israel	1995–present	Syria	Safe haven to members	1995–2010
				Safe haven to leaders	1995–2010
				Open offices	1995–2010
				Transport of military equipment, military advice	2000–2010

(continued)

Target	Nonstate Armed Group	Period Active	Supporters	Type of Support	Period of Support
Israel	Palestinian Islamic Jihad (PIJ)	1995–present	Iran	Training	2000–2010
				Weapons and logistics aid	2000–2010
Israel	Popular Front for the Liberation of Palestine - General Command (PFLP-GC)	1989–present	Iran	Financial aid	1986
			Libya	Weapons and logistics aid	1986–1989
				Training camps	1986–1989
			Syria	Safe haven to members	1989–2010
				Open offices	1989–2010
				Weapons and logistics aid	1989–2010
				Financial aid	1989–2010
Israel	Popular Front for the Liberation of Palestine (PFLP)	1989–2001	South Yemen	Safe havens to members	1989–1990
				Training camp	1989–1990
			Syria	Safe havens to members	1989–2001
				Training camp	1989–2001
				Open offices	1989–2001
				Weapons and logistics aid	1989–2001
				Financial aid	1989–2001
Côte d'Ivoire (Ivory Coast)	Movement for Justice and Peace (MJP)	2002	Liberia	Safe havens to members	2002
				Weapons and logistics aid	2002
			Burkina Faso	Weapons and logistics aid	2002
Lebanon	Lebanese Army (Aoun)	1989–1990	Iraq	Weapons and logistics aid	1989–1990
Lebanon	Lebanese Forces - Hobeika faction	1986	Israel	Safe havens to members	1986
				Safe havens to leadership	1986
				Transport of military equipment, military advice	1986

Liberia	Liberians United for Reconciliation and Democracy (LURD)	2000–2003	Guinea	Safe haven to members	2000–2003
			Guinea	Safe haven to leaders	2000–2003
				Open offices	2000–2003
				Weapons and logistics Aid	2000–2003
			Ivory Coast	Safe haven to members	2000–2003
			Sierra Leone	Safe haven to members	2000–2003
				Troops	2000–2003
Liberia	Movement for Democracy in Liberia (MODEL)	2003–2003	Ivory Coast	Safe haven to members	2003
				Training camp	2003
				Weapons and logistics Aid	2003
Liberia	National Patriotic Front of Liberia (NPFL)	1989–1997	Libya	Safe haven to members	1989–1994
				Safe haven to leaders	1989–1994
				Training camp	1989
				Training	1989–1994
				Weapons and logistics Aid	1989–1994
				Financial aid	1989–1994
			Ivory Coast	Safe haven to members	1989–1997
				Safe haven to leaders	1989–1990
				Open offices	1989–1990
				Weapons and logistics Aid	1989–1997
				Financial aid	1989–1997
				Transport	1989–1997
			Burkina Faso	Training camp	1991–1997
				Training	1991–1997

(continued)

Target	Nonstate Armed Group	Period Active	Supporters	Type of Support	Period of Support
Liberia	National Patriotic Front of Liberia (NPFL)	1989–1997	Burkina Faso	Transport	1991–1997
				Troops	1991
Macedonia, FYR	National Liberation Army (UCK)	2001–2001	Albania	Safe haven to members	2001
				Safe haven to leaders	2001
Mali	Arab Islamic Front of Azawad (FIAA)	1994–1994	Libya	Safe haven to members	1994
				Training camp	1994
				Training	1994
				Weapons and logistics Aid	1994
Mali	Northern Mali Tuareg Alliance for Change (ATNMC)	2007–2009	Libya	Safe haven to members	2007–2009
				Safe haven to leaders	2007–2009
				Weapons and Logistics Aid	2007–2008
				Financial aid	2007–2008
Mauritania	Popular Front for the Liberation of Saguia el-Hamra and Río de Oro (POLISARIO)	1975–1978	Algeria	Safe haven to members	1975–1978
				Safe haven to leaders	1975–1978
				Training camp	1975–1978
				Weapons and Logistics Aid	1978
			USA	Safe haven to leaders	1975–1978
				Open offices	1975–1978
Moldova	Pridnestrovian Moldavian Republic (PMR)	1992–1997	Russia (Soviet Union)	Troops	1992

Country	Organization		Supporter	Type of support	Years
Morocco	Popular Front for the Liberation of Saguia el-Hamra and Río de Oro (POLISARIO)	1975–1989	USA	Safe haven to members	1975–1989
				Safe haven to leaders	1975–1989
				Open offices	1975–1989
			Algeria	Safe haven to members	1975–1989
				Safe haven to leaders	1975–1989
				Open offices	1975–1989
				Weapons and logistics Aid	1975–1989
Mozambique	Mozambican National Resistance (Renamo)	1977–1992	South Africa	Safe haven to members	1977–1992
				Safe haven to leaders	1977–1992
				Open offices	1977–1992
				Weapons and logistics Aid	1977–1992
				Financial aid	1977–1992
Myanmar (Burma)	All Burma Students' Democratic Front (ABSDF)	1990–present	Thailand	Safe haven to members	1990–1994
				Training camp	1990–1994
Myanmar (Burma)	Communist Party of Burma (CPB)	1948–1988	China	Safe haven to members	1966–1975
				Training	1966–1975
				Weapons and logistics Aid	1966–1975
				Financial aid	1966–1975
Myanmar (Burma)	God's army	2000–2000	Thailand	Safe haven to leaders	2000
Myanmar (Burma)	Karen National Union (KNU)	1966–present	Thailand	Safe haven to members	1966–1989
				Training camp	1966–1989
				Weapons and logistics Aid	1966–1989
				Financial aid	1966–1989
			USA	Safe haven to members	2006–2010

(continued)

Target	Nonstate Armed Group	Period Active	Supporters	Type of Support	Period of Support
Myanmar (Burma)	United Wa State Army (UWSA)	1997–1997	China	Weapons and logistics Aid	1997
Nepal	Communist Party of Nepal - Maoist (CPN-M)	1996–2006	India	Weapons and logistics Aid	1996–2001
Nicaragua	Contras / Nicaraguan Democratic Force (FDN)	1982–1990	Honduras	Safe haven to members	1982–1986
				Training camp	1982–1986
				Weapons and logistics Aid	1983
			USA	Safe haven to leaders	1982–1987
				Training	1983–1987
				Weapons and logistics Aid	1983–1987
				Financial aid	1982–1987
			Argentina	Training	1983
			Israel	Weapons and logistics Aid	1983–1987
			Saudi Arabia	Financial aid	1984–1987
			Taiwan	Financial aid	1984–1985
			Venezuela	Financial aid	1984–1985
			Guatemala	Financial aid	1984–1985
Nicaragua	Sandinista National Liberation Front (FSLN)	1977–1979	Panama	Safe haven to members	1978–1979
				Weapons and logistics Aid	1977–1979
			Costa Rica	Safe haven to leaders	1979
				Training camp	1977–1979

Country	Group	Years	Supporter	Type of support	Year(s)
Nigeria	Republic of Biafra	1967–1970	France	Open offices	1967–1970
			Israel	Weapons and logistics Aid	1967–1970
			Israel	Weapons and logistics Aid	1968–1970
				Financial aid	1968
			Portugal	Weapons and logistics Aid	1968
			Ivory Coast	Transport	1968–1970
North Yemen	National Democratic Front (NDF)	1979-1982	Yemen People's Republic	Safe haven to members	1979–1982
				Safe haven to leaders	1979–1982
				Training	1979–1982
				Weapons and logistics Aid	1979–1982
				Financial aid	1979–1982
				Troops	1979
North Yemen	Royalists	1962–1970	Israel	Weapons and logistics Aid	1964–1966
			Saudi Arabia	Weapons and logistics Aid	1962–1970
				Financial aid	1962–1970
				Transport	1962–1970
Oman	Popular Front for the Liberation of Oman (PFLO)	1969–1975	Yemen People's Republic	Safe haven to members	1969–1975
				Training	1969–1975
				Weapons and logistics Aid	1969–1975
				Financial aid	1969–1975
				Transport	1969–1975
			China	Training	1969
				Weapons and logistics Aid	1969
Oman	State of Oman/Free Oman	1957–1957	Saudi Arabia	Weapons and logistics Aid	1957

(continued)

Target	Nonstate Armed Group	Period Active	Supporters	Type of Support	Period of Support
Pakistan	Balochistan Republican Army (BRA)	2008–2009	Afghanistan	Safe haven to leaders	2008–2009
				Training camp	2008–2009
				Transport	2008–2009
			India	Weapons and logistics Aid	2008–2009
				Financial aid	2008–2009
			USA	Financial aid	2008–2009
Pakistan	Mukti Bahini	1971–1971	India	Training camp	1971
				Training	1971
				Weapons and logistics Aid	1971
				Troops	1971
Pakistan	Tehrik-i-Taliban Pakistan (TTP)	2008–present	India	Training	2009–2010
				Weapons and logistics Aid	2008–2010
				Financial aid	2008–2010
			USA	Weapons and logistics Aid	2010
				Financial aid	2010
			Israel	Weapons and logistics Aid	2010
				Financial aid	2010
Panama	Military faction (forces of Moisés Giroldi)	1989–1989	USA	Financial aid	1989
				Troops	1989
Papua New Guinea	The Bougainville Revolutionary Army (BRA)	1989–1996	Solomon Islands	Safe haven to members	1991–1996
				Open offices	1991–1996
Peru	National Liberation Army (ELN)	1965–1965	Cuba	Safe haven to members	1965
				Safe haven to leaders	1965
				Training camp	1965

Country	Group		Sponsor	Type of support	Year
Peru	Revolutionary Left Movement (MIR)	1965–1965	Cuba	Safe haven to members	1965
				Safe haven to leaders	1965
				Training camp	1965
Peru	Tupac Amaru Revolutionary Movement (MRTA)	1989–1993	Nicaragua	Safe haven to members	1989–1990
				Safe haven to leaders	1989–1990
				Training camp	1989–1990
				Weapons and logistics Aid	1989–1990
				Financial aid	1989–1990
			Cuba	Training camp	1990–1991
				Training	1990–1991
				Weapons and logistics Aid	1989–1993
				Financial aid	1989–1993
Philippines	Communist Party of the Philippines (CPP)	1969–2012	China	Weapons and logistics Aid	1974–1986
Philippines	Mindanao Independence Movement (MIM)	1970–1971	Malaysia	Safe haven to members	1970–1971
				Safe haven to leaders	1970–1971
				Training camp	1970–1971
				Training	1970–1971
Portugal	Mozambique Liberation Front (Frelimo)	1964–1974	Tanzania	Safe haven to members	1965–1973
				Safe haven to leaders	1964–1967
				Open offices	1964–1967
				Training camp	1964–1967
				Training	1964–1965
				Weapons and logistics Aid	1965

(continued)

Target	Nonstate Armed Group	Period Active	Supporters	Type of Support	Period of Support
Portugal	National Front for the Liberation of Angola (FNLA)	1961–1975	Zaire	Safe haven to members	1962–1974
				Training camp	1962–1974
				Troops	1962–1974
			China	Training	1962–1974
				Weapons and logistics Aid	1962–1974
				Training	1962–1974
Portugal	People's Movement for the Liberation of Angola (MPLA)	1961–1974	South Africa	Training	1961–1974
			Soviet Union	Weapons and logistics Aid	1961–1974
				Financial aid	1961–1974
				Training	1961–1974
			Cuba	Weapons and logistics Aid	1961–1974
				Troops	1961–1974
			China	Weapons and logistics Aid	1961–1962
				Financial aid	1961–1962
Russia (Soviet Union)	Ukrainian Insurgent Army (UPA)	1946–1950	Germany	Weapons and logistics Aid	1946–1950
Russia (Soviet Union)	United Democratic Resistance Movement (BDPS)	1946–1948	USA	Safe haven to members	1948
				Weapons and logistics Aid	1948
Rwanda	Rwandan Patriotic Front (FPR)	1990–1994	Uganda	Safe haven to members	1990–1994
				Training camp	1990–1994
				Training	1990–1994
				Weapons and logistics Aid	1990–1994
				Financial aid	1990–1994
				Transport	1990–1994

Target country	Group	Years	Supporter	Type of support	Years
Senegal	Movement of Democratic Forces of Casamance (MFDC)	1990–2003	Guinea-Bissau	Weapons and logistics Aid	1998–2003
Serbia (Yugoslavia)	Kosovo Liberation Army (UCK)	1998–1999	Albania	Training	1998–1999
			USA	Training	1998–1999
				Weapons and logistics Aid	1998–1999
Sierra Leone	Armed Forces Revolutionary Council (AFRC)	1997–2000	Liberia	Safe haven to members	1997–2000
				Safe haven to leaders	1997–2000
				Weapons and logistics Aid	1997–2000
				Financial aid	1997–2000
				Transport	1997–2000
				Troops	1997–2000
Sierra Leone	Revolutionary United Front (RUF)	1991–2001	Libya	Safe haven to members	1991
				Safe haven to leaders	1991
				Open offices	1991
				Training camp	1991
				Training	1991
				Weapons and logistics Aid	1991–2001
				Financial aid	1991–2001
			Burkina Faso	Safe haven to members	1991
				Safe haven to leaders	1991
				Open offices	1991
				Training camp	1991
				Training	1991

(continued)

Target	Nonstate Armed Group	Period Active	Supporters	Type of Support	Period of Support
Sierra Leone	Revolutionary United Front (RUF)	1991–2001	Burkina Faso	Weapons and logistics Aid	1991–2001
				Financial aid	1991–2001
				Transport	2000
			Liberia	Troops	1991–2001
				Safe haven to members	1993–2001
				Safe haven to leaders	1993–2001
				Open offices	1997–2001
				Training camp	1997–2001
				Training	1991–2000
				Weapons and logistics Aid	1997–2001
				Financial aid	1997–2001
				Transport	1991–2000
				Troops	1997–2001
Somalia	Alliance for the Re-liberation of Somalia (ARS/UIC)	2006–2008	Eritrea	Safe haven to leaders	2007–2008
				Open offices	2007
				Weapons and logistics Aid	2006–2008
				Financial aid	2006–2008
			Djibouti	Weapons and logistics Aid	2006
				Financial aid	2006
			Yemen	Weapons and logistics Aid	2006
				Financial aid	2006
			Saudi Arabia	Weapons and logistics Aid	2006
				Financial aid	2006

			Syria	Weapons and logistics Aid	2006
				Financial aid	2006
			Iran	Weapons and logistics Aid	2006
				Financial aid	2006
			Egypt	Weapons and logistics Aid	2006–2008
				Financial aid	2006
			Libya	Financial aid	2006
Somalia	Hizbul-Islam	2009–present	Eritrea	Weapons and logistics Aid	2009–2010
Somalia	Somali National Movement (SNM)	1983–1991	Ethiopia	Safe haven to members	1983–1988
				Safe haven to leaders	1983–1988
				Open offices	1983–1988
				Training camp	1983–1988
				Weapons and logistics Aid	1983 and 1987–1988
Somalia	Somali Patriotic Movement (SPM)	1989–1991	Kenya	Safe haven to leaders	1989–1991
Somalia	Somali Reconciliation and Restoration Council (SRRC)	2001–2004	Ethiopia	Open offices	2001
				Training	2002
				Financial aid	2002
Somalia	Somali Salvation Democratic Front (SSDF)	1982–1984	Ethiopia	Safe haven to members	1982–1984
				Safe haven to leaders	1982–1984
				Open offices	1982–1984
				Training camp	1982–1984
				Weapons and logistics Aid	1982–1984
				Financial aid	1982–1984

(continued)

Target	Nonstate Armed Group	Period Active	Supporters	Type of Support	Period of Support
Somalia	United Somali Congress / Somali National Alliance (USC/SNA)	1991–1996	Malaysia	Financial aid	1996
South Africa	African National Congress (ANC)	1981–1988	Angola	Safe haven to members	1981–1988
				Training camp	1981–1988
			Tanzania	Safe haven to members	1981–1988
				Open offices	1981–1988
			Mozambique	Safe haven to members	1981–1988
			Cuba	Training	1981–1984
			Russia (Soviet Union)	Training	1981–1988
South Africa	South West Africa People's Organization (SWAPO)	1966–1988	Angola	Safe haven to members	1966–1988
				Safe haven to leaders	1966–1988
				Open offices	1966–1988
				Training camp	1966–1988
			Russia (Soviet Union)	Training	1975–1988
				Weapons and logistics Aid	1975–1988
Spain	Basque Homeland and Freedom (ETA)	1978–2011	Cuba	Training	1978
			Libya	Training camp	1970–1983
			France	Safe haven to leaders	1968–1984
				Safe haven to members	1968–1984
Sri Lanka	Eelam People's Revolutionary Liberation Front (EPRLF)	1985–1985	India	Safe haven to members	1985
				Open offices	1985
				Training	1985
				Weapons and logistics Aid	1985

Country	Organization		Supporter	Support type	
Sri Lanka	Liberation Tigers of Tamil Eelam (LTTE)	1984–2009	India	Safe haven to members	1984–1987
				Safe haven to leaders	1984–1987
				Training Camp	1984–1987
				Weapons and logistics Aid	1984–1987
				Financial Aid	1984–1987
			North Korea	Weapons and logistics Aid	1994–2009
				Transport	1994–1997
Sri Lanka	Tamil Eelam Liberation Organization (TELO)	1984–1985	India	Safe haven to members	1984–1985
				Safe haven to leaders	1984–1985
				Open offices	1984–1985
				Training camp	1984–1985
				Training	1984–1985
Sudan	Anya Nya	1963–1972	Ethiopia	Safe haven to members	1963–1972
				Safe haven to leaders	1963–1972
			Israel	Weapons and logistics Aid	1967–1972
				Financial aid	1967–1972
			Uganda	Safe haven to members	1963–1972
				Safe haven to leaders	1963–1972
Sudan	Justice and Equality Movement (JEM)	2003–2011	Libya	Safe haven to leaders	2010
Sudan	National Democratic Alliance (NDA)	1996–2005	Egypt	Safe haven to leaders	2005
				Open offices	2005
Sudan	Sudan Liberation Movement/Army - Unity (SLM/A-Unity)	2007–2008	Chad	Safe haven to members	2008
			United Kingdom	Safe haven to members	2007–2008
				Open offices	2007–2008

(continued)

Target	Nonstate Armed Group	Period Active	Supporters	Type of Support	Period of Support
Sudan	Sudan Liberation Movement/Army (SLM/A)	2003–2009	Israel	Open offices	2008–2009
				Financial aid	2008–2009
			USA	Open offices	2003–2007
			Eritrea	Financial aid	2003–2005
				Transport	2003–2005
Sudan	Sudan People's Liberation Movement/ Army (SPLM/A)	1983–2014	Israel	Weapons and logistics Aid	2002
				Financial aid	1986–2004
Sudan	Sudanese Communist Party	1971–1971	Egypt	Safe haven to members	1971
Syria	Muslim Brotherhood	1979–1982	Iraq	Safe haven to members	1980–1982
Tajikistan	United Tajik Opposition (UTO)	1992–1999	Afghanistan	Safe haven to members	1996–1998
				Open offices	1996–1998
				Training camp	1996–1998
				Transport	1996–1998
			Pakistan	Training	1993–1997
				Financial aid	1995–1997
			Iran	Financial aid	1996–1998
Thailand	Communist Party of Thailand (CPT)	1974–1982	Laos	Safe haven to members	1974–1982
				Safe haven to leaders	1974–1982
				Open offices	1974–1982
				Training camp	1974–1982
				Training	1974–1982
				Weapons and logistics Aid	1974–1982
				Financial aid	1974–1982
				Transport	1974–1982

Country	Group	Active	Sponsor	Type of support	Period
Thailand	Communist Party of Thailand (CPT)	1974–1982	Cambodia	Safe haven to members	1974–1982
				Safe haven to leaders	1974–1982
				Open offices	1974–1982
Thailand	Patani insurgents	2003–present	Malaysia	Safe haven to members	2003–2010
				Safe haven to leaders	2003–2010
				Open offices	2003–2010
				Financial aid	2003–2010
Trinidad and Tobago	Jamaat al-Muslimeen	1990–1990	Libya	Training camp	1990
				Weapons and logistics Aid	1990
				Financial aid	1990
Tunisia	Résistance Armée Tunisienne	1980–1980	Libya	Safe haven to members	1980
				Training camp	1980
Turkey	Devrimci Sol	1991–1992	Syria	Training	1992
Turkey	Kurdistan Workers' Party (PKK)	1984–present	Syria	Safe haven to members	1987–1998
				Safe haven to leaders	1984–1998
				Training camp	1984–1992
			Iran	Safe haven to members	1994–2004
				Safe haven to leaders	2000–2002
				Training camp	1995–2000
				Weapons and logistics Aid	1992–2000
			Greece	Open offices	1995–1998
				Training camp	1994–1996

(continued)

Target	Nonstate Armed Group	Period Active	Supporters	Type of Support	Period of Support
Uganda	Front for National Salvation (Fronasa)	1979–1979	Tanzania	Safe haven to members	1979–1979
				Training camp	1979–1979
				Training	1979–1979
				Weapons and logistics Aid	1979–1979
Uganda	Lord's Army	1988–1988	Sudan	Safe haven to members	1988–1988
				Training camp	1988–1988
				Weapons and logistics Aid	1988–1988
Uganda	National Resistance Army (NRA)	1981–1986	Libya	Training camp	1981–1986
				Financial aid	1981–1985
Uganda	Uganda Freedom Movement (UFM)	1982–1982	Libya	Training	1982
				Weapons and logistics Aid	1982
Uganda	Uganda National Liberation Front (UNLF)	1979–1979	Tanzania	Safe haven to leaders	1979
				Troops	1979
Uganda	Uganda National Rescue Front - II (UNRF II)	1997–2002	Sudan	Safe haven to members	1997–2002
				Safe haven to leaders	1998–2002
				Training camp	1997–2002
				Weapons and logistics Aid	1997
Uganda	West Nile Bank Front (WNBF)	1996–1996	Sudan	Weapons and logistics Aid	1996
Uganda	Uganda People's Army (UPA)	1987–1992	United Kingdom	Safe haven to leaders	1988
			Sudan	Safe haven to leaders	1990
United Kingdom	Communist Party of Malaya (CPM)	1948–1957	Thailand	Safe haven to members	1948–1957
				Safe haven to leaders	1948–1957
United Kingdom	National Organisation of Cypriot Fighters (EOKA)	1955–1959	Greece	Weapons and logistics Aid	1955–1959

Sponsor	Group	Period	Recipient	Support	Year
United Kingdom	North Kalimantan Liberation Army	1962–1962	Indonesia	Safe haven to members	1962
				Training	1962
				Weapons and logistics Aid	1962
United Kingdom	Provisional IRA (PIRA)	1971–2005	Libya	Safe haven to members	1972–1991
				Training camp	1972–1991
				Training	1972–1992
				Weapons and logistics Aid	1972–1973 and 1985–1991
				Financial Aid	1986–1991
United States	al-Qaeda	2001–present	Iran	Safe haven to members	2002–2010
				Safe haven to leaders	2002–2010
					2001–2010
			Afghanistan	Safe haven to members	2001–2002
				Safe haven to leaders	2001–2002
				Training camp	2001–2002
United States	Pathet Lao	1963–1973	North Vietnam	Safe haven to members	1963–1973
				Training	1963–1973
				Weapons and logistics Aid	1963–1973
Uzbekistan	Islamic Movement of Uzbekistan (IMU)	1999–2000	Afghanistan	Safe haven to members	1999–2000
				Safe haven to leaders	1999–2000
				Open offices	1999–2000
				Training camp	1999–2000
				Training	1999–2000
Uzbekistan	Jihad Islamic Group (JIG)	2004–2004	Pakistan	Training camp	2004

(continued)

Target	Nonstate Armed Group	Period Active	Supporters	Type of Support	Period of Support
Yemen	Democratic Republic of Yemen	1994–1994	USA	Safe haven to leaders	1994
Zimbabwe	Zimbabwe African People's Union (Zapu)	1964–1974	Zambia	Safe haven to members	1964–1974
				Open offices	1964–1974
			Botswana	Safe haven to members	1966–1974
				Safe haven to leaders	1966–1974
			United Kingdom	Safe haven to members	1966
			Russia (Soviet Union)	Training	1964–1966
			Sweden	Financial aid	1969–1974
Zimbabwe	Zimbabwe African National Union (ZANU)	1973–1976	Zambia	Safe haven to members	1973–1976
				Safe haven to leaders	1973–1975
				Open offices	1973–1975
				Training camp	1973–1975
			Botswana	Safe haven to members	1973–1976
			Mozambique	Safe haven to members	1975
				Open offices	1975
				Training camp	1975
			United Kingdom	Open offices	1973–1976
			Sweden	Financial aid	1973–1976
Zimbabwe	Patriotic Front	1976–1979	Zambia	Training camp	1976–1979
			Sweden	Financial aid	1976–1979

The Entire Cases of De Facto Support, 1945–2010

Target	Nonstate Armed Group	Period Active	Supporters	Type of Support	Period of Support
Afghanistan	Hizb-i Islami-yi Afghanistan	1980–1991	Saudi Arabia	Financial Aid	1980–1991
Afghanistan	Taliban	1995–2012	Pakistan	Safe havens to members	2002–2010
				Safe havens to leadership	2002–2010
				Open offices	2002–2010
				Training camp	2002–2010
				Training	2006–2007
				Weapons and logistics aid	2006
Afghanistan	United Islamic Front for Salvation of Afghanistan (UIFSA)	1996–2001	United Kingdom	Open offices	2001
Algeria	Al-Qaeda in the Islamic Maghreb (AQIM)	1999–2012	Mali	Safe havens to members	1999–2010
				Training camp	1999–2010
			Spain	Safe havens to members	2007–2010
			Pakistan	Training	
Algeria	Armed Islamic Group of Algeria (GIA)	1993–2003	Switzerland	Safe havens to members	2002–2003
			United Kingdom	Safe havens to members	1993–2003
				Open offices	2002–2003
Azerbaijan	Military faction (forces of Suret Husseinov)	1993	Afghanistan	Training	
			Russia (Soviet Union)	Safe havens to leadership	1993

Country		Group	Supporter	Type of support	Dates
Azerbaijan	1994–2005	Republic of Nagorno-Karabakh	Armenia	Safe havens to members	1994–2005
				Safe havens to leadership	
				Open offices	
				Weapons and logistics aid	
				Financial aid	
				Transport of military equipment, military advice	
			Russia (Soviet Union)	Safe havens to members	1994–2005
				Safe havens to leadership	
				Open offices	
				Training camp	
				Training	
				Weapons and logistics aid	
				Financial aid	
				Transport of military equipment, military advice	
Bangladesh	2005–present	Purba Banglar Communist Party - Janajuddha (PBCP - Janajudhha)	India	Safe havens to leadership	2008–2010
				Open offices	2008–2010
				Transport of military equipment, military advice	2009–2010
			Myanmar (Burma)	Transport of military equipment, military advice	2009–2010
Bangladesh	2005–present	Purba Banglar Communist Party (PBCP)	India	Safe havens to members	2005–present
				Safe havens to leadership	2005–present

(continued)

Target	Nonstate Armed Group	Period Active	Supporters	Type of Support	Period of Support
Bangladesh	Purba Banglar Communist Party (PBCP)	2005–present	India	Open offices	2008–2010
				Weapons and logistics aid	2010
				Transport of military equipment, military advice	2009
			Pakistan	Weapons and logistics aid	2010
Bosnia-Herzegovina	Autonomous Province of Western Bosnia	1993–1995	Croatia	Transport of military equipment, military advice	1993–1995
Bosnia-Herzegovina	Croatian Republic of Bosnia-Herzegovina	1993–1994	USA	Safe havens to members	1993–1994
				Safe havens to leadership	
				Open offices	
				Financial aid	
Burundi	National Council for the Defense of Democracy – Forces for the Defense of Democracy (CNDD-FDD)	1998–2003	Tanzania	Safe havens to members	1998–2003
				Training camp	
Burundi	National Liberation Front (Frolina)	1997–2000	Tanzania	Safe havens to members	1997–2000
				Training camp	
				Weapons and logistics aid	
Burundi	Palipehutu	1991–2000	Tanzania	Safe havens to members	1991–1992
Burundi	Palipehutu-National Forces of Liberation (Palipehutu-FNL)	1997–2008	Tanzania	Safe havens to members	1997–2008
Cameroon	Union of the Peoples of Cameroon (UPC)	1960–1961	Switzerland	Safe havens to leadership	1960

Country	Group	Dates	Host	Support type	Year(s)
Central African Republic	Convention of Patriots for Justice and Peace (CPJP)	2009–2011	Chad	Safe havens to leadership	2009
Central African Republic	Forces of Francois Bozize	2002	France	Safe havens to leadership	2002
Central African Republic	Union of Democratic Forces for Unity (UFDR)	2006	Benin	Safe havens to leadership	2006
Chad	National Liberation Front of Chad (FROLINAT)	1966–1970	Sudan	Safe havens to leadership	1966
Chad	Chadian National Front (FNT)	1992–1994	Sudan	Safe havens to members	1992–1994
Chad	Islamic Legion	1989–1990	Sudan	Safe havens to members	1989–1990
Chad	Movement for Democracy and Development (MDD)	1991–1999	Niger	Safe havens to members	1991–1997
Chad	Movement for Democracy and Development (MDD)		Nigeria	Safe havens to members	1991–1997
Chad	Movement for National Salvation of Chad (MOSANAT)	1989	Nigeria	Safe havens to members	1989
Chad	Movement for National Salvation of Chad (MOSANAT)		Sudan	Safe havens to members	1989
Chad	Movement for National Salvation of Chad (MOSANAT)		Ethiopia	Safe havens to members	1989
Chad	Revolutionary Forces of 1 April	1989	Sudan	Safe havens to members	1989
Chad	Revolutionary Forces of 1 April			Safe havens to leadership	1989
Chad	Union of Forces for Democracy and Development (UFDD)	2006–2007	France	Open offices	2007
Chad	Union of Forces for Democracy and Development (UFDD)		United Kingdom	Open offices	2007
China	East Turkestan Islamic Movement (ETIM)	1990–present	Afghanistan	Safe havens to members	2004–2010
China	East Turkestan Islamic Movement (ETIM)			Training camp	2002–2008
China	East Turkestan Islamic Movement (ETIM)		Pakistan	Safe havens to members	2001–2010
China	East Turkestan Islamic Movement (ETIM)			Safe havens to leadership	2002–2003
China	East Turkestan Islamic Movement (ETIM)			Open offices	2002–2010

(continued)

Target	Nonstate Armed Group	Period Active	Supporters	Type of Support	Period of Support
China	Taiwanese insurgents	1947	Japan	Safe havens to leadership	1947
Colombia	Revolutionary Armed Forces of Colombia (FARC)	1964–present	Panama	Safe havens to members	1997–2010
				Transport of military equipment, military advice	1997–2010
			Ecuador	Safe havens to members	1997–2010
				Transport of military equipment, military advice	1997–2010
			Venezuela	Safe havens to members	1997–2010
				Transport of military equipment, military advice	1997–2010
Colombia	National Liberation Army (ELN)	1966–2008	Bolivia	Safe havens to members	1999–2001
Colombia	Popular Liberation Army (EPL)	1984–present	Ecuador	Safe havens to members	1990–2006
				Open offices	
Costa Rica	National Liberation Army (NLA)	1948	Dominican Republic	Training	1948
			Honduras	Training	1948
			Guatemala	Weapons and logistics aid	1948
Djibouti	Front for Restoration of Unity and Democracy - Ahmed Dini (FRUD-AD)	1999	Eritrea	Safe havens to members	1999
Djibouti	Front for Restoration of Unity and Democracy (FRUD)	1991–1994	Ethiopia	Safe havens to members	1991–1994
			Eritrea	Safe havens to members	1991

Country	Group	Years	Sponsor	Type of aid	Years
DR Congo (Zaire)	Alliance of Democratic Forces for the Liberation of Congo (AFDL)	1996–1997	Rwanda	Financial aid	1996–1997
			Uganda	Financial aid	1996–1997
			Angola	Financial aid	1996–1997
Egypt	Al-Gama'a al-Islamiyya (Islamic Group)	1993–1998	United Kingdom	Financial aid	1993–1998
El Salvador	Ejército Revolucionario del Pueblo (ERP)	1979	USA	Financial aid	1979
El Salvador	Military faction (forces of Benjamin Mejia)	1972	Venezuela	Safe havens to leadership	1972
Ethiopia	Al-Itihaad al-Islamiya (AIAI)	1993–1999	Kenya	Safe havens to members	1993–1999
				Financial aid	1993–1999
			Libya	Safe havens to members	1993–1999
			Yemen	Safe havens to members	1993–1999
Ethiopia	Al-Itihaad al-Islamiya (AIAI)	1993–1999	Saudi Arabia	Weapons and logistics aid	1993–1999
				Financial aid	1993–1999
			Pakistan	Weapons and logistics aid	1993–1999
				Financial aid	1993–1999
			Sudan	Financial aid	1993–1999
			United Arab Emirates	Financial aid	1993–1999
			Djibouti	Financial aid	1993–1999
Ethiopia	Al-Shabaab	2008–present	Kenya	Safe havens to members	2010
Ethiopia	Eritrean Liberation Front (ELF)	1964–1980	Egypt	Safe havens to members	1964–1970
				Open offices	
			Sudan	Safe havens to leadership	1964–1980
			Saudi Arabia	Safe havens to leadership	1964–1980

(continued)

Target	Nonstate Armed Group	Period Active	Supporters	Type of Support	Period of Support
Ethiopia	Eritrean People's Liberation Front (EPLF)	1973–1991	Sudan	Financial aid	1970–1980
Ethiopia	Oromo Liberation Front (OLF)	1977–present	Kenya	Safe havens to members	1977–2010
			Somalia	Training camp	
				Safe havens to members	1977–1999
France	Algerian National Movement (MNA)	1955–1957	Belgium	Safe havens to members	1955–1957
France	Khmer Issarak	1946–1953	Thailand	Safe havens to members	1948–1953
				Weapons and logistics aid	
				Financial aid	
Georgia	Republic of Abkhazia	1992–1993	Russia (Soviet Union)	Weapons and logistics aid	1992–1993
			Turkey	Financial aid	1992–1993
Georgia	Zviadists	1992–1993	Russia (Soviet Union)	Safe havens to members	1992–1993
				Safe havens to leadership	
Guatemala	Guatemalan National Revolutionary Unity (URNG)	1982–1995	Mexico	Safe havens to members	1982–1990
				Open offices	1982–1990
				Transport of military equipment, military advice	1991–1993
Guatemala	Revolutionary Organization of Armed People (ORPA)	1979–1981	El Salvador	Weapons and logistics aid	1980–1981
Guinea	Rally of Democratic Forces of Guinea (RFDG)	2000–2001	Liberia	Safe havens to members	2000–2001
Haiti	National Revolutionary Front for the Liberation (FLRN)	2004	Dominican Republic	Safe havens to members	2004

Country	Group	Years active	Host country	Type of support	Year
India	Communist Party of India– Maoist (CPI-M)	2005–2011	Burma	Training camp	2010
India	Garo National Liberation Army (GNLA)	2010–2012	Bangladesh	Safe havens to members; Safe havens to leadership	2010
India	Maoist Communist Centre of India (MCC)	1992–2004	Nepal	Safe havens to members; Training camp; Weapons and logistics aid	2001–2004
India	Naga National Council (NNC)	1956–1968	United Kingdom	Safe havens to leadership	1960–1968
India	National Democratic Front of Bodoland–Ranjan Daimary (NDFB - RD)	2009–present	Bangladesh	Safe havens to members; Safe havens to leadership	2009–2010
India	National Socialist Council of Nagaland–Isak-Muivah (NSCN - IM)	1992–2000	Bangladesh; Thailand	Training camp; Safe havens to leadership; Weapons and logistics aid	1993; 1992–2000
India	National Socialist Council of Nagaland–Khaplang (NSCN - K)	2005–present	Myanmar (Burma)	Safe havens to members; Safe havens to leadership; Open offices; Training camp	2005–2010
India	People's Liberation Army (PLA)	1982–present	Myanmar (Burma); Bangladesh	Safe havens to members; Safe havens to leadership; Training camp; Safe havens to leadership; Training camp	1982–2010; 2006; 1982–2010; 2005–2010; 2008–2010

(continued)

Target	Nonstate Armed Group	Period Active	Supporters	Type of Support	Period of Support
India	People's Liberation Army of Manipur (PREPAK)	2008–2009	Bangladesh	Safe havens to members	2008–2009
			Myanmar	Safe havens to members	2008–2009
				Training camp	2008
India	People's United Liberation Front (PULF)	2000–2008	Pakistan	Training camp	2008
India	People's War Group (PWG)	1990–2004	Nepal	Safe havens to members	2001–2004
				Safe havens to leadership	2001
				Training camp	2001
			Sri Lanka	Weapons and logistics aid	1991 and 2001–2002
India	Sikh insurgents	1983–1993	Canada	Open offices	1983
India	National Democratic Front of Bodoland (NDFB)	1993–2010	Bhutan	Safe havens to members	1993–2003
				Safe havens to leadership	
				Open offices	
				Training camp	
			Bangladesh	Safe havens to members	1993–2010
				Safe havens to leadership	
				Training camp	
			Myanmar	Safe havens to members	2003–2010
				Safe havens to leadership	
				Open offices	
				Training camp	

Country	Group	Group years	Host country	Type of support	Support years
			Nepal	Safe havens to members	2003–2010
			China	Weapons and logistics aid	2008–2010
India	Tripura National Volunteers (TNV)	1979–1988	Bangladesh	Safe havens to members	1984–1988
India	United Liberation Front of Assam (ULFA)	1990–2010	Myanmar (Burma)	Safe havens to members, leaders	1990–2010
				Open offices, Training camp	2003–2010
			Cambodia	Weapons and logistics aid	1993
India	United National Liberation Front (UNLF)	1994–2009	Myanmar (Burma)	Safe havens to leadership	2001–2002
				Training camp	1995–2004
			Bangladesh	Safe havens to leadership	2006
				Training camp	2003–2009
Indonesia	Free Aceh Movement (GAM)	1990–2005	Malaysia	Safe havens to members	1990–2005
				Safe havens to leadership	
				Open offices	
				Weapons and logistics aid	
				Financial aid	
				Transport of military equipment, military advice	
			Singapore	Safe havens to members	1990–2005
				Safe havens to leadership	
				Open offices	
				Financial aid	
			Australia	Safe havens to members	1990–2005
				Safe havens to leadership	1990–2005
			Australia	Open Offices	2001–2005
				Financial aid	1990–2005

(continued)

Target	Nonstate Armed Group	Period Active	Supporters	Type of Support	Period of Support
Indonesia	Free Aceh Movement (GAM)	1990–2005	USA	Open offices	2001–2005
				Financial aid	1995–2006
			Thailand	Weapons and logistics aid	1990–2005
				Transport of military equipment, military advice	
Indonesia	Free Aceh Movement (GAM)	1990–2005	Sweden	Financial aid	1990–2005
			Denmark	Financial aid	2000–2005
			Norway	Financial aid	1999–2005
			Sweden	Safe havens to leadership	1965–1981
			USA	Weapons and logistics aid	1958–1959
				Financial aid	
				Transport of military equipment, military advice	
			Singapore	Transport of military equipment, military advice	1958
Indonesia	Republic of South Moluccas	1950	Netherlands	Safe havens to members	
				Safe havens to leadership	1950
				Financial aid	
Indonesia	Revolutionary Front for an Independent East Timor (Fretilin)	1975–1998	Sweden	Safe havens to leadership	1975–1998

Country	Organization	Period	State	Type of support	Years
Indonesia	Revolutionary Government of the Republic of Indonesia (PRRI)	1958–1961	USA	Weapons and logistics aid	1958–1959
				Financial aid	
				Transport of military equipment, military advice	
			Singapore	Transport of military equipment, military advice	1958
Iran	Kurdistan Democratic Party of Iran (KDPI)	1946–1996	Iraq	Safe havens to members	1946–1996
				Safe havens to leadership	
				Open offices	
				Weapons and logistics aid	
				Financial aid	
				Transport of military equipment, military advice	
Iran	Party of Free Life of Kurdistan (PJAK)	2004–present	USA	Weapons and logistics aid	1946–1979
			USA	Safe havens to members	2010
				Safe havens to leadership	2010
				Open offices	2010
				Transport of military equipment, military advice	2004–2010
			Azerbaijan	Safe havens to members	2004–2010
			Iraq	Safe havens to members	2004–2010
				Safe havens to leadership	
				Open offices	
				Transport of military equipment, military advice	

(continued)

Target	Nonstate Armed Group	Period Active	Supporters	Type of Support	Period of Support
Iran	Mujahedin-e Khalq (MEK)	1979–2001	France	Safe havens to members Safe havens to leadership Open offices	1979–1988
			Turkey	Safe havens to members	1991–1992
Iraq	Al-Mahdi Army	2004–2008	Iran	Safe havens to members, leaders Open offices Training camp Training Weapons and logistics aid Financial aid Transport of military equipment, military advice	2004–2008
Iraq	Ansar al-Islam	2004–2014	Spain	Safe havens to members	2004–2010
			Germany	Safe havens to members	2004–2010
			Norway	Safe havens to members Safe havens to leadership	2004–2010
			Iran	Safe havens to members Safe havens to leadership Open offices	2004–2010
			Jordan	Safe havens to members Safe havens to leadership Open offices	2004–2010

Country	Group	Years	Supporter	Support	Years
Iraq	Ansar al-Islam	2004–2014	Saudi Arabia	Safe havens to members	2004–2010
				Safe havens to leadership	
				Open offices	
			Afghanistan	Safe havens to members, leaders	2004–2010
				Training camp, training	
				Transport of military equipment, military advice	
Iraq	Islamic State of Iraq (ISI)	2006–present	Syria	Recruitment	2004
				Transport of military equipment	
			Lebanon	Recruitment	2004
			Jordan	Recruitment	2004
			Saudi Arabia	Recruitment	2004
				Financial Aid	2004–2010
Iraq	Kurdistan Democratic Party (KDP)	1961–1991	USA	Safe havens to members	1961–1991
				Safe havens to leadership	
				Open offices	
				Training	
				Weapons and logistics aid	

(continued)

Target	Nonstate Armed Group	Period Active	Supporters	Type of Support	Period of Support
Iraq	Kurdistan Democratic Party (KDP)	1961–1991	United Kingdom	Safe havens to members	1961–1991
				Safe havens to leadership	
				Open offices	
			Turkey	Financial aid	1995
				Transport of military equipment, military advice	1995
			Israel	Safe havens to members	1961–1991
				Safe havens to leadership	
				Training	
				Weapons and logistics aid	
				Financial aid	
				Transport of military equipment, military advice	
Iraq	Kurdistan Democratic Party-Provisional Command (KDP-QM)	1977–1978	Iran	Safe havens to members	1977–1978
				Safe havens to leadership	

Country	Group	Years	Sponsor	Support	Years
Iraq	Patriotic Union of Kurdistan (PUK)	1976–1996	United Kingdom	Safe havens to members Safe havens to leadership Open offices	1976–1996
			Iran	Safe havens to members Safe havens to leadership Open offices Weapons and logistics aid Financial aid Transport of military equipment, military advice	1976–1996
			Syria	Safe havens to members Safe havens to leadership Open offices Training camp Training Weapons and logistics aid Financial aid	1976–1996
			Libya	Weapons and logistics aid Financial aid	1976–1996
Iraq	Supreme Council for the Islamic Revolution in Iraq (SCIRI)	1982–1996	United Kingdom	Safe havens to members Safe havens to leadership Open offices	1982–1996
			France	Safe havens to members, leaders Open offices	1982–1996

(continued)

Target	Nonstate Armed Group	Period Active	Supporters	Type of Support	Period of Support
Iraq	Supreme Council for the Islamic Revolution in Iraq (SCIRI)	1982–1996	Switzerland	Safe havens to members Safe havens to leadership Open offices	1982–1996
			Austria	Safe havens to members Safe havens to leadership Open offices	1982–1996
			Iran	Safe havens to members Safe havens to leadership Open offices Financial aid	1982–1996
			Saudi Arabia	Safe havens to members Safe havens to leadership Open offices	1982–1996
			Kuwait	Safe havens to members Safe havens to leadership Open offices	1982–1996
Israel	Fatah	1959–present	United Kingdom	Safe havens to members	1990–2007
			Turkey	Safe haven to members	1967–1970
			Lebanon	Safe haven to leaders Open offices Training camp	2005–2010
			Italy	Open Offices	1959–1972

Country	Group	Years	Supporter	Type of support	Years
Israel	Hamas	1993–present	United Kingdom	Financial aid	1993–2010
			United States	Financial aid	1993–2010
Israel	Palestinian Islamic Jihad (PIJ)	1995–present	Sudan	Transport of military equipment, military advice	2000–2010
Israel	Popular Front for the Liberation of Palestine– General Command (PFLP-GC)	1968–present	Sweden	Safe haven to members	1988–1989
			Germany	Safe haven to members	1988–1989
			Lebanon	Safe haven to members	1969–2010
				Open offices	
				Training camps	
Ivory Coast	Ivorian Popular Movement of the Great West (MPIGO)	2002–2003	Burkina Faso	Safe havens to members	2002–2003
			Liberia	Safe havens to members	2002–2003
Kenya	Military faction (forces of Hezekiah Ochuka)	1982	Tanzania	Safe havens to leadership	1982
Lebanon	Amal	1983–1984	Iraq	Financial aid	1983–1984
Lebanon	Lebanese Arab Army (LAA)	1976	Libya	Safe havens to members	1976
Lebanon	Lebanese Forces	1989	United Kingdom	Financial aid	1989
Liberia	Liberians United for Reconciliation and Democracy (LURD)	2000–2003	USA	Safe havens to leadership	2003
				Financial aid	2000–2003
Liberia	National Patriotic Front of Liberia (NPFL)	1989–1997	USA	Safe havens to members	1989–1990
				Financial aid	1989–1997
			Sierra Leone	Safe havens to members	1989–1997

(continued)

Target	Nonstate Armed Group	Period Active	Supporters	Type of Support	Period of Support
Macedonia, FYR	National Liberation Army (UCK)	2001	USA	Safe havens to members Safe havens to leadership Financial aid	2001
			Albania	Safe havens to members Safe havens to leadership Open offices Training camp Training Weapons and logistics aid Financial aid Transport of military equipment, military advice	2001
			Croatia	Safe havens to members Safe havens to leadership Weapons and logistics aid Financial aid Transport of military equipment, military advice	2001
Malaysia	Communist Party of Malaya (CPM)	1956–1957	Thailand	Training camp Financial aid	1957

Country	Group		Host country	Type of support	
Mauritania	Al-Qaeda in the Islamic Maghreb (AQIM)	2008–2012	Spain	Safe haven to members	2008–2010
			Mali	Safe haven to members	2008–2010
			Pakistan	Training camp	2008–2010
				Training	
Morocco	Popular Front for the Liberation of Saguia el-Hamra and Rio de Oro (POLISARIO)	1975–1989	France	Safe haven to members	1975–1989
				Safe haven to leaders	
			Italy	Safe haven to members	1975–1989
				Safe haven to leaders	
			Algeria	Safe haven to members	1975–1989
				Safe haven to leaders	
				Open offices	
				Weapons and logistics Aid	
			Libya	Weapons and logistics Aid	1975–1989
Mozambique	Mozambican National Resistance (RENAMO)	1977–1992	USA	Safe haven to members, leaders	1977–1992
				Open offices, Weapons, Logistics and Financial aid	
			Canada	Safe haven to members, leaders	1977–1992
			United Kingdom	Safe haven to members, leaders	1977–1992
				Open offices	
			Portugal	Safe haven to members, leaders	1977–1992
				Open offices	
			Kenya	Safe haven to members, leaders	1977–1992

(continued)

Target	Nonstate Armed Group	Period Active	Supporters	Type of Support	Period of Support
Mozambique	Mozambican National Resistance (RENAMO)	1977–1992	South Africa	Safe haven to members, leaders Open offices, Training, Training Camp, Weapons and logistics Aid Financial aid	1977–1992
Myanmar (Burma)	Arakan National Liberation Party (ANLP)	1964–1972	Bangladesh	Safe haven to members Training camp	1964–1972
Myanmar (Burma)	Mujahid Party	1948–1961	Pakistan	Safe haven to members	1948–1961
Myanmar (Burma)	New Mon State Party (NMSP)	1959–present	Thailand India	Safe haven to members Weapons and logistics Aid Training camp	1959 1959–1990 1959–1994
Myanmar (Burma)	Rohingya Solidarity Organisation (RSO)	1991–present	Bangladesh Saudi Arabia Afghanistan India Pakistan	Training Financial aid Training Financial aid Training Financial aid Training Financial aid Training Financial aid	1991–1994 1991–1994 1991–1994 1991–1994 1991–1994

Country	Group	Conflict years	Supporter	Support type	Support years
Nepal	Communist Party of Nepal– Maoist (CPN-M)	1996–2006	Malaysia	Training	1991–1994
				Financial aid	1996–2006
			India	Safe haven to members	1996–2005
				Safe haven to leaders	1996–2006
				Training camp	1996–2006
				Transport	
Nepal	Nepali Congress	1960–1962	India	Safe haven to members, leaders	1960–1962
Nicaragua	Contras / Nicaraguan Democratic Force (FDN)	1982–1990	Honduras	Open offices	1983–1984
				Transport	1986–1987
			Panama	Financial aid	1984–1987
			Switzerland	Financial aid	1984–1987
Nicaragua	Sandinista National Liberation Front (FSLN)	1977–1979	Cuba	Safe haven to members	1977–1979
			Honduras	Safe haven to members	1977–1979
			Costa Rica	Safe haven to members	1978–1979
				Safe haven to leaders	1977–1979
Niger	Air and Azawak Liberation Front (FLAA)	1991–1993	Mali	Safe haven to members	1991–1993
Niger	Democratic Front for Renewal (FDR)	1995–1995	Mali	Safe haven to members	1995
			Nigeria	Safe haven to members	1995
Nigeria	Boko Haram	2009–present	Niger	Safe haven to members, leaders	2009–2010
			Cameroon	Safe haven to members	2009–2010
			Chad	Safe haven to members	2009–2010
			Algeria	Safe haven to members, leaders	2009–2010
				Training, Financial Aid	

(continued)

Target	Nonstate Armed Group	Period Active	Supporters	Type of Support	Period of Support
Nigeria	Boko Haram	2009–present	Somalia	Safe haven to leaders, training	2009–2010
			Mauritania	Training	2009–2010
			Mali	Training	2009–2010
			Afghanistan	Training	2009–2010
Pakistan	Balochistan Liberation Army (BLA)	2004–2009	United Arab Emirates	Financial aid	2004–2006
Pakistan	Balochistan Republican Army (BRA)	2008–2009	Afghanistan	Transport	2008–2009
Pakistan	Muttahida Qaumi Movement (MQM)	1990–1996	United Kingdom	Safe haven to leaders	1991–1996
				Open offices	
				Financial aid	
			Canada	Safe haven to leaders	1994–1996
				Open offices	1995–1996
				Financial aid	1995–1996
			USA	Open offices	1995–1996
				Financial aid	1995–1996
			South Africa	Open offices	1995–1996
				Financial aid	1995–1996
Pakistan	Tehreek-e-Nafaz-e-Shariat-e-Mohammadi (TNSM)	2007	Afghanistan	Safe haven to members	2007
Pakistan	Tehrik-i-Taliban Pakistan (TTP)	2008–present	Afghanistan	Safe haven to members	2008–2010
			Saudi Arabia	Financial aid	2009
Papua New Guinea	Bougainville Revolutionary Army (BRA)	1989–1996	Solomon Islands	Transport	1989–1996

Country	Group	Years	Host country	Type of aid	Years
Paraguay	Opposition coalition (Febreristas, Liberals, and Communists)	1947–1947	Argentina	Safe haven to members	1947
Peru	Revolutionary Left Movement (MIR)	1965–1965	Bolivia	Safe haven to members	1965
				Safe haven to leaders	
				Transport	
Peru	Shining Path (Sendero Luminoso)	1963–2007	Bolivia	Safe haven to members	1989–2007
			Colombia	Financial aid	1975–2007
Peru	Tupac Amaru Revolutionary Movement (MRTA)	1989–1993	El Salvador	Safe haven to members	1989–1993
			Colombia	Safe haven to members	1989–1993
				Training camp	
				Training	
				Weapons and logistics Aid	
				Financial aid	
				Training	
				Weapons and logistics Aid	
				Financial aid	
			Ecuador	Safe haven to members	1989–1993
			Bolivia	Safe haven to members	1989–1993
				Safe haven to leaders	
			Chile	Safe haven to members	1989–1993
				Safe haven to leaders	
				Training	
				Weapons and logistics Aid	
				Financial aid	
			Panama	Weapons and logistics Aid	1989–1993

(continued)

Target	Nonstate Armed Group	Period Active	Supporters	Type of Support	Period of Support
Philippines	Abu Sayyaf Group (ASG)	1993–present	Afghanistan	Safe haven to members Safe haven to leaders Training Financial aid	1993–2010
Philippines	Moro National Liberation Front (MNLF)	1972–2007	Malaysia Afghanistan Libya	Safe haven to members Safe haven to leaders Financial aid Training Financial aid	1972–1993 1972–1993 1972–1993
Russia (Soviet Union)	Association of the Latvian Fatherland Guards (LTS(p)A)	1946–1946	Sweden	Safe haven to leaders	1946
Russia (Soviet Union)	Forces of the Caucasus Emirate	2007–2009	Turkey	Safe havens for members	2009
Russia (Soviet Union)	Forest Brothers	1946–1948	Sweden	Safe haven to leaders	1946–1948
Russia (Soviet Union)	Latvian National Guerrilla Organisation (LNPA)	1946	Sweden	Safe haven to leaders	1946
Rwanda	Army for the Liberation of Rwanda (ALIR)	1996–2000	Democratic Republic of Congo (Zaire) Burundi	Safe haven to members Training camp Safe haven to members	1996–2000 1996–2000 1996–2000
Rwanda	Democratic Forces for the Liberation of Rwanda (FDLR)	1990–2012	USA	Safe haven to leaders	2009–2010

Country	Armed group	Period	Supporter	Type of support	Year
Rwanda	Rwandan Patriotic Front (FPR)	1990–1994	Belgium	Safe haven to leaders	1990–1994
				Open offices	
Senegal	Movement of Democratic Forces of Casamance (MFDC)	1990–2003	Guinea-Bissau	Safe haven to members	1995–2003
			The Gambia	Safe haven to members	1990–2003
				Transport	1990–1994
			France	Open offices	1990–2003
Serbia (Yugoslavia)	Kosovo Liberation Army (UCK)	1998–1999	Albania	Weapons and logistics Aid	1996–1999
Sierra Leone	Armed Forces Revolutionary Council (AFRC)	1997–2000	Guinea	Safe haven to leaders	1998
Sierra Leone	Revolutionary United Front (RUF)	1991–2001	Liberia	Safe haven to members	1991–1996
				Safe haven to leaders	
				Open offices	
				Training camp	
				Training	
				Weapons and logistics Aid	
				Financial aid	
			Ukraine	Weapons and logistics Aid	1991–2001
Somalia	Alliance for the Re-liberation of Somalia (ARS/UIC)	2006–2008	Djibouti	Safe haven to members, leaders	2008
				Open offices	
			Yemen	Safe haven to leaders	2007
			Egypt	Safe haven to leaders	2008
			Saudi Arabia	Financial aid	2006
			Sweden	Safe haven to members	2008

(continued)

Target	Nonstate Armed Group	Period Active	Supporters	Type of Support	Period of Support
Somalia	Hizbul-Islam	2009–present	USA	Safe haven to members	2010
				Financial aid	
Somalia	United Somali Congress / Somali Salvation Alliance (USC/SSA)	1990–1991	United Kingdom	Safe haven to members	1990–1991
			Italy	Safe haven to members	1990
South Africa	African National Congress (ANC)	1981–1988	Zambia	Safe haven to leaders	1981–1988
				Open offices	
South Africa	South West Africa People's Organization (SWAPO)	1966–1988	Zambia	Safe haven to members	1966–1988
				Training camp	
Spain	Basque Homeland and Freedom (ETA)	1978–2011	France	Safe haven to members	1978–2011
				Safe haven to leaders	1978–1992
Sri Lanka	Liberation Tigers of Tamil Eelam (LTTE)	1984–2009	Myanmar (Burma)	Open offices	1993–1996
				Weapons and logistics Aid	1999–2000
			Thailand	Open offices	1996–2009
				Weapons and logistics Aid	1991–2009
				Financial aid	1996–2009
				Transport	1995–2009
			United Kingdom	Open offices	1984–2001
				Financial aid	1984–2007
			Canada	Open offices	2007–2008
				Financial aid	1987–2008
			Australia	Open offices	1984–2007
				Financial aid	1984–2007

Country	Group		Sponsor	Support	Dates
Sri Lanka	Liberation Tigers of Tamil Eelam (LTTE)	1984–2009	France	Open offices, financial aid	1996–2007
			Cambodia	Weapons and logistics Aid	1994–2009
			Malaysia	Weapons and logistics Aid	1994–1996
				Transport	1991–1996
			Vietnam	Weapons and logistics Aid	1999–2000
			Singapore	Weapons and logistics Aid	1994–1996
			Ukraine	Weapons and logistics Aid	1994–1996
			USA	Financial aid	1998–2008
			Indonesia	Transport	1990–2009
Sudan	Anya Nya	1963–1972	United Kingdom	Safe haven to members, leaders	1963–1972
			Congo	Safe haven to members, leaders	1963–1972
				Open offices	
				Training	
			Uganda	Safe haven to members, leaders	1963–1972
				Open offices	
				Training	
			Kenya	Safe haven to members	1963–1972
			Ethiopia	Safe haven to members	1963–1972
				Safe haven to leaders	
Sudan	Sudan Liberation Movement/Army (SLM/A)	2003–2009	Chad	Safe haven to members	2007–2009
			Ukraine	Weapons and logistics Aid	2009
			Eritrea	Weapons and logistics Aid	2009
				Transport	2009
			France	Financial aid, Safe Haven to leaders	2003–2009

(continued)

Target	Nonstate Armed Group	Period Active	Supporters	Type of Support	Period of Support
Syria	Muslim Brotherhood	1979–1982	Jordan	Safe haven to members	1979–1982
Tajikistan	Forces of Khudoberdiyev	1998–1998	Uzbekistan	Safe haven to members	1998
				Safe haven to leaders	
				Training	
				Weapons and logistics Aid	
Tajikistan	Islamic Movement of Uzbekistan (IMU)	2010–2011	Pakistan	Safe haven to members	2010
				Safe haven to leaders	
				Open offices	
				Training camp	
			Afghanistan	Safe haven to members	2010
				Safe haven to leaders	
				Open offices	
				Training camp	
				Training	
			Saudi Arabia	Financial aid	2010
Tajikistan	United Tajik Opposition (UTO)	1992–1999	Afghanistan	Safe haven to members	1992–1995
				Safe haven to leaders	
				Open offices	
				Training camp	
				Transport	
			Pakistan	Weapons and logistics Aid	1996–1998
				Safe haven to leaders	1992–1997
			Iran	Safe haven to leaders	1992–1998

Country	Group	Period	Host country	Type of support	Year
Thailand	Communist Party of Thailand (CPT)	1974–1982	Laos	Safe haven to members	1974–1982
				Safe haven to leaders	
				Open offices	
				Training camp	
				Training	
				Weapons and logistics Aid	
				Financial aid	
				Transport	
			Cambodia	Safe haven to members	1974–1982
				Safe haven to leaders	
				Open offices	
Thailand	Patani insurgents	2003–present	Malaysia	Safe haven to members	2003–2010
				Safe haven to leaders	
				Open offices	
				Financial aid	
Tunisia	Résistance Armée Tunisienne	1980–1980	Algeria	Safe haven to members	1980
Turkey	Devrimci Sol	1991–1992	Netherlands	Safe haven to leaders	1991–1992
			France	Safe haven to members	1991
				Open offices	1992
			Lebanon	Training camp	1992
			United Kingdom	Financial aid	1992
Turkey	Kurdistan Workers' Party (PKK)	1984–present	Syria	Safe haven to members	1999–2010
			Iraq	Safe haven to members	1984–2010
				Safe haven to leaders	1984–2010

(continued)

Target	Nonstate Armed Group	Period Active	Supporters	Type of Support	Period of Support
Turkey	Kurdistan Workers' Party (PKK)	1984–present	Lebanon	Safe haven to leaders	1984–1992
				Training camp	1984–1992
			Belgium	Open offices	1993–1999
				Training camp	1996–1998
			Netherlands	Training camp	2004
Uganda	Allied Democratic Forces (ADF)	1996–2007	Saudi Arabia	Training camp	2007
				Financial aid	2007
Uganda	Uganda People's Democratic Army (UPDA)	1986–1988	Sudan	Safe haven to members	1986–1988
				Safe haven to leaders	
Uganda	West Nile Bank Front (WNBF)	1996–1996	Democratic Republic of Congo (Zaire)	Safe haven to members	1996
			Sudan	Open offices	1996
				Open offices	1996
Uganda	Uganda National Rescue Front (UNRF)	1981–1983	Sudan	Safe haven to leaders	1981–1983
			Zaire	Safe haven to leaders	1981–1983
United Kingdom	Provisional IRA (PIRA)	1971–2005	Colombia	Safe haven to members	1992–2002
				Training camp	2001–2002
			Lebanon	Training camp	1972–1982
			Ireland	Financial aid	1971–2005
			USA	Weapons, logistics, Funds	1981–1985

United States	Al-Qaeda	2001–present			
			United Kingdom	Safe haven to members	2001–2010
				Safe haven to leaders	
				Open offices	
				Financial aid	2001–2010
			Belgium	Safe haven to members	2001–2010
				Training camp	
				Weapons and logistics Aid	
				Financial aid	
			France	Safe haven to members	2001–2010
			Spain	Safe haven to members	2001–2010
				Safe haven to leaders	
				Financial aid	
			Germany	Safe haven to members	2001–2010
				Financial aid	
			Turkey	Safe haven to members	2001–2003
			Netherlands	Financial aid	2001
			Italy	Financial aid	2001–2002
			Saudi Arabia	Safe haven to members	2001–2010
				Financial aid	
			Pakistan	Safe haven to members	2002–2010
				Safe haven to leaders	
				Training camp	
			Afghanistan	Safe haven to leaders	2002–2010

(continued)

Target	Nonstate Armed Group	Period Active	Supporters	Type of Support	Period of Support
Uzbekistan	Islamic Movement of Uzbekistan (IMU)	1999–2000	Tajikistan	Safe haven to members / Open offices / Training camp	1999–2000
Uzbekistan			Saudi Arabia	Financial aid	1999–2000
Uzbekistan	Jihad Islamic Group (JIG)	2004–2004	Germany	Weapons and logistics Aid / Financial aid	2004
Yemen	Al-Qaeda in Arabic Peninsula (AQAP)	2009–present	Saudi Arabia	Financial Aid	2009–2010
Zimbabwe	Zimbabwe African People's Union (Zapu)	1964–1974	Tanzania	Training camp	1964–1974
Zimbabwe	Zimbabwe African National Union (ZANU)	1973–1976	Tanzania	Safe haven to members / Training camp	1973–1976
Zimbabwe	Patriotic Front	1976–1979	Tanzania	Safe haven to leaders	1976

Notes

1. Niccolò Machiavelli, *The Prince* (1532/2005), translated by Peter Bondenella, Vol. 19, p. 63.

2. The Thugs were a group of murderers inspired by a specific cult of Hinduism that operated from the thirteenth to the nineteenth centuries. They used a noose or handkerchiefs to strangulate their victims. They specifically targeted travelers across India and were suppressed by the arrival of British rulers. See Rapoport (1984) for a detailed treatment of the Thugs as one of the ancient terrorist organizations using religion as a motivation for killing.

3. The Assassins were based on a cult of Shi'a Islam, under the leadership of Hassan-i Sabbah in the early twelfth century. They threatened the Sunni Seljuk state, a Turkish state founded within Persian territories. Their main strategy was to assassinate key political figures by knife. Sabbah founded a state in Alamut, a region in the northwestern part of modern Iran. The state collapsed as a result of the Mongolian invasions. See Rapoport (1984).

4. These figures are calculated using the newly collected dataset on state support of rebel groups under the project titled "Dangerous Companions: Cooperation between States and Nonstate Armed Groups (NAGs)." The NAGs data set (San-Akca 2015, ver.4) constitutes the empirical basis of *States in Disguise*. Chapter 3 talks extensively about the new data, variables coded and the coding-related issues. The project website is http://nonstatearmedgroups.ku.edu.tr.

5. I thank the anonymous reviewer of Oxford University Press for highlighting this point.

6. For several Western states, such as Belgium and Germany, used as an operational base for the PKK, see Buckley (1993), Fisher (1993), Agence France Press (1996), and Agence France Press (2004).

7. I return to this issue later in the chapter.

8. See Fukuyama (2004), Krasner and Pascual (2005), Lesser (1999), Rotberg (2002), Cohen (2002), and Rice (2008) for the commonly held view that weak states are the most significant breeding grounds for nonstate violence. Also, see Patrick (2006) for a review of the literature on addressing the problem of weak states as the top issue in counterinsurgency and counterterrorism efforts. For a debate on failed states and their influence on terrorism, see Cohen (2002).

9. This figure has been mentioned and Laquer was cited in Patrick (2006).

10. See "In the Spotlight: Revolutionary Armed Forces of Colombia," Center for Defense Information Terrorism Project (2002). Available at http://www.cdi.org/terrorism/farc.cfm. Accessed on January 10, 2009.

11. See "In the Spotlight: Al-Gama'a Al-Islamiyya," Center for Defense Information Terrorism Project (2002). Available at http://www.cdi.org/terrorism/farc.cfm. Accessed on January 10, 2009.

12. The Dangerous Companions Project (DCP) and the NAGs Dataset use the definition and rebel groups identified by the Uppsala Conflict Data Program (UCDP)/Peace Research Institute Oslo (PRIO) Armed Conflict Dataset (ACD), ver.4 (2015). The ACD Codebook is available at http://www.pcr.uu.se/research/ucdp/datasets/ucdp_prio_armed_conflict_dataset/.

13. Note that most of these groups use violent and peaceful means simultaneously. The rebels' motives for utilizing peaceful propaganda, and their effectiveness, might be the subjects of further research.

14. Both Uganda and Rwanda allowed their troops to fight alongside the rebels against the Mobutu regime of the Democratic Republic of Congo (DRC) in 1996, and later on against the Kabila regime. For an interesting analysis of the DRC and the rebel movements assisted by its neighboring countries, see Onishi (1998).

15. See United Nations (UN) Resolution 2131 (XX), Article 2. The resolution on 'Declaration on the Inadmissibility of Intervention in the Domestic Affairs of States and the Protection of Their Independence and Sovereignty,'" December 21, 1965. Available at http://legal.un.org/avl/pdf/ha/ga_2131-xx/ga_2131-xx_e.pdf. Accessed on May 16, 2016.

16. Check fn.4 citing NAGs Dataset.

17. Byman (2005b) adopts a similar approach by naming such support as passive support, which means that a government knowingly turns a blind eye to rebels for various reasons, such as risk posed to leaders of these governments, or institutional constraints they face in taking particular actions required to control the activities of these groups. Chapter 3 talks in detail about how de facto support differs from passive support.

18. An invaluable body of research is available that examines the effects of external support for rebels on interstate relations. See Gleditsch et al. (2008), Salehyan (2009), and Carment et al. (2009).

19. Liberalism, in its broad sense, refers to a school of thought in the study of international relations that takes into consideration interstate trade, domestic institutions (such as regime type), and intergovernmental organizations (IGOs), to explain conflict and cooperation among states. In the present context, I use liberalism to identify the strand of the literature that emphasizes domestic political survival motives of leaders as an explanation for foreign policy choices. See Baldwin (1993) for a detailed examination of liberalism, and how it differs from realism, in studying international relations.

20. See Lake and Powell (1999) for an application of the strategic choice model to making foreign policy choices in general.

21. The balance of power theory is understood here as an extension of realism. Originated by Morgenthau (1963), the balancing behavior argues that states balance against strong powers. Walt (1987) refined this theory, arguing that states not only balance against powerful states, but also against threats or adversaries.

22. Saideman (2002) provides a similar argument for realism's explanation of external state support for ethnic insurgencies.

23. See Bueno de Mesquita (2002) for a review of the linkage literature. This literature and its relationship to the book are explained in the next section.

24. There are some exceptions. For a theoretical debate, see Salehyan (2010) and Conrad (2011). For an empirical analysis, see Maoz and San-Akca (2012).

25. One exception is the work of Salehyan et al. (2011), which takes into consideration the strength of rebel groups in explaining external state support onset for rebels..

26. An exception is Cunningham et al. (2009a). Yet it is limited to two types of support: implicit and explicit, which makes it difficult to conduct analysis about support level.

27. See fn. 4

28. All sources used for data collection and coding are available on the website of the DCP. Available at http://nonstatearmedgroups.ku.edu.tr/index.php.

CHAPTER 2

1. This figure is calculated based on the proportion of the total number of internal and internationalized internal conflicts to the total number of conflicts in the post-1945 period, coded by the UCDP/PRIO ACD, ver. 4 (2015). The other two types of conflict ACD tracks are interstate and extra-systemic conflicts, which show states as parties to conflict. See ACD Codebook. Available at http://www.pcr.uu.se/digitalAssets/124/124920_1codebook_ucdp_prio-armed-conflict-dataset-v4_2015.pdf.

2. See Maoz (1990) for a detailed analysis of foreign policy decisionmaking and various factors at the individual, domestic, and international levels, which influence it.

3. According to Maoz (1990), the stimulus for a foreign policy decision emerges with the rise of either a motive or an opportunity. The motive, in his opinion, emerges with the perception of a threat to a nation's assets, yet we know that foreign policy decisions can also be motivated by a rise in domestic threats. Maoz adds a third component to the conditions for a leader to begin to develop a particular foreign policy: time pressure.

4. See Dassel and Reinhardt (1999) for a review of the literature on diversionary theory of war and its empirical findings. They argue that domestic strife will lead to foreign aggression only if it threatens the interests of the armed forces. Civilian politicians might benefit from rallying support for foreign aggression, yet they are rarely the ones who initiate the aggression in the first place. Among scholars who investigate the link between internal political turmoil and external war, Maoz (1996) identifies two main causal paths. One is in line with the diversionary use of force theory. He argues that states experiencing revolution might engage in an external war only in the initial times of a revolutionary regime. Second, he argues that states experiencing revolutions are perceived as threats by their neighbors, who are not clear about the intentions of a new

regime. Since a newly established regime is vulnerable, outside adversaries see an opportunity in seeking to settle old disputes with the revolutionary state.

5. Bueno de Mesquita and Siverson (1995) argue that "leaders subject themselves to a domestic political hazard that threatens the very essence of office holding" (p. 852). They further investigate how this hazard is mitigated in nondemocracies versus democracies. Regardless of whether it is a democracy or not, war is not a desirable outcome of interstate rivalry.

6. Carr (1954) and Morgenthau (1963) are proponents of classical realism, which focuses on national capacities and the ability of statesmen to manage and extract domestic resources to achieve international goals. Yet they do not systematically explain the ways in which variations in extraction capacity influence foreign policy decisions. Furthermore, extraction is only one method of increasing investment in military expenditures in general. The literature on "guns versus butter" (warfare versus welfare expenses) gauges arms acquisition as a matter of resource allocation. A detailed discussion of resource allocation is found in the literature on deterrence and arms races. See Snyder (1961), Brodie (1965), Mearsheimer (1983), Huth (1988), Jervis (1989), Sagan (1989), Powell (1993), Huth and Russett (1993), and Glaser (2000) for examples in this vein. Pursuing extraction, governments could increase their revenue via various means, such as taxing, establishing monopolies, and imposing tariffs and customs fees. In the case of allocation, a government could shift resources from health, education, and other areas of welfare spending, to military expenditures (Powell 1993). A discussion of the various ways in which governments could increase their revenues is beyond the scope of this book. See Lamborn (1983) and Tarschys (1988) for a detailed analysis of resource extraction strategies.

7. Literature on the diversionary theory and its critique is vast. I will not go into the details of how and when leaders use diversionary tactics. Rather, my aim is to show why all types of risks to internal survival might not automatically lead to diversion from a domestic threat to an external scapegoat. See Levy and Mabe (2004) and Morgan and Bickers (1992) for further work on what kind of domestic opposition can be addressed by external war. Levy and Mabe (2004) argue that when a segment of domestic opposition anticipates the loss of benefits at the end of a war, they try to prevent the war. Morgan and Bickers introduce a significant revision to the argument of the diversionary use of force. They argue that leaders will respond more seriously to domestic opposition that comes from those segments of society that are critical for maintaining the leader's ruling coalition than when it comes from other segments. Although they do not directly argue that domestic opposition must be greater than external opposition, their argument marks a first step in understanding variation within the domestic opposition that a leader faces and the ways this variation influences foreign policy choices.

8. This lack of data is also evident in the highly reputed article titled, "Ethnicity, Insurgency, and Civil War" (2003) by Fearon and Laitin. The authors mention external support as one of the facilitating factors for the onset of an insurgency, yet they fail to empirically test the external support argument. My purpose here is not to denigrate the contribution by Fearon, Laitin, and other scholars I mentioned with reference to the lack of data on state support of rebel groups. Rather, I try to point out the ways through which we can advance the invaluable insights we have learnt so far by an extensive dataset on state and rebel group relations.

9. The theoretical framework does not account for all four outcomes. Rather, the purpose here is to create a reference point to place the support of rebels among possible foreign policy instruments and to lay out the internal and external circumstances within which a leader resorts to rebels as a foreign policy instrument, as opposed to direct use of force.

10. Nincic (2005) examines the link between the domestic context and external environments of "renegade" regimes, or internationally deviant states, and argues that the conventional ways of dealing with deviant states, such as economic sanctions, do not serve the purpose. He stresses that the external actors' responses to these regimes serve them at home, leading to the emergence of "rally—round-the-flag" sentiments, even for those who initially oppose the regime. See pages 24–26 for an interesting statement of this link.

11. The logic of delegation was offered and examined in detail by Salehyan (2010) from the perspective of principle-agent theory. Despite the invaluable insights produced, the systematic knowledge of the state support of rebels against adversaries remains limited due to the lack of empirical analysis based on detailed data of myriad cases of state support of rebels.

12. Identity is not specifically attributable to the constructivist school of thought. There is an extensive body of literature on violence and political psychology, focusing mostly on internal nationalist violence, such as revolutions and propagandas, in the field of Comparative Politics. See Gurr (1970), Hardin (1995), and Bates et al. (1998) for examples. This body of research uses norms, ideas, and culture that make up identity to explain revolution, ethnic conflict, and civil war. In addition, some studies of political participation (Inglehart 1990, 1997; Putnam 1993) and ethnic conflict (Geertz 1963; Fearon and Laitin 2000) build their primary explanations about violent and nonviolent participation on ideational components, such as culture. In the field of International Relations, Huntington ("The Clash of Civilizations?" [1996]) and Fukuyama ("The End of History and the Last Man" [1992]) use cultural components as the drivers behind international change.

13. See Klotz and Lynch (2007) for a detailed discussion of constructivism and the venues of research according to this school of thought. For a discussion of mutual construction of material and ideational interests , see pp. 86–104. See Carlton (1990) and Colley (1992) for an historical assessment of the role that ideology, a component of the ideational identity, plays in identifying one's enemy. See Haas (2005) for an explanation of ideology's influence on threat perception.

14. I focus on the ideational identity that helps define states' interests at home, yet within the literature of constructivism works are found that emphasize the significance of international norms, and how these norms guide the external behavior of states. The scholarly research on humanitarian intervention and, in particular, the nonuse of chemical and biological weapons, examines both the creation of these norms in the international realm and how these norms, in turn, shape the external behaviors of states. See Finnemore (1993), Berger (1996), Jepperson et al. (1996), Finnemore (1996), Legro (1997), Goldtsein et al. (2000), and Finnemore and Sikkink (2001). Also see Risse and Sikkink (1999) and Risse and Ropp (1999) for an interesting review of the spread of international norms to the domestic realm.

15. Examining alliances in the Middle East between 1955 and 1979, Walt (1987) finds that alliances between states have been motivated largely by a commonly perceived threat rather than a common ideology.

16. The weak state argument has been extensively discussed in Chapter 1.

17. See Buzan (1983) for a treatment of different levels of state strength, with respect to two dimensions: domestic strength and external strength. He argues that it is possible to have domestically weak, but externally strong, states, as well as domestically strong and externally weak ones. Testing this is beyond the scope of this book. Future research might examine state strength from the two angles and discuss its implications for the formation of state-rebel group alliances.

CHAPTER 3

1. The DCP is available at http://nonstatearmedgroups.ku.edu.tr. The codebook in Appendix 2 provides detailed information about the team involved and the coding protocol.

2. See UCDP/PRIO ACD Codebook, ver. 4 (2015).

3. Maoz (1996) and Maoz and Russett (1993) talk extensively about the criteria to identify politically relevant dyads. In addition, Maoz (1996) identifies pairs of indirectly contiguous states that share a colonial or imperial past. See pp. 122–123 in Maoz (1996) for a detailed explanation of political relevancy. See Lemke and Reed (2001) for a comparison of the statistical results for conflict analysis by using all the dyads in the world, versus politically relevant dyads. They conclude there are no significant differences across findings. Using politically relevant dyads makes statistical analysis with a large population of cases manageable.

4. See Appendix 1 for an exemplary data table.

5. See Minorities at Risk Project (MAR) (2005). Available at http://www.cidcm.umd.edu/mar/ Accessed on August 26, 2015.

6. The Global Terrorism Database is hosted by the National Consortium for the Study of Terrorism and Responses to Terrorism (START) at the University of Maryland. Available at http://www.start.umd.edu/gtd/.

7. See International Terrorism: Attributes of Terrorist Events (ITERATE) Data. Available at http://library.duke.edu/data/collections/iterate.html. Although ITERATE dataset has a variable coding state support, the groups are limited to the ones, which conduct international terrorism. Since it is an incident-based data set, there are, understandably, missing data on state support in every case of terrorist attack.

8. The sources used to collect the required information are published under the profile of each NAG on the website of the DCP. Available at http://nonstatearmedgroups.ku.edu.tr.

9. In the following section, I describe the major types of support coded. For other variables used in the empirical analysis of this book, such as ideational characteristics, and more, see Appendix 2, which provides the codebook of the NAGs dataset.

10. See Associated Press International (1997).

11. See BBC (1996).

12. For a detailed analysis of Israel's engagement with Lebanon, and the activities of the Palestinian groups that have found safe havens in that country since the late 1960s, see Maoz (2006), pp. 171–230.

13. For a full description of the development of this measure, see Maoz (2007).

14. See the Political Instability Task Force Problem Set Codebook, 1955–2008 for a detailed description of each instability incident (Marshall et. al. 2015). Available at http://www.systemicpeace.org/inscrdata.html. Accessed on May 20, 2015.

15. A more elaborate and proper measurement of political ideology could have been achieved by examining each state for each year, in terms of its place on an ideological scale, ranging from left to right on the basis of its major governing ideology (if democracy, the ideology of the major political party adheres to; if autocracy, the ideology the leadership adheres to). Yet, the time required to complete this book and an already ambitious data collection and coding effort, which constitutes the empirical core of this book, prevented me from engaging in another extensive coding project.

16. See Appendix 3 for a list of states governed by communist/socialist regimes. I thank Nick Schroeder for sharing the dataset from his honor's thesis, on states that have been governed by communist single-party regimes, while I was studying at University of California, Davis.

17. See Marshall and Jaggers (2002) Polity IV Project: Political Regime Characteristics and Transitions, 1800–2007, available at http://www.systemicpeace.org/polity/polity4.htm.

18. The Ethnic Power Relations (EPR) dataset is hosted by the GROWup portal, which matches UCDP/PRIO Armed Conflict data on nonstate armed groups with corresponding ethnic groups in each target state. However, at the time of the coding of the NAGs dataset, ethnic identities of groups were not yet available. Therefore, each NAG's ethnic identity was coded according to EPR identities by the DCP team.

19. Whether the minority group in a potential supporter state is politicized or not, and how that would influence transnational ethnic kin, is a separate debate and not the focus of the theoretical argument in this book. See Saideman (1997, 2001) for a detailed treatment of how the domestic efforts of minorities influence support for transnational ethnic kin, when these ethnic groups are mobilized and armed to fight against their target state.

20. Extensive research is available on this topic. See Cederman et al. (2009, 2013) for a detailed analysis of transnational ethnic kin and their influence on ethnic insurgencies, including the acquisition of external resources.

21. Table 3.2 lists the rebel groups coded in the NAGs Dataset, including their objectives and ideational characteristics. For space considerations, it is presented on the website of the DCP at http://nonstatearmedgroups.ku.edu.tr/

22. See Tiller (1997) for a detailed analysis of the ideologies that guide American politics.

CHAPTER 4

1. See Appendix 4 presenting the entire cases of intentional support between 1945 and 2010.

2. This figure is an estimated total for the entire six decades. Only during the period between 1973 and 1977 did the Pakistani army hit Balochistan the hardest—3,300 army troops and 5,300 militants lost their lives. See Khan (2009).

3. See BBC News 2012. http://www.bbc.com/news/world-asia-17182978. Accessed on May 20, 2015.

4. See U.S. Congress. House. 2012. https://rohrabacher.house.gov/press-release-rohrabacher-introduces-bill-recognizing-baluchistans-right-self-determination. Accessed on May 13, 2015.

5. See Gall (2011). http://www.nytimes.com/2011/08/24/world/asia/24baluch.html?_r=1. Accessed on December 4, 2015.

6. Note that this figure is based on the entire population of supporter states in the NAGs dataset. The data used for the analysis of the book contains information on sixty-nine supporter states, which are members of the politically relevant groups of target states as explained in detail in chapter 3.

7. See Cleveland (2004) for an excellent narration of the developments in both the domestic and the international environments of Egypt, Syria, Jordan, Iraq, and Lebanon. Cleveland provides a detailed analysis of the context within which Palestinian militant groups were organized.

8. The graph does not include all the armed groups, who fought or have been fighting against Israel. It records data for groups that were involved in conflicts leading to a minimum of twenty-five battle-related deaths. Thus, it lists the major Palestinian groups, such as Hamas, Fatah, and Hezbollah.

9. See "Islamic Jihad" (Haaretz). Available http://www.haaretz.com/misc/tags/Islamic%20Jihad-1.477032. Accessed on July 5, 2015.

10. Hamas published its official foundation charter in 1988, but it was founded in Gaza as the local political arm of the Muslim Brotherhood. Its adherents came from the ranks of the Muslim Brotherhood throughout the 1970s subsequent to the Israeli occupation of Gaza after the Six-Day War in 1967. See Briggs (2006).

11. It is commonly accepted that Hezbollah emerged as a resistance movement against the Israeli occupation of southern Lebanon. My goal is not to discuss the causes behind the emergence of rebel groups and reach a conclusion about their specific objectives. Rather, my focus is on what happens after they emerge with respect to their acquisition of external resources from other states. Therefore, the language used in this book is purposefully neutral, neither favoring nor stigmatizing any militant rebel group or state.

12. Report of Staff Survey Mission to Ethiopia, Iran, and the Arabian Peninsula, House Committee on International Relations, Dec. 1977 (pp. 135–136); for 1976–1979 Department of Defense, Security Assistance Program, Congressional Presentation Document FY 1979. The report was mentioned in *Middle East Research and Information Project (MERIP) Reports* 71 (October) and is cited in Barak 2003 (p. 315).

13. SAVAK stands for Sāzemān-e Ettelā'āt va Amniyat-e Keshvar, which means the Organization of Intelligence and National Security in Persian.

14. See Appendix 2 for the detailed coding protocol. Chapter 3 presents an extensive discussion of the NAGs dataset and the Dangerous Companions Project and some preliminary findings from the descriptive analysis of the data.

15. Turning a blind eye to a rebel group's activities was labeled as "passive support" in Byman 2005b. De facto support is coded when there was not observed evidence of government sponsorship since it is very difficult to determine whether or not a government was turning a blind eye for the high number of cases coded in the NAGs dataset. The coding criteria are discussed in detail in chapter 3.

16. The construction of the population of cases is explained in detail in chapter 3.

17. Note that these figures are limited to analysis of data only with supporters in the PRGs of target states. Chapter 3 presents overall figures for the entire NAGs dataset.

18. I thank Zeev Maoz for making the data available. Two datasets have a more direct measure of inter-state rivalries yet they are not updated to allow coverage of all cases until 2010 (Goertz and Diehl 1995; Thompson 2001).

19. I thank Nick Schroeder for sharing his dataset from his honor's thesis on states that had once or have been governed by single-party communist regimes.

20. The Correlates of War (COW) Database is available at http://correlatesofwar.org. The COW Database hosts multiple datasets, including interstate alliances data, system membership data, and national capabilities data.

21. The ATOP dataset (version 3.0) codes whether a state adheres to a neutrality or nonaggression pact as well. I incorporate only offense and defense pacts since they require a relatively stronger commitment from allies.

22. See ATOP codebook. http://atop.rice.edu/download/ATOPcdbk.pdf. Accessed on May 10, 2015.

23. The COW Project. 2011. "State System Membership List, ver.2011." http://correlatesofwar.org.

24. See Long and Freese (2006), pp.197–198 for a detailed explanation of the parallel regression, or proportional odds, assumption.

25. When estimating the decision to support rebels, continuous years of no support and cubic splines have been included in the analyses but not included in the table to save space.

26. Odds ratios that are smaller than zero means that the probability of occurrence is less likely than that of nonoccurrence. Odds ratios larger than 1 mean that the probability of occurrence is more likely than that of nonoccurrence.

27. It is possible to calculate the percent change in the probability of occurrence of the dependent variable with list coefficient command in Stata. Stata has post-estimation tools to report and interpret the results from a logit analysis. See "Statistical Computing Seminars: Logistic Regression with Stata." http://www.ats.ucla.edu/stat/stata/seminars/stata_logistic/. Accessed on September 5, 2015.

28. Saideman (1997, 2001, 2002) includes various capacity measures and domestic vulnerability indicators in testing hypotheses about the decision of states to support ethnic rebels. Yet the data on external support are very limited; thus, they do not allow for testing hypotheses related to support level.

29. Distance between capital cities of targets and supporters have been included as a control variable across all models, yet not reported since the coefficients are almost zero, and they did not have much influence on support likelihood, although statistically significant. Extractive capacity also turned out to be statistically significant, with almost a coefficient of "0." It is also not reported in the table although included in the analysis. The significance level for joint external and internal threat variable tuned out to be 0.053 and ideational ties in the external threat model turned out to be 0.052. Both are rounded down to 0.05.

30. Distances between capital cities of targets and supporters have been included as a control variable across all models, yet not reported since the coefficients are almost zero, and they did not have much influence on support likelihood, although statistically significant. Extractive capacity also turned out to be statistically significant, with a coefficient of almost "0."

CHAPTER 5

1. See Appendix 5 presenting all cases of de facto support.

2. There is a significant body of research on the conditions under which internal conflict is externalized (Salehyan 2009; Gledistch et al. 2008). It is beyond the scope of this book to develop a theory to capture the reverse causal relationship between external support of rebels and inter-state conflict.

3. Future work will engage in simultaneous equation modeling to examine the two-way causal interaction between external threat and state support of rebels.

4. See Human Rights Watch. 2013. http://www.hrw.org/sites/default/files/reports/chad-1213summary_english.pdf. Accessed on May 12, 2015.

5. See BBC Worldwide Monitoring. (2007).

6. The conditions under which states support rebels that target other states have been extensively examined in chapter 4. As noted, the findings point to a more complex set of interactions between states and rebels than that can be captured by the principle-agent approach.

7. Chapter 3 and Appendix 2 (Codebook) discuss the variables related to measuring the precision level for each support variable. A precision level of 1 corresponds to a strong confidence and 4 corresponds to the lowest confidence level in the source used to code the data. The cases with a precision level of 4 are excluded in the analysis of RSM in this chapter.

8. See Agence France Press (1999) and "BBC Monitoring South Asia (2008).

9. See Daily Mirror (Sri Lanka) (2008).

10. The findings on the relationship between democracy and domestic repression are quite diverse. Davenport (2007a, 2007b) finds that democracies do sometimes resort to violence internally.

11. Adopted from the Correlates of War Project, "State System Membership List" (2011). Available at http://correlatesofwar.org.

CHAPTER 6

1. See Walsh (2009). Available at http://www.guardian.co.uk/world/2009/apr/14/sharia-law-in-pakistans-swat-valley. Accessed on April 28, 2009.

2. See BBC News (2007). Available at http://news.bbc.co.uk/2/hi/uk_news/7078332.stm. Accessed on April 28, 2009.

3. See BBC Monitoring Middle East (2014) for further information on Western support of FSA.

Bibliography

Agence France Presse. 1996. "Missing Kurds Found at PKK Training Camp in Belgium." 23 November.

Agence France Presse. 1999. "Sri Lanka Warns Britain over Tiger Threats." 2 September.

Agence France Presse. 2004. "Dutch Police Raid Kurdish Training Camp." 12 November.

Albright, Joseph. 1985. "Blacks Armed Soon, Predict ANC Chiefs." *Courier-Mail*. 3 September.

Arquilla, John, David Ronfeldt, and Michele Zanini. 1999. "Networks, Netwar, and Information-Age Terrorism." In *Countering the New Terrorism*. Edited by Ian O. Lesser, Bruce Hoffman, John Arquilla, David Ronfeldt, Michele Zanini, and Brian Michael Jenkins, 39–84. Santa Monica, CA: RAND.

Art, Robert J. 2000. "The Political Uses of Force: The Four Functions of Force." In *International Politics: Enduring Concepts and Contemporary Issues*. Edited by Robert J. Art and Robert Jervis, 131–138. New York: Addison Wesley Longman.

Associated Press International. 1997. "Tamil Tigers, from a Rag-Tag Band to a Fighting Force." Associated Press Worldstream, 15 October.

Associated Press International. 1999. "AMMAN: 10 Years." (November 21).

Atzili, Boaz. 2010. "'State Weakness' and 'Vacuum of Power' in Lebanon." *Studies in Conflict and Terrorism* 33(8): 757–782.

Atzili, Boaz, and Wendy Pearlman. 2012. "Triadic Deterrence: Coercing Strength, Beaten by Weakness." *Security Studies* 21(2): 301–335.

Aydin, Aysegul. 2012. *Foreign Powers and Intervention in Armed Conflicts*. Stanford, CA: Stanford University Press.

Aydin, Aysegul, and Patrick M. Regan. 2011. "Networks of Third-Party Interveners and Civil War Duration." *European Journal of International Relations* 18 (June): 573–597.

Azar, Edward E., and Chung-in Moon. 1988. *National Security in the Third World: The Management of Internal and External Threats*. Aldershot, UK: Edward Elgar.

Balch-Lindsay, Dylan, and Andrew J. Enterline. 2000. "Killing Time: The World Politics of Civil War Duration, 1820–1992." *International Studies Quarterly* 44(4): 615–642.

Baldwin, David A., ed. 1993. *Neorealism and Neoliberalism: The Contemporary Debate*. New York: Columbia University Press.

Baloch, Shehzad. 2012. "Will Support US, Nato or Indian Intervention: Brahamdagh Bugti." *The Express Tribune*, 22 February. http://tribune.com.pk/story/340137/will-support-foreign-interventionwhether-by-us-nato-or-india-barahmdagh/ (December 16, 2015).

Bapat, Navin A. 2006. "State Bargaining with Transnational Terrorist Groups." *International Studies Quarterly* 50(2): 215–232.

Bapat, Navin A. 2007. "The Internationalization of Terrorist Campaigns." *Conflict Management and Peace Science* 24(2): 265–280.

Bapat, Navin A. 2012. "Understanding State Sponsorship of Militant Groups." *British Journal of Political Science* 42(1): 1–29.

Barak, Oren. 2003. "Lebanon: Failure, Collapse, and Resuscitation." In *State Failure and State Weakness in a Time of Terror*. Edited by Robert I. Rotberg, 305–339. Washington, DC: Brooking Institution Press.

Barnett, Michael N. 1996. "Identity and Alliances in the Middle East." In *The Culture of National Security: Norms and Identity in World Politics*. Edited by Peter J. Katzenstein, 400–447. New York: Columbia University Press.

Bates, Robert H., Avner Greif, Margaret Levi, and Jean-Laurent Rosenthal, eds. 1998. *Analytic Narratives*. Princeton, NJ: Princeton University Press.

BBC. 1996. "Qom Meeting of Fundamentalist Groups: Lebanon Training Camps to Move to Somalia." BBC Summary of World Broadcasts, 17 March.

BBC. 2007. "Chad: UK Branch of Rebel UFDD Movement Calls Meeting." BBC Worldwide Monitoring, 22 May.

BBC. 2007. "UK Considers Pakistan Aid Package." BBC News, November 5. http://news.bbc.co.uk/2/hi/uk_news/7078332.stm (April 28, 2009).

BBC. 2008. "'Global Onslaught' Severely Affects Tamil Tiger Activities: Sri Lankan Paper." BBC Monitoring South Asia, 2 May.

BBC. 2010. "Experts Warn of Alliance between Al-Qa'idah, Nigeria's Boko Haram." BBC Monitoring Middle East, 15 June.

BBC. 2012. "Waking Up to the War in Balochistan." BBC News, February 29. http://www.bbc.com/news/world-asia-17182978 (December 17, 2015).

BBC. 2014. "Jordan Reportedly Alarmed over Obama Plan to Arm "Moderates" in Syria." BBC Monitoring Middle East, 12 September.

Beck, Nathaniel, Johnathan N. Katz, and Richard Tucker. 1998. "Taking Time Seriously." *American Journal of Political Science* 42(4): 1260–1288.

Berger, Thomas U. 1996. "Norms, Identity, and National Security in Germany and Japan." In *The Culture of National Security: Norms and Identity in World Politics*. Edited by Peter J. Katzenstein, 317–356. New York: Columbia University Press.

Bonner, Raymond. 1998. "Tamil Guerrillas in Sri Lanka: Deadly and Armed to the Teeth." *New York Times*. March 7. http://www.nytimes.com/1998/03/07/world/tamil-guerrillas-in-sri-lanka-deadly-and-armed-to-the-teeth.html?pagewanted=all (August 15, 2008).

Braithwaite, Alex, and Quan Li. 2007. "Transnational Terrorism Hot Spots: Identification and Impact Evaluation." *Conflict Management and Peace Science* 24(4): 281–296.

Brecher, Michael. 1993. *Crises in World Politics: Theory and Reality.* Oxford: Pergamon.

Briggs, Billy. 2006. "Islamic Child of the First Intifada Whose Stated Aim Is to Wipe Nation Off the Map." *The Herald,* January 27. https://www.highbeam.com/doc/1P2-23620731.html (December 16, 2007).

Brodie, Bernard. 1965. *National Security Policy and Economic Stability.* New Haven, CT: Yale University Press.

Brophy-Baermann, Bryan, and John A. C. Conybeare. 1994. "Retaliating against Terrorism: Rational Expectations and the Optimality of Rules vs. Discretion." *American Journal of Political Science* 38(1): 196–210.

Brown, Larisa. 2015. "UK Troops to Train Syrian Army in Fight against IS." *Daily Mail.* 27 March.

Brown, Michael E., ed. 1996. *The International Dimensions of Internal Conflict.* Cambridge, MA: MIT Press.

Buchanan, Allen. 1992. "Self-Determination and the Right to Secede." *Journal of International Affairs* 45(2): 347–365.

Buckley, D. 1993. "Kurds to Hold Hostages for Weeks." *Courier-Mail,* 21 August.

Bueno de Mesquita, Bruce. 2002. "Domestic Politics and International Relations." *International Studies Quarterly* 46(1): 1–9.

Bueno de Mesquita, Bruce, and David Lalman. 1990. "Domestic Opposition and Foreign War." *American Political Science Review* 84(3): 747–765.

Bueno de Mesquita, Bruce, and Randolph M. Siverson. 1995. "War and the Survival of Political Leaders: A Comparative Case Study of Regime Types and Political Accountability." *American Political Science Review* 89(4): 841–855.

Bueno de Mesquita, Bruce, Alastair Smith, Randolph M. Siverson, and James D. Morrow. 2003. *The Logic of Political Survival.* Cambridge, MA: MIT Press.

Bueno de Mesquita, Ethan. 2005. "Conciliation, Counterterrorism, and Patterns of Terrorist Violence." *International Organization* 59(1): 145–176.

Buzan, Barry. 1983. *People, States, and Fear: The National Security Problem in International Relations.* Chapel Hill: University of North Carolina Press.

Buzan, Barry, and George Lawson. 2015. *The Global Transformation: History, Modernity and the Making of International Relations.* Cambridge, UK: Cambridge University Press.

Byman, Daniel L. 2005a. *Deadly Connections: States That Sponsor Terrorism.* Cambridge, UK: Cambridge University Press.

Byman, Daniel L. 2005b. "Passive Sponsors of Terrorism." *Survival* 47(4): 117–144.

Byman, Daniel L. 2005c. *Going to War with the Allies You Have: Allies, Counterinsurgency, and the War on Terrorism.* Carlisle, PA: Strategic Studies Institute, U.S. Army War College.

Byman, Daniel, Peter Chalk, Bruce Hoffman, William Rosenau, and David Brannan. 2001. *Trends in Outside Support for Insurgent Movements.* Santa Monica, CA: RAND.

Byman, Daniel, and Sarah E. Kreps. 2010. "Agents of Destruction? Applying Principal-Agent Analysis to State-Sponsored Terrorism." *International Studies Perspective* 11(1): 1–18.

Campbell, Kurt M., and Michele A. Floumoy. 2001. *To Prevail: An American Strategy for the Campaign against Terrorism.* Washington, DC: Center for Strategic and International Studies.

Carlton, Eric. 1990. *War and Ideology.* London: Routledge.

Carment, David, and Patrick James. 2000. "Explaining Third-Party Intervention in Ethnic Conflict: Theory and Evidence." *Nations and Nationalism* 6: 173–202.

Carment, David, Patrick James, and Zeynep Taydas. 2009 "The Internationalization of Ethnic Conflict: State, Society, and Synthesis." *International Studies Review* 11 (1): 63–86.

Carr, Edward H. 1954. *The Twenty Years' Crisis.* London: Macmillan.

Caverley, Jonathan D. 2014. *Democratic Militarism: Voting, Wealth, and War.* Cambridge: Cambridge University Press.

Cederman, Lars-Erik, Luc Girardin, and Kristian Skrede Gleditsch. 2009. "Ethnonationalist Triads: Assessing the Influence of Kin Groups on Civil Wars." *World Politics* 61(3): 403–437.

Cederman, Lars-Erik, Brian Min, and Andreas Wimmer. 2010. "Ethnic Power Relations Dataset: Version 1 [Computer File]." http://hdl.handle.net/1902.1/11796 .

Cederman, Lars-Eric, Kristian Skrede Gleditsch, Idean Salehyan, and Julian Wucherpfenning. 2013. "Transborder Ethnic Kin and Civil War." *International Organization* 67(2): 389–410.

Center for Defense Information-Terrorism, Military and Security Policy Research Organization. 2002. "In the Spotlight: Al-Gama'a Al-Islamiyya." Center for Defense Information Terrorism Project. December 2, http://www.cdi.org/ terrorism/farc.cfm (January 10, 2009).

Cetinyan, Rupen. 2002. "Ethnic Bargaining in the Shadow of Third-Party Intervention." *International Organization* 56: 645–677.

Chann, Sewell. 2015. "Ninth Person Is Arrested in Belgium Over Paris Attacks." New York Times, December 24. http://www.nytimes.com/2015/12/25/world/europe/paris-attacks-belgium.html?_r=1 (December 30, 2015).

Checkel, Jeffrey T. 1998. "The Constructive Turn in International Relations Theory." *World Politics* 50(2): 324–348.

Chenoweth, Erica. 2010. "Democratic Competition and Terrorist Activity." *Journal of Politics* 72(1): 16–30.

Chiozza, Giacomo. 2002. "Is There a Clash of Civilizations? Evidence from Patterns of International Conflict Involvement, 1946–97." *Journal of Conflict Resolution* 47(3): 251–278.

Clark, David. H. 2001. "Trading Butter for Guns: Domestic Imperatives for Foreign Policy Substitution." *Journal of Conflict Resolution* 45(5): 636–660.

Cleveland, William L. 2004. *A History of the Modern Middle East.* Boulder, CO: Westview.

Cline, Ray S., and Yonah Alexander. 1984. *Terrorism: The Soviet Connection.* New York: Crane and Russak.

Clunan, Anne, and Trinkunas A. Harold, eds. 2010. *Ungoverned Spaces: Alternatives to State Authority in an Era of Softened Sovereignty.* Stanford, CA: Stanford University Press.

Cohen, Stephen P. 2002. "The Nation and the State of Pakistan." *Washington Quarterly* 25(3): 109–122.

Colley, Linda. 1992. *Britons: Forging the Nation, 1707–1837.* New Haven, CT: Yale University Press.

Collins, Stephen. D. 2004. "Dissuading State Support of Terrorism: Strikes or Sanctions? (An Analysis of Dissuasion Measures Employed Against Libya)." *Studies in Conflict & Terrorism* 27(1): 1–18.

Conrad, Justin. 2011. "Interstate Rivalry and Terrorism: An Unprobed Link." *Journal of Conflict Resolution* 55 (4): 529–555.

Correlates of War Project. 2011. "State System Membership List, v2011." http://correlatesofwar. org (Mach 10, 2016).

Crenshaw, Martha. 1990. "Is International Terrorism Primarily State-Sponsored?" In *International Terrorism: Characteristics, Causes, and Controls*. Edited by Charles W. Kegley, 163–169. New York: St. Martin's.

Crenshaw, Martha. 2001. "Democracy, Commitment Problems and Managing Ethnic Violence: The Case of India and Sri Lanka." In *The Democratic Experience and Political Violence*. Edited by David C. Rapoport and Leonard Weinberg, 135–160. London: Frank Cass.

Cunningham, David. 2010. "Blocking Resolution: How External States Can Prolong Civil War." *Journal of Peace Research* 47(2): 115–127.

Cunningham, David E., Kristian Skrede Gleditsch, and Idean Salehyan. 2009a. "Non-state Actor Data: Version 3.3 [Computer File]." http://privatewww.essex.ac.uk/~ksg/eacd.html (February 10, 2016).

Cunningham, David E., Kristian Skrede Gleditsch, and Idean Salehyan. 2009b. "It Takes Two: A Dyadic Analysis of Civil War Duration and Outcome." *Journal of Conflict Resolution* 53(4): 570–597.

Daily Mirror. 2008. "Targeting the LTTE's Global Network." Daily Mirror (Sri Lanka). 3 May.

Dakroub, Hussein. 1995. "In Lebanon, Fundamentalists Change Tactics as Influence Wanes." *Associated Press International*. October 30.

Dassel, Kurt, and Eric Reinhardt. 1999. "Domestic Strife and the Initiation of Violence at Home and Abroad." *American Journal of Political Science* 43(1): 56–85.

Davenport, Christian. 1995. "Multi-dimensional Threat Perception and State Repression: An Inquiry into Why States Apply Negative Sanctions." *American Journal of Political Science* 39(3): 683–713.

Davenport, Christian. 2007a. "State Repression and Political Order." *Annual Review of Political Science* 10: 1–23.

Davenport, Christian. 2007b. "State Repression and Tyrannical Peace." *Journal of Peace Research* 44(4): 485–504.

Davenport, Christian, and David A. Armstrong II. 2004. "Democracy and the Violation of Human Rights: A Statistical Analysis from 1976 to 1996." *American Journal of Political Science* 48(3): 538–554.

Davis, David R., and Will H. Moore. 1997. "Ethnicity Matters: Transnational Ethnic Alliances and Foreign Policy Behavior." *International Studies Quarterly* 41: 171–184.

Debos, Marielle. 2011. "Living by the Gun in Chad: Armed Violence as a Practical Occupation." *Journal of Modern African Studies* 49(3): 409–428.

Deutsch, Karl W. 1964. "External Involvement in Internal Wars." In *Internal War: Problems and Approaches*. Edited by Harry Eckstein, 100–110. New York: Free Press of Glencoe.

Deutsche Presse-Agentur. 1997. "Angolan Tanks and Troops Enter Congo's Oil Town Pointe Noir." 15 October.

De Waal, Alex. 2006. "Chad in the Firing Line." *Index on Censorship* 35(1): 58–65.

Dowden, Richard. 1992. "Chad Looks to Paris as Habre Returns in Force." *The Independent*. January 4.

Encarnación, Omar G. 2007. "Democracy and Dirty Wars in Spain." *Human Rights Quarterly*, 29(4): 950–972.

Enders, Walter, and Todd Sandler. 2006. "Distribution of Transnational Terrorism among Countries by Income Class and Geography after 9/11." *International Studies Quarterly* 50(2): 367–393.

Eubank, William L., and Leonard Weinberg. 1994. "Does Democracy Encourage Terrorism?" *Terrorism and Political Violence* 6(4): 417–443.

Eubank, William L., and Leonard Weinberg. 1998. "Terrorism and Democracy: What Recent Events Disclose." *Terrorism and Political Violence* 10(1): 108–118.

Eubank, William L., and Leonard Weinberg. 2001. "Terrorism and Democracy: Perpetrators and Victims." *Terrorism and Political Violence* 13(1): 155–164.

Eyerman, Joe. 1998. "Terrorism and Democratic States: Soft Targets or Accessible Systems." *International Interactions* 24(2): 151–170.

Farah, Douglas. 2000. "Liberia Reportedly Arming Guerrillas: Rebel Control of Sierra Leone Diamond-Mining Areas Crucial to Monrovia, Sources Say." *Washington Post*, June 18. http://www.highbeam.com/doc/1P2-519818.html. (December 16, 2015).

Farah, Douglas. 2001. "Commander Poison Sheds Name, and His Taste for War." *Washington Post*, June 4. https://www.washingtonpost.com/archive/politics/2001/06/04/commander-poison-sheds-name-and-his-taste-for-war/503741f7-402c-49b4-8e2a-8605025d676a/. (December 14, 2015).

Fearon, James D. 1994. "Domestic Political Audiences and the Escalation of International Disputes." *American Political Science Review* 88: 577–599.

Fearon, James D. 1995. "Rationalist Explanations for War." *International Organization* 49(3): 379–414.

Fearon, James D. 1997. "Signaling Foreign Policy Interests: Tying Hands versus Sinking Costs." *Journal of Conflict Resolution* 41(1): 68–90.

Fearon, James D., and David D. Laitin. 2000. "Violence and the Social Construction of Ethnic Identity." *International Organization* 54(4): 845–877.

Fearon, James D., and David D. Laitin. 2003. "Ethnicity, Insurgency, and Civil War." *American Political Science Review* 97(1): 75–90.

Fearon, James D., Kimuli Kasara, and David D. Laitin. 2007. "Ethnic Minority Rule and Civil War Onset." *American Political Science Review* 101(1): 187–193.

Findley, Michael G., and Tze Kwang Teo. 2006. "Rethinking Third-Party Interventions into Civil Wars: An Actor-Centric Approach." *The Journal of Politics* 68 (4): 828–837.

Finnemore, Martha. 1993. "International Organizations as Teachers of Norms: The United Nations Educational, Scientific, and Cultural Organization and Science Policy." *International Organization* 47(4): 565–597.

Finnemore, Martha. 1996. "Review: Norms, Culture, and World Politics; Insights from Sociology's Institutionalism." *International Organization* 50(2): 325–347.

Finnemore, Martha, and Kathryn Sikkink. 2001. "Taking Stock: The Constructivist Research Program in International Relations and Comparative Politics." *Annual Review of Political Science* 4(1): 391–416.

Fisher, Marc. 1993. "Turkish Businesses, Offices Hit as Kurds Attack in 29 Cities." *Washington Post*. June 25. https://www.highbeam.com/doc/1P2-952870.html (December 14, 2015).

Fukuyama, Francis. 1992. *The End of History and the Last Man*. London: Hamish Hamilton.

Fukuyama, Francis. 2004. *State-Building: Governance and World Order in the 21st Century*. Ithaca, NY: Cornell University Press.

Gall, Carlotta. 2011. "Pakistan's Bitter, Little-Known Ethnic Rebellion." *New York Times*, August 23. http://www.nytimes.com/2011/08/24/world/asia/24baluch.html?_r=0. (December 15, 2015).

Gambill, Gary. 2002. "Sponsoring Terrorism: Syria and the PFLP-GC." *Middle East Intelligence Bulletin* 4(9).

Ganley, Elaine. 2013. "World Powers to Meet on Syrian Rebel Demands." *Associated Press*. 19 June.

Garfinkle, Adam. 2005. "A Conversation with Condoleezza Rice." *American Interest* 1(1): 47–50.

Gasiorowski, Mark J. 1988. "Regime Legitimacy and National Security: The Case of Pahlavi Iran." In *National Security in the Third World: The Management of Internal and External Threats*. Edited by Edward E. Azar and Chung-in Moon, 227–250. Aldershot, UK: Edward Elgar.

Geertz, Clifford. 1963. *Agricultural Involution: The Process of Ecological Change in Indonesia*. Chicago: University of Chicago Press.

Gelpi, Christopher F. 1997. "Democratic Diversions: Governmental Structure and the Externalization of Domestic Conflict." *Journal of Conflict Resolution* 41(2): 255–282.

Gilmour, Anna. 2011a. "Ecuadorian Police Detain Suspected FARC Arms Smugglers." *IHS Global Insight*, 4 March.

Gilmour, Anna. 2011b. "Ecuador Activates Two Military Encampments on Colombian Border." *IHS Global Insight*, 31 January.

Glaser, Charles L. 2000. "The Causes and Consequences of Arms Races." *Annual Review of Political Science* 3: 251–276.

Gleditsch, Kristian S., and Michael D. Ward. 2001. "Measuring Space: A Minimum Distance Database and Applications to International Studies." *Journal of Peace Research* 38(6): 739–758.

Gleditsch, Nils Peter, Peter Wallensteen, Mikael Eriksson, Margareta Sollenberg, and Havard Strand. 2002. "Armed Conflict, 1946–2001: A New Dataset." *Journal of Peace Research* 39(5): 625–637.

Gleditsch, Kristian Skrede. 2007. "Transnational Dimensions of Civil War." *Journal of Peace Research* 44(3): 293–309

Gleditsch, Kristian Skrede, and Kyle Beardsley. 2004. "Nosy Neighbors: Third-Party Actors in Central American Conflicts." *Journal of Conflict Resolution* 48(3): 379–402.

Gleditsch, Kristian Skrede, Idean Salehyan, and Kenneth A. Schultz. 2008. "Fighting at Home, Fighting Abroad: How Civil Wars Lead to International Disputes." *Journal of Conflict Resolution* 52(4): 479–506.

Goertz, G., and P. F. Diehl. 1995. "The Initiation and Termination of Enduring Rivalries: The Impact of Political Shocks." *American Journal of Political Science* 39(1): 30–52.

Golani, Motti. 1995. "The Historical Place of the Czech-Egyptian Arms Deal, Fall 1955." *Middle Eastern Studies* 31(4): 803–827.

Goldstein, Judith, and Robert O. Keohane. 1993. "Ideas and Foreign Policy: An Analytical Framework." In *Ideas and Foreign Policy: Beliefs, Institutions, and Political Change*. Edited by Judith Goldstein and Robert O. Keohane, 3–30. Ithaca, NY: Cornell University Press.

Goldstein, Judith, Miles Kahler, Robert O Keohane, and Anne-Marie Slaughter, eds. 2000. *Legalization and World Politics*. Cambridge, MA: MIT Press.

Gulick, Edward V. 1955. *Europe's Classical Balance of Power: A Case History of the Theory and Practice of One of the Great Concepts of European Statecraft*. Ithaca, NY: Cornell University Press.

Gunter, M. Michael. 2004. "The Kurdish Question in Perspective." *World Affairs* 166(4): 197–205.

Gurr, Tedd Robert. 1970. *Why Men Rebel*. Princeton, NJ: Princeton University Press.

Haaretz. 2015. "Islamic Jihad." Haaretz | Israel News, August 19. http://www.haaretz.com/misc/tags/Islamic%20Jihad-1.477032. (December 17, 2015).

Haas, Mark L. 2005. *The Ideological Origins of Great Power Politics, 1789–1989*. Ithaca, NY: Cornell University Press.

Hardin, Russell. 1995. *One for All: The Logic of Group Conflict*. Princeton, NJ: Princeton University Press.

Harik, Judith Palmer. 2004. *Hezbollah: The Changing Face of Terrorism*. London: I. B. Tauris.

Hartzell, Caroline, Matthew Hoddie, and Donald Rothchild. 2001. "Stabilizing the Peace After Civil War: An Investigation of Some Key Variables." *International Organization* 55(1): 183–208.

Hastings, Justin V. 2010. *No Man's Land: Globalization, Territory, and Clandestine Groups in Southeast Asia*. Ithaca, NY: Cornell University Press.

Henderson, Errol A. 1997. "Culture or Contiguity: Ethnic Conflict, the Similarity of States, and the Onset of War, 1820–1989." *Journal of Conflict Resolution* 41(5): 649–668.

Henderson, Errol A., and Richard Tucker. 2001. "Clear and Present Strangers: The Clash of Civilizations and International Conflict." *International Studies Quarterly* 45(2): 317–338.

Heraclides, Alexis. 1992. "Secession, Self-Determination and Nonintervention: In Quest of a Normative Symbiosis." *Journal of International Affairs* 45(2): 399–420.

Heraclides, Alexis. 1997. "Ethnicity, Secessionist Conflict and the International Society: Towards Normative Paradigm Shift." *Nations and Nationalism* 3(4): 493–520.

Herbst, Jeffrey. 1989. "The Creation and Maintenance of National Boundaries in Africa." *International Organization* 43(4): 673–692.

Hoffman, Bruce. 1998. *Inside Terrorism*. New York: Columbia University Press.

Hooper, Simon. 2007. "PKK's decades of violent struggle." *CNN International Edition*, October 11. http://edition.cnn.com/2007/WORLD/europe/10/10/pkk.profile/index.html (June 2, 2015).

Holsti, Kalevi J. 1996. *The State, War and the State of War*. Cambridge, UK: Cambridge University Press.

Hopf, Ted. 2002. *Social Construction of International Politics: Identities and Foreign Policies, Moscow 1955–1999*. Ithaca, NY: Cornell University Press.

Horstmann, Alexander. 2011. "Sacred Spaces of Karen Refugees and Humanitarian Aid Across the Thailand-Burma Border." *ASEAS – Austrian Journal of South-East Asian Studies* 4(2): 254–272.

Högbladh, Stina, Thérèse Pettersson, and Lotta Themnér. 2011. "External Support in Armed Conflict, 1975–2009. Presenting New Data." Presented at the 52nd Annual International Studies Association Convention, Montreal.

Huband, Mark. 1992. "Chadian Troops Back Down after Threat to Storm Palace." *The Guardian*, 24 April.

Human Rights Watch . 2013. "The Plain of the Dead: The Chad of Hissène Habré, 1982–1990." http://www.hrw.org/sites/default/files/reports/chad1213summary_english.pdf (December 17, 2015).

Huntington, Samuel P. 1993. "The Clash of Civilizations?" *Foreign Affairs* 72(3): 22–49.

Huntington, Samuel P. 1996. *The Clash of Civilizations and the Remaking of World Order.* New York: Simon & Schuster.

Hurst, Grant. 2012. "Ecuadorian Police Uncover Suspected Arsenal of Colombian FARC Guerrillas." *IHS Global Insight*, 2 August.

Huth, Paul K. 1988. *Extended Deterrence and the Prevention of War.* New Haven, CT: Yale University Press.

Huth, Paul K., and Bruce Russett. 1993. "General Deterrence between Enduring Rivals: Testing Three Competing Models." *American Political Science Review* 87(1): 61–73.

Ikenberry, John G. 2000. "America's Liberal Grand Strategy: Democracy and National Security in the Post-war Era." In *American Democracy Promotion: Impulses, Strategies, and Impacts.* Edited by Michael Cox, John G. Ikenberry, and Takashi Inogochi, 103–126. Oxford: Oxford University Press.

Ikenberry, G. John. 2006. *Liberal Order and Imperial Ambition: Essays on American Power and International Order.* London: Polity Press.

Inglehart, Ronald. 1990. *Culture Shift in Advanced Industrial Society.* Princeton, NJ: Princeton University Press.

Inglehart, Ronald. 1997. *Modernization and Postmodernization: Cultural, Economic, and Political Change in 43 Societies.* Princeton, NJ: Princeton University Press.

Jackman, Robert W. 1993. *Power without Force: The Political Capacity of Nation-States.* Ann Arbor: University of Michigan Press.

Jackson, Robert H. 1996. *Quasi-States: Sovereignty, International Relations and the Third World.* New York: Cambridge University Press.

Jayamaha, Dilshika. 2000. "AP Photos COL101-102." *Associated Press Worldstream*, 11 December.

Jepperson, Ronald L., Alexander Wendt, and Peter J. Katzenstein. 1996. "Norms, Identity, and Culture in National Security." In *The Culture of National Security: Norms and Identity in World Politics.* Edited by Peter J. Katzenstein, 33–76. New York: Columbia University Press.

Jervis, Robert. 1989. "Rational Deterrence: Theory and Evidence." *World Politics* 41(2): 183–207.

Kalyvas, Stathis N., and Laia Balcells. 2010. "International System and Technologies of Rebellion: How the End of Cold War Shaped Internal Conflict." *American Political Science Review* 104(3): 415–429.

Karsh, Efraim. 1987–1988. "Military Power and Foreign Policy Goals: The Iran-Iraq War Revisited." *International Affairs* 64(1): 83–95.

Katzenstein, Peter, ed. 1996. *The Culture of National Security: Norms and Identity in World Politics.* New York: Columbia University Press.

Kegley, Charles W., ed. 1990. *International Terrorism: Characteristics, Causes, and Controls.* New York: St. Martin's.

Khan, Adeel. 2009. "Renewed Ethnonationalist Insurgency in Balochistan, Pakistan: The Militarized State and Continuing Economic Deprivation." *Asian Survey* 49(6): 1071–1091.

Klotz, Audie, and Cecelia Lynch. 2007. *Strategies for Research in Constructivist International Relations.* Armonk, NY: M. E. Sharpe.

Krasner, Stephen D., and Carlos Pascual. 2005. "Addressing State Failure." *Foreign Affairs* 84(4): 153–163.

Kreutz, Joakim. 2010. "How and When Armed Conflicts End: Introducing the UCDP Conflict Termination Dataset." *Journal of Peace Research* 47(2): 243–250.

Kubalkova, Vendulka, Nicholas Onuf, and Paul Kowert. 1998. "Constructing Constructivism." In *International Relations in a Constructed World*. Edited by Vendulka Kubalkova, Nicholas Onuf, and Paul A. Kowert, 3–21. Armonk, NY: M. E. Sharpe.

Lake, David A., and Robert Powell. 1999. "International Relations: A Strategic-Choice Approach." In *Strategic Choice and International Relations*. Dited by David. A. Lake and Robert Powell, 3–20. Princeton, NJ: Princeton University Press.

Lamborn, Alan C. 1983. "Power and the Politics of Extraction." *International Studies Quarterly* 27(2): 125–146.

Lebow, Richard Ned. 2008. *A Cultural Tehory of International Relations*. Cambridge, UK: Cambridge University Press.

Lebow, Richard Ned. 2010. *Why Nations Fight*. Cambridge, UK: Cambridge University Press.

Leeds, Brett Ashley. 2005. "Alliance Treaty Obligations and Provisions Codebook (ATOP): Version 3." http://atop.rice.edu/download/ATOPcdbk.pdf (June 20, 2015).

Leeds, Brett Ashley, Jeffrey M. Ritter, Sara McLaughlin Mitchell, and Andrew G. Long. 2002. "Alliance Treaty Obligations and Provisions, 1815–1944." *International Interactions* 28: 237–260.

Legro, Jeffrey W. 1997. "Which Norms Matter? Revisiting the 'Failure' of Internationalism." *International Organization* 51(1): 31–64.

Lemke, Douglas, and William Reed. 2001. "The Relevance of Politically Relevant Dyads." *Journal of Conflict Resolution* 45(1): 126–144.

Lesser, Ian O. 1999. "Countering the New Terrorism: Implications for Strategy." In *Countering the New Terrorism*. Edited by Ian O. Lesser, Bruce Hoffman, John Arquillaet, David Ronfeldt, Michele Zanini, and Brian Michael Jenkins, 85–144. Santa Monica, CA: RAND.

Lesser, Ian O., Bruce Hoffman, John Arquilla, David Ronfeldt, Michele Zanini, and Brian Michael Jerkins. 1999. *Countering the New Terrorism*. Santa Monica, CA: RAND.

Levitt, Matthew, and Dennis Ross. 2007. *Hamas: Politics, Charity, and Terrorism in the Service of Jihad*. New Haven, CT: Yale University Press.

Levy, Jack S. 1988. "Domestic Politics and War." *Journal of Interdisciplinary History* 18(4): 653–673.

Levy, Jack. S. 1989. "The Diversionary Theory of War: A Critique." In *Handbook of War Studies*. Edited by Manus I. Midlarsky, 259–288. Boston: Unwin Hyman.

Levy, Jack S., and Lily I. Vakili. 1992. "Diversionary Action by Authoritarian Regimes: Argentina in the Falkalnds / Malvinas Case." In *Internationalization of Communal Strife*. Edited by Manus. I. Midlarsky, 118–149. New York: Routledge.

Levy, Jack S., and William F. MabeJr. 2004. "Politically Motivated Opposition to War." *International Studies Review* 6(4): 65–83.

Lewis, Neil A. 1987. "Washington Talk: Working Profile; Chester Crocker: Inside, Making Policy on Africa." *New York Times*, June 9. http://www.nytimes.com/1987/06/09/us/washington-talk-working-profile-chester-crocker-inside-making-policy-on-africa.html (August 28, 2007).

Li, Quan. 2005. "Does Democracy Promote or Reduce Transnational Terrorist Incidents?" Journal of Conflict Resolution 49 (2): 278–97.

Li, Quan, and Drew Schaub. 2004. "Economic Globalization and Transnational Terrorist Incidents: A Pooled Time Series Analysis." *Journal of Conflict Resolution* 48(2): 230–258.,

Linnee, Susan. 1985. "TODAY'S FOCUS: Basque Separatists Pose Problems for Governing Socialists." *Associated Press*, 6 August.

Little, Dougles. 1985. *Malevolent Neutrality: The United States, Great Britain and the Origins of the Spanish Civil War*. Ithaca, NY: Cornell University Press.

Little, Richard. 2013. "Intervention and Non-intervention in International Society: Britain's Responses to the American and Spanish Civil Wars." *Review of International Studies* 39 (5): 1111–1129.

Long, J. Scott, and Jeremy Freese. 2006. *Regression Models for Categorical Dependent Variables Using Stata*. College Station, TX: Stata.

Lust-Okar, Ellen. 2005. *Structuring Conflict in the Arab World: Incumbents, Opponents, and Institutions*. Cambridge, UK: Cambridge University Press.

Machiavelli, Niccolò. 1532/2005. *The Prince*. New York: Oxford University Press.

Mackinlay, John. 2000. "Defining Warlords." In *Peacekeeping and Conflict Resolution*. Edited by Tom Woodhouse and Oliver Ramsbotham, 48–63. London: Frank Cass.

Mann, Joseph. 2007. "The Conflict with Israel according to Neo-Ba'ath Doctrine." *Israel Affairs* 13(1): 116–130.

Maoz, Zeev. 1983. "Resolve, Capabilities, and the Outcome of Interstate Disputes, 1816–1976." *Journal of Conflict Resolution* 27(2): 195–229.

Maoz, Zeev. 1990. *National Choices and International Processes*. Cambridge, UK: Cambridge University Press.

Maoz, Zeev. 1996. *Domestic Sources of Global Change*. Ann Arbor: University of Michigan Press.

Maoz, Zeev. 2006. *Defending the Holy Land: A Critical Analysis of Israel's Security and Foreign Policy*. Ann Arbor: University of Michigan Press.

Maoz, Zeev. 2007. "The Formation of International Networks: How Cooperation Emerges from Conflict." Presented at the annual meeting of the American Political Science Association, Chicago. http://citation.allacademic.com/meta/p209115_index.html (January 12, 2016).

Maoz, Zeev, and Bruce Russett. 1993. "Normative and Structural Causes of Democratic Peace, 1946-1986." *American Political Science Review* 87(3): 624–638.

Maoz, Zeev, Lesley G. Terris, Ranan D. Kuperman, and Ilan Talmud. 2007. "What Is the Enemy of My Enemy? Causes and Consequences of Imbalanced International Relations, 1816–2001." *Journal of Politics* 69(1): 100–115.

Maoz, Zeev, and Belgin San-Akca. 2012. "Rivalry and State Support of Non-state Armed Groups (NAGs), 1946–2001." *International Studies Quarterly* 56(4): 720–734.

Maoz, Zeev, and Errol A. Henderson. 2013. "The World Religion Dataset, 1945–2010: Logic, Estimates, and Trends." *International Interactions* 39(3): 265–291. http://www.correlatesofwar.org/data-sets/world-religion-data (January 7, 2016).

Marquis, Christopher. 2004. "Bush Imposes Sanctions on Syria, Citing Ties to Terrorism." *New York Times*, May 12. http://www.nytimes.com/2004/05/12/world/bush-imposes-sanctions-on-syria-citing-ties-to-terrorism.html?_r=0 (December 9, 2015).

Marshall, Monty G., and Keith Jaggers. 2002. "Polity IV Project: Political Regime Characteristics and Transitions, 1800–2007." http://www.systemicpeace.org/polity/polity4.html (November 4, 2015).

Marshall Monty G., Ted Robert Gurr, and Barbara Harff. 2015. "Political Instability Task Force: State Failure Problem Set, 1955–2014." Vienna, VA: Societal-Systems Research. http://www.systemicpeace.org/inscrdata.html (January 24, 2016).

Mastanduno, Michael, David A. Lake, and G. John Ikenberry. 1989. "Toward a Realist Theory of State Action." *International Studies Quarterly* 33(4): 457–474.

Matfess, Hilary. 2015. "Nigeria's Oil Curse." *Al Jazeera America*, November 25. http://america.aljazeera.com/opinions/2015/11/nigerias-oil-curse.html (December 14, 2015).

McBeth, John. 2003. "A Futile Fight." *Far Eastern Economic Review* 166(22): 16.

McElroy, Claudia. 1998. "Dapper Islamist Cuts Revolutionary Cord." *The Guardian Foreign Page*, 14 April.

McLean, Phillip. 2002. "Colombia: Failed, Failing, or Just Weak?" *Washington Quarterly* 25(3): 123–134.

Mearsheimer, John J. 1983. *Conventional Deterrence*. Ithaca, NY: Cornell University Press.

Mearsheimer, John J. 1994. "The False Promise of International Institutions." *International Security* 19(3): 5–49.

Micholus, Edward F., et al. 2007. "International Terrorism: Attributes of Terrorist Events (ITERATE) Data." http://library.duke.edu/data/collections/iterate.html (February 10, 2016).

Middle East Research and Information Project. 1974. "Repression in Iran." *Merip Reports* 25 (Feb): 18–19.

Middle East Research and Information Project. 1975. "The Kurds Trust a Bad Ally" *Merip Reports* 38 (Jun): 25–26.

Middle East Research and Information Project. 1978. "Documents: US Arms Sales to Iran." *Merip Reports* 71 (Oct): 22–23.

Mideast Mirror. 1993. "Official Account of the Arrest of Arab American Pair as Hamas Agent-Couriers." 1 February.

Miles, William F. S. 1995. "Tragic Tradeoffs: Democracy and Security in Chad." *Journal of Modern African Studies* 33(1): 53–65.

Minorities at Risk Project (MAR). 2005. "Minorities at Risk Dataset." College Park, MD: Center for International Development and Conflict Management. Retrieved from http://www.cidcm.umd.edu/mar/ (August 26, 2008).

Mintz, Alex. 1989. "Guns versus Butter: A Disaggregated Analysis." *American Political Science Review* 83(4): 1285–1293.

Missbach, Antje. 2013. "The Waxing and Waning of the Acehnese Diaspora's Long-Distance Politics." *Modern Asian Studies* 47(3): 1055–1082.

Mitchell, Charlet. 1981. "African National Congress Guerrillas Winning Propaganda War." *United Press International*. August 11.

Moghadam, Tanaz. 2008. "Revitalizing Universal Jurisdiction: Lessons from Hybrid Tribunals Applied to the Case of Hissene Habre." *Columbia Human Rights Law Review*. Spring, 2008.

Moore, John Norton. 1969. "The Control of Foreign Intervention in Internal Conflict." *Virginia Journal of International Law* 9: 209–342.

Morgan, Acher. 1985. "Basque Demands Met but Terrorism Could Go on Foreever." *Globe and Mail*, April 13.

Morgan, T. Clifton, and Kenneth N. Bickers. 1992. "Domestic Discontent and the External Use of Force." *Journal of Conflict Resolution* 36(1): 25–52.

Morgenthau, Hans J. 1959. "The Nature and Limits of a Theory of International Relations." In *Theoretical Aspects of International Relations*. Edited by William T. R. Fox. Notre Dame, IN: University of Notre Dame Press.

Morgenthau, Hans J. 1963. *Politics among Nations: The Struggle for Power and Peace*. New York: Alfred A. Knopf.

Morgenthau, Hans J. 1967. "To Intervene or Not to Intervene." *Foreign Affairs* 45(3): 425–436.

Morrow, James D. 1985. "A Continuous Outcome Expected Utility Theory of War." *Journal of Conflict Resolution* 29: 473–502.

Morrow, James D. 1989. "Capabilities, Uncertainty, and Resolve: A Limited Information Model of Crisis Bargaining." *American Journal of Political Science* 33: 941–972.

Mutawi, Samir A. 2002. *Jordan in the 1967 War.* Cambridge, UK: Cambridge University Press.

Nadarajah, Suthaharan, and Dhananjayan Sriskandarajah. 2005. "Liberation Struggle or Terrorism? The Politics of Naming the LTTE." *Third World Quarterly* 26(1): 87–100.

National Center for the Study of Terrorism and Responses to Terrorism (START). 2013. "Global Terrorism Database." http://www.start.umd.edu/start/ (May 12, 2015).

Nau, Henry. 2000. "America's Identity, Democracy Promotion and National Interests: Beyond Realism, Beyond Idealism." In *American Democracy Promotion: Impulses, Strategies, and Impacts.* Edited by Michael Cox, G. John Ikenberry, and Takashi Inogochi, 127–148. Oxford: Oxford University Press.

New York Times. 1972a. "Arab Sources Say USSR Has Recently Begun to Supply Weapons." 18 October.

New York Times. 1972b. "Highly Placed Pro-commando Sources Say on Sept. 21 That Recent Shipment of Soviet Weapons. . . .". 21 September.

Nincic, Miroslav. 1982. "Understanding International Conflict: Some Theoretical Gaps." *Journal of Peace Research* 19(1): 49–60.

Nincic, Miroslav. 2005. *Renegade Regimes: Confronting Deviant Behaviour in World Politics.* New York: Columbia University Press.

Olson, Robert. 1973. "Al-Fatah in Turkey: Its Influence on the March 12 Coup." *Middle East Studies* 9(2): 197–205.

Onapajo, Hakeem, Ufo Okeke Uzodike, and Ayo Whetho. 2012. "Boko Haram Terrorism in Nigeria: The International Dimension." *South African Journal of International Affairs* 19(3): 337–357.

O'Neill, B. E. (1980). "Insurgency: A Framework for Analysis." In *Insurgency in the Modern World.* Edited by Bard E. O'Neill, W. R. Heaton and D. J. Alberts. Boulder, Colorado: Westview Press.

Onishi, Norimitsu. 1998. "Congo Gets More Help in Africa in Rebel War." *New York Times,* August 23. http://www.nytimes.com/1998/08/23/world/congo-gets-more-help-in-africa-in-rebel-war.html (July 20, 2007).

Oren, Michael B. 2002. *Six Days of War: June 1967 and the Making of the Modern Middle East.* New York: Oxford University Press.

Orobator, S. E. 1984. "Civil Strife and International Involvement: The Case of Chad, 1964–1983." *Africa: Rivista trimestrale di studi e documentazione dell'Istituto Italiano per l'Africa e l'Oriente* 39(2): 300–316.

Owen, John M., IV. 2010. *Clash of Ideas in World Politic: Transnational Networks, States, and Regime Change, 1510–2010.* Princeton, NJ: Princeton University Press.

Patrick, Steward M. 2006. "Weak States and Global Threats: Fact or Fiction?" *Washington Quarterly* 29(2): 27–53.

Perlmutter, Amos. 1981. "A Palestinian Entity?" *International Security* 5(4): 103–116.

Perry, A. 2006. "How Sri Lanka's Rebels Build a Suicide Bomber." *Time,* May 12. http://content.time.com/time/world/article/0,8599,1193862,00.html (November 4, 2015).

Pettersson, Thérése, and Peter Wallensteen. 2015. "Armed Conflicts, 1946–2014." *Journal of Peace Research* 52(4): 536–550.

Piazza, James A. 2007. "Draining the Swamp: Democracy Promotion, State Failure, and Terrorism in 19 Middle Eastern Countries." *Studies in Conflict & Terrorism* 30(6): 521–539.

Posen, Barry R. 2001. "The Struggle against Terrorism: Grand Strategy, Strategy, and Tactics." *International Security* 26(3): 39–55.

Powell, Robert. 1993. "Guns, Butter, and Anarchy." *American Political Science Review* 87(1): 115–132.

Putnam, Robert D. 1988. "Diplomacy and Domestic Politics: The Logic of Two-Level Games." *International Organization* 42(3): 427–460.

Putnam, Robert D. 1993. "The Prosperous Community: Social Capital and Public Life." *The American Prospect* 4(13): 35–42.

Ramos, Jennifer M. 2013. *Changing Norms through Actions: The Evolution of Sovereignty.* Oxford: Oxford University Press.

Rapoport, David C. 1984. "Fear and Trembling: Terrorism in Three Religious Traditions." *American Political Science Review* 78(3): 658–677.

Regan, Patrick M. 1996. "Conditions of Successful Third-Party Intervention in Intrastate Conflicts." *Journal of Conflict Resolution* 40 (2): 336–359.

Regan, Patrick. 1998. "Choosing to Intervene: Outside Interventions in Internal Conflicts." *The Journal of Politics* 60 (3): 754–779.

Regan, Patrick M. 2000. *Civil Wars and Foreign Powers: Outside Intervention in Intrastate Conflict.* Ann Arbor: University of Michigan Press.

Regan, Patrick M. 2002. "Third-Party Interventions and the Duration of Intrastate Conflicts." *Journal of Conflict Resolution* 46(1): 55–73.

Regan, Patrick M., and Aysegul Aydin. 2006. "Diplomacy and Other Forms of Intervention in Civil War." *Journal of Conflict Resolution* 50(5): 736–756.

Regan, Patrick M., Richard Frank, and Aysegul Aydin. 2009. "Diplomatic Interventions and Civil Wars: A New Dataset." *Journal of Peace Research* 46(1): 135–146.

Reiter, Dan. 1996. *Crucible of Beliefs: Learning, Alliances, and World Wars.* Ithaca, NY: Cornell University Press.

Reno, William. 1999. *Warlord Politics and African States.* London: Lynne Rienner.

Rice, Condoleezza. 2008. "Rethinking the National Interest." *Foreign Affairs* 87(4): 2–26.

Risse, Thomas, and Stephen C. Ropp. 1999. "International Human Rights Norms and Domestic Change: Conclusions." In *The Power of Human Rights: International Norms and Domestic Change.* Edited by Thomas Risse, Stephen C. Ropp, and Kathryn Sikkink, 234–278. New York: Cambridge University Press.

Risse, Thomas, and Kathryn Sikkink. 1999. "The Socialization of International Human Rights Norms into Domestic Practices: Introduction." In *The Power of Human Rights: International Norms and Domestic Change.* Edited by Thomas Risse, Stephen C. Ropp, and Kathryn Sikkink, 1–38. New York: Cambridge University Press.

Rosecrance, Richard N. 1963. *Action and Reaction in World Politics.* Boston: Little, Brown.

Rotberg, Robert I. 2002. "The New Nature of Nation-State Failure." *Washington Quarterly* 25(3): 85–96.

Rotberg, Robert I. 2003. "Failed States, Collapsed States, Weak States: Causes and Indicators." In *State Failure and State Weakness in a Time of Terror.* Edited by Robert. I. Rotberg, 1–28. Cambridge, MA: World Peace Foundation.

Rothchild, Donald. 2002. "The Effects of State Crisis on African Interstate Relations (and Comparisons with Post-Soviet Eurasia)." In *Beyond State Crisis? Postcolonial Africa and Post-Soviet Eurasia in Comparative Perspective*. Edited by Mark R. Beissinger and Crawford Young, 189–217. Washington, DC: Woodraw Wilson Center Press.

Rupert, James. 2000. "In Freetown, Graham Greene's Hotel Checks Out." *Washington Post*, July 10. https://www.highbeam.com/doc/1P2-536921.html (December 13, 2015).

Russett, Bruce M., John R. Oneal, and Michaelene Cox. 2000. "Clash of Civilizations, or Realism and Liberalism Déja Vu? Some Evidence." *Journal of Peace Research* 37(5): 583–608.

Sagan, Scott. 1989. *Moving Targets: Nuclear Strategy and National Security*. Princeton, NJ: Princeton University Press.

Saideman, Stephen M. 1997. "Explaining the International Relations of Secessionist Conflicts: Vulnerability versus Ethnic Ties." *International Organization* 51(4): 721–753.

Saideman, Stephen M. 2001. *The Ties That Divide: Ethnic Politics, Foreign Policy, and International Conflict*. New York: Columbia University Press.

Saideman, Stephen M. 2002. "Discrimination in International Relations: Analyzing External Support for Ethnic Groups." *Journal of Peace Research* 39(1): 27–50.

Saideman, Stephen M. and Erin K. Jenne. 1992. "The International Relations of Ethnic Conflict." In *The Internationalization of Communal Strife*. Edited by Manus I. Midlarsky, 26–279. London: Routledge.

Salehyan, Idean, and Kristian Skrede Gleditsch. 2006. "Refugees and the Spread of Civil War." *International Organization* 60 (2): 335–366.

Salehyan, Idean. 2007. "Transnational Rebels: Neighboring States as Sanctuary for Rebel Groups." *World Politics* 59(2): 217–242.

Salehyan, Idean. 2008a. "The Externalities of Civil Strife: Refugees as a Source of International Conflict." *American Journal of Political Science* 52(4): 787–801.

Salehyan, Idean. 2008b. "No Shelter Here: Rebel Sanctuaries and International Conflict." *Journal of Politics* 70(1): 54–66.

Salehyan, Idean. 2009. *Rebels without Borders: Transnational Insurgencies in World Politics*. Ithaca, NY: Cornell University Press.

Salehyan, Idean. 2010. "The Delegation of War to Rebel Organizations." *Journal of Conflict Resolution* 54(3): 493–515.

Salehyan, Idean, Kristian Skrede Gleditsch, and David E. Cunningham. 2011. "Explaining External Support for Insurgent Groups." *International Organization* 65(4): 709–744.

Samii, Abbas William. 1997. "The Shah's Lebanon Policy: The Role of SAVAK." *Middle Eastern Studies* 33(1): 66–91.

San-Akca, Belgin. 2009. "Supporting Non-state Armed Groups: A Resort to Illegality?" *Journal of Strategic Studies* 32(4):589–613.

San-Akca, Belgin. 2014. "Democracy and Vulnerability: An Exploitation Theory of Democracies by Terrorists." *Journal of Conflict Resolution* 58(7): 1285–1310.

San-Akca, Belgin. 2015. "Dangerous Companions: Cooperation between States and Nonstate Armed Groups (NAGs Dataset): Vol. 04/2015." nonstatearmedgroups.ku.edu.tr (April 20, 2016).

Sandler, Todd, and Harvey E. Lapan. 1988. "The Calculus of Dissent: An Analysis of the Terrorists' Choice of Targets." *Synthese* 76(2): 245–261.

Schenker, David. 2006. "The Syria Accountability and Lebanese Sovereignty Restoration Act of 2003: Two Years On." Washington Institute Policy Analysis (June 2006).

http://www.washingtoninstitute.org/policy-analysis/view/the-syria-accountability-and-lebanese-sovereignty-restoration-act-of-2003-t (December 9, 2015).

Schultz, Kenneth A. 2010. "The Enforcement Problem in Coercive Bargaining: Interstate Conflict over Rebel Support in Civil Wars." *International Organization* 64(2): 281–312.

Schulze, Kirsten E., 2007. "GAM: Indonesia, GAM, and the Acehnese Population in a Zero-Sum Trap." In *Terror, Insurgency, and the State: Ending Protracted Conflicts.* Edited by Marianne Heiberg, Brendan O'Leary, and John Tirman, 83–122. Philadelphia: University of Pennsylvania Press.

Schweitzer, Yoram. 2004. "Neutralizing Terrorism-Sponsoring States: The Libyan 'Model.'" *Strategic Assessment* 7(1): 7–14.

Schweller, Randall L. 1994. "Bandwagoning for Profit: Bringing the Revisionist State Back In." *International Security* 19(1): 72–107.

Sharrock, David. 2007. "IRA Baron Charged on Tax". *Weekend Australian*, November 9.

Shear, Micheal D., Helene Cooper, and Eric Schmitt. 2015. "Obama Administration Ends Effort to Train Syrians to Combat ISIS." *New York Times*, 10 October. http://www.nytimes.com/2015/10/10/world/middleeast/pentagon-program-islamic-state-syria.html?_r=1 (November 12, 2015).

Shemesh, Moshe. 2006. "The Fida'iyyun Organization's Contribution to the Descent to the Six-Day War." *Israel Studies* 2(1): 1–34.

Simon, Marc V., and Harvey Starr. 1996. "Extraction, Allocation, and the Rise and Decline of States: A Simulation Analysis of Two-Level Security Management." *Journal of Conflict Resolution* 40(2): 272–297.

Singer, J. David, Stuart Bremer, and John Stuckey. 1972. "Capability Distribution, Uncertainty, and Major Power War, 1820–1965." In *Peace, War and Numbers.* Edited by Bruce Russett, 19–48. Beverly Hills, CA: SAGE.

Siqueira, Kevin, and Todd Sandler. 2006. "Terrorists versus the Government: Strategic Interaction, Support, and Sponsorhsip." *Journal of Conflict Resolution* 50(6): 878–898.

Smith, Alastair. 1995. "Alliance Formation and War." *International Studies Quarterly* 39(4): 405–425.

Smith, Tony. 2000. "National Security Liberalism and American Foreign Policy." In *American Democracy Promotion: Impulses, Strategies, and Impacts.* Edited by Michael Cox, G. John Ikenberry, and Takashi Inogochi, 85–102. Oxford: Oxford University Press.

Snyder, Glenn H. 1961. *Deterrence and Defense: Toward a Theory of National Security.* Princeton, NJ: Princeton University Press.

Starr, Harvey. 1994. "Revolution and War: Rethinking the Linkage between Internal and External Conflict." *Political Research Quarterly* 47(2): 481–507.

Stavenhagen, Rodolfo. 1996. *Ethnic Conflicts and the Nation-State.* New York: St. Martin's.

Stohl, M. 2007. "Swamps, Hot Spots, Dick Cheney and the Internationalization of Terrorist Campaigns." *Conflict Management and Peace Science* 24(4): 257–264.

Strindberg, Anders. 2000. "The Damascus-Based Alliance of Palestinian Forces: A Primer." *Journal of Palestinian Studies* 29(3): 60–76.

Tarschys, Daniel. 1988. "Tributes, Tariffs, Taxes, and Trade: The Changing Sources of Government Revenue." *British Journal of Political Science* 18(1): 1–20.

Thomson, Janice E. 1994. *Mercanaries, Pirates, and Sovereigns: State-Building and Extraterritorial Violence in Early Modern Europe.* Princeton, NJ: Princeton University Press.

Thompson, William R. 2001. "Identifying Rivals and Rivalries in World Politics." *International Studies Quarterly* 45 (4): 557–586.

Tiller, Mark. 1997. *Big Ideas: An Introduction to Ideologies in American Politics*. New York: St. Martin's.

United Nations General Assembly. 1965. "Declaration on the Inadmissibility of Intervention in the Domestic Affairs of States and the Protection of Their Independence and Sovereignty." Resolution Number 2131 (December 21). http://www.un-documents.net/a20r2131.htm (June 20, 2015).

U.S. Congress. House. 2012. *Rohrabacher Introduces Bill Recognizing Baluchistan's Right to Self- Determination*. 17 February. Press Release. https://rohrabacher.house.gov/press-release-rohrabacher-introduces-bill-recognizing-baluchistans-right-self-determination (May 13, 2015).

van Bruinessen, Martin. 1986. "The Kurds between Iran and Iraq." *MERIP Reports* 141 (July–August): 14–27.

Wagner, R. Harrison. 2000. "Bargaining and War." *American Journal of Political Science* 44(3): 469–484.

Waldman, Matt. 2010. "The Sun in the Sky: The Relationship between Pakistan's ISI and Afghan Insurgents." Carr Center for Human Rights Policy, Kennedy School of Government, Harvard University, Cambridge, MA (June).

Walsh, Declan. 2009. "Pakistan Bows to Demand for Sharia Law in Taliban-Controlled Swat Valley." *The Guardian*, April 14. http://www.guardian.co.uk/world/2009/apr/14/sharia-law-in-pakistans-swat-valley (April 28, 2009).

Walt, Stephen M. 1985. "Alliance Formation and the Balance of World Power." *International Security* 9(4): 3–41.

Walt, Stephen M. 1987. *The Origins of Alliances*. Ithaca, NY: Cornell University Press.

Walt, Stephen M. 1996. *Revolution and War*. Ithaca, NY: Cornell University Press.

Waltz, Kenneth N. 1959. *Man, the State, and War: A Theoretical Analysis*. New York: Columbia University Press.

Waltz, Kenneth N. 1979. *Theory of International Politics*. New York: Random House.

Weber, Max. 1946. "Politics as a Vocation." In *From Max Weber: Essays in Sociology*. Translated by H. H. Gerth and C. Wright Mills. Oxford: Oxford University Press, pp.77–128.

Wendt, Alexander. 1992. "Anarchy Is What States Make of It: The Social Construction of Power Politics." *International Organization* 46(2): 391–425.

Wendt, Alexander, and Michael N. Barnett. 1993. "Dependent State Formation and Third World Militarization." *Review of International Studies* 19(4): 321–347.

Wilkenfeld, Jonathan. 1968. "Domestic and Foreign Conflict Behavior of Nations." *Journal of Peace Research* 5(1): 56–69.

Williams, Richard. 2006. "Generalized Ordered Logit/ Partial Proportional Odds Models for Ordinal Dependent Variables." *Stata Journal* 6(1): 58–82.

Wilner, Alex S. 2012. "Apocalypse Soon? Deterring Nuclear Iran and Its Terrorist Proxies." *Comparative Strategy* 31(1): 18–40.

Zartman, I. William, ed. 1995. *Collapsed States: The Disintegration and Restoration of Legitimate Authority*. London: Lynne Rienner.

Zelkovitz, Ido. 2015. "Militancy and Religiosity in the Service of National Aspiration: Fatah's Formative Years." *Israel Affairs* 21(4): 668–690.

Index